Ecological Education in Everyday Life

ALPHA 2000

Edited by Jean-Paul Hautecoeur

Access to quality basic adult education is a concern in many countries throughout the world. In this innovative study, sixteen researchers from ten different countries in the Western and Arab worlds look at adult education, and discuss how an ecological approach to education – focusing on the cultural traditions and natural environments of communities – can be more useful than education in specialized institutions. Education, they argue, should involve the transmission of knowledge and know-how within an environment appropriate to the students.

This interdisciplinary collection of essays is a follow-up to preceding works of research on literacy, published in the ALPHA series in Quebec and at UNESCO over the past twenty years. In their humanist, ecological vision of the world, the contributors aim to provide alternatives to neo-capitalist thinking, and promote local education and development through international cooperation.

JEAN-PAUL HAUTECOEUR is an independent consultant from Montreal.

Ecological Education in Everyday Life

ALPHA 2000

Edited by Jean-Paul Hautecoeur

UNIVERSITY OF TORONTO PRESS
Toronto Buffalo London

© UNESCO Institute for Education 2002
Published by University of Toronto Press
Toronto Buffalo London

and by the UNESCO Institute for Education
in collaboration with the Canadian Commission for UNESCO

Printed in Canada

ISBN 0-8020-3668-6 (cloth)
ISBN 0-8020-8496-6 (paper)

Printed on acid-free paper

National Library of Canada Cataloguing in Publication Data

Main entry under title:

Ecological education in everyday life : ALPHA 2000

Co-published by the UNESCO Institute for Education in
collaboration with the Canadian Commission for UNESCO.
Includes bibliographical references.
ISBN 0-8020-3668-6.   ISBN 0-8020-8496-6 (pbk.)

I. Environmental education   I. Hautecoeur, Jean-Paul, 1943–
II. Canadian Commission for Unesco.   III. Unesco Institute for Education.

GE70.E27 2002   363.7   C2001-903933-6

Translation from the French by Peter Sutton and Carolyn Perkes

University of Toronto Press acknowledges the financial assistance to
its publishing program of the Canada Council for the Arts and the
Ontario Arts Council.

University of Toronto Press acknowledges the financial support for
its publishing activities of the Government of Canada through the
Book Publishing Industry Development Program (BPIDP).

I should like to live in a world without artificial and unnecessary noise ...
A world which placed great stress on the idea of renewal and despised the notion of novelty.
A world in which every living object, tree and animal was sacred and never destroyed, except with regret and because of absolute necessity ...
A world in which the very idea of competition was stigmatized as base.

Marguerite Yourcenar

Contents

Foreword   ix

    Open Carriage   xiii
       Lisa Zucker, Canada

INTRODUCTION
    Ecological Approaches in Basic Education   3
       Jean-Paul Hautecoeur, Canada

PART ONE
Shifting the Education Paradigm   19

    Ecological Education in the Living Environment   21
       Laila Iskandar Kamel, Egypt

    Abundance As a Central Idea in Ecological Approaches
    in Education   44
       Munir Fasheh, Palestinian Territories

    Ecology and Basic Education among the
    Indigenous Peoples of Canada   51
       Serge Wagner, Canada

    From Reaching In to Reaching Out: El-Warsha 1987–1999   71
       Hassan El-Geretly, Egypt

    The Creation of Knowledge through Environmental Education   82
       Paolo Orefice, Italy

An Ecological Culture for Teachers 94
Viara Gurova, Bulgaria

PART TWO
Stimulating Participation through Social Action 107

Education for Regional Sustainable Development 109
Jan Keller, Czech Republic

Environmental Adult Education in the Czech Republic 122
Michal Bartos, Czech Republic

Literacy Practices in Local Activities: An Ecological Approach 137
David Barton, United Kingdom

Addressing Alexandria's Environmental Problems 150
Adel Abu Zahra, Egypt

The Campaign against the MAI in Canada 159
Brian Sarwer-Foner, Canada

PART THREE
For Sustainable Endogenous Development 177

Sustainable Development Literacy in Central Appalachia 179
Anthony Flaccavento, United States

Sustainable Community Development with
Human Dimensions: The Basaisa Experience 200
Salah Arafa, Egypt

Revitalizing a Depopulating Region in Hungary 217
Valeria Nagy Czanka and Ildiko Mihaly, Hungary

Agricultural Development and the Preservation
of Indigenous Knowledge 227
Ismail Daiq and Shawkat Sarsour, Palestinian Territories

CLOSING REMARKS
The Nuweiba Seminar 243
Jean-Paul Hautecoeur

Notes on Contributors 259

Foreword

Three Questions

ALPHA 2000 explores the links between ecology and community education in the everyday context. It explores the links between adult basic education, as it has been defined in previous ALPHA publications,[1] and sustainable living.

Since education above all means making links, it is fundamentally ecological. But reality is not fundamental, and current education barely ecological. Usually it destroys 'natural' links with experience, cultural heritage, community, and environment. The question posed at the start of our research venture was *how to restore links with people's experience in their natural, social, and cultural environment.*

The link between education and sustainable living is no longer current either. Adult education and training have above all turned towards adaptation to the new world economic order, as though that were going to do away with poverty. The second question that concerns us is *how to survive in a world of growing impoverishment.* Or, *how to link the struggle against poverty with the renewal of resources as a whole.*

There is another link to be discovered and created – of a more spiritual, ethical, and civic nature – between individuals, communities, peoples, genders, and North and South. The answers to the previous questions depend on the nature of the links that will be created, or destroyed, between different human groups, and between humans and the other species on our planet. The third question drawing us together is *how to learn to live together while respecting differences.*

Who Are We?

We are researchers, educators, local and regional development workers, or a mixture of all of them, from three regions: the Arab States, Europe, and North America. Our expectations were to learn from the experiences of others, to gain a better understanding through dialogue, to thereby improve local education and development projects, and, if possible, to strengthen actions through co-operation.

An initial research group – let us call it the 'Northern Group' – met during a seminar in Brno, in the Czech Republic, in September 1998. A second group was formed at a seminar in Cairo in December 1998: the 'Southern Group.' All the researchers were set the same task: to answer the questions set out in this Foreword on the basis of their own experience. They agreed to meet in the spring, in Sinai, to present their papers and to try to begin putting together a joint publication.

Finally, a score of researchers met in Nuweiba, in Sinai, in March 1999. Their monographs make up the chapters of this book. The discussions held at the Nuweiba seminar are taken up in the concluding chapter.

ALPHA

ALPHA was an action-research program of the UNESCO Institute for Education, entitled 'Literacy Strategies in Industrialized Countries' (now ended). In reality, this program has for a long time been opened up to a range of adult basic education practices.[2] Literacy is understood as part of the learning taking place in endogenous community development projects. The aims of this biennial action-research program are international cooperation in the field of adult basic education, support for experimental socio-educational practices, and international dissemination of its research work.[3]

The ALPHA program used to cover intellectual cooperation between what has been conventionally called 'East and West' in Europe. Since the International Conference on Adult Education held in Hamburg in 1997, the program has embraced North-South cooperation. The theme of ALPHA 2000, ecological education, demanded that the program be opened up to the rest of the world.

Not all regions were represented in the ALPHA 2000 research team. We started with the involvement of the Arab Region because it was under-represented in the projects of the UNESCO Institute. But also, by coincidence, an Egyptian team volunteered to join in the coordination of the UNESCO project, in particular in the arrangement of two seminars on Egyptian soil. If Egypt is finally over-represented in the table of contents, this is because of the withdrawal of some of the Arab participants from Morocco, Tunisia, Yemen, and Saudi Arabia. In the European group, we also lost the participation of researchers from France, Poland, and the Czech Republic. We deeply regret this loss.

ALPHA projects could not be conducted without the support of governmental partners and non-governmental organizations, or the collaboration of numerous researchers. ALPHA 2000 benefited from the support of the following bodies:

Canadian Commission for UNESCO
Community and Institutional Development (CID), Egypt
International Development and Research Centre (IDRC), Egypt
Jan Hus Foundation of the Czech Republic
Mendel University of Agriculture and Forestry, Brno, Czech Republic
Ministry of the Environment of the Czech Republic
National Literacy Secretariat of the Government of Canada

We have been especially assisted in the coordination of the research and the process of publication by:

Stanislav Hubik, Professor at the University of Agriculture, Brno, Czech Republic
Laila Iskandar Kamel, Director of CID, Egypt
Carolyn Perkes, translator-reviser, English edition, Montreal, Canada
Brian Sarwer-Foner, editorial assistant, English edition, Montreal, Canada
Peter Sutton, translator, United Kingdom
Serge Wagner, Professor at Université du Québec à Montréal, Canada
Lisa Zucker, sculptor, Canada

We thank all the authors for their willing collaboration, and the institutions that enabled them to take part.

J.P.H.

Notes

1 ALPHA (from *alphabétisation*) is the acronym of a publication series on literacy and basic education research applied to the North American and European regions. Initiated in Quebec in the late seventies and directed since that time by the present author, it rapidly became an international activity connected mainly with community organizations and their fieldwork. Published only in French until 1988 by the Quebec Ministry of Education, ALPHA was then also co-published in English by the UNESCO Institute for Education in Hamburg and Culture Concepts in Canada. The whole series comprises seventeen titles. More than two hundred authors participated in their realization.
2 J.-P. Hautecoeur, 'The Story of ALPHA – in Three Parts (1978–1999),' *International Review of Education* (forthcoming).
3 S. Wagner, *The ALPHA Programme (1993–1999) – Literacy Strategies in Industrialized Countries – of the UNESCO Institute for Education (UIE): Elements of Evaluation* (Hamburg: UNESCO Institute for Education, 1999).

Open Carriage

Lisa Zucker, address to the Board of Governors,
UNESCO Institute for Education, Hamburg, 1999

It is a great pleasure and privilege to present the instalation of my bronze sculpture, *Open Carriage*, here at the UNESCO Institute in Hamburg (see cover photo). When I began to think of which piece to propose to the Institute, I thought of this one because it recalls that great symbol of the Industrial Revolution, the 'iron horse,' the train, and in turn the railway lines which democratized travel and communication, at least in the West. People and mail bags circulated more freely than ever before, in keeping with the highest ideals of basic education. The advent of this wonderful new technology, affectionately referred to as 'horsepower,' also brought about the popularization of the printing press, long since thought of by Gutenberg, and with it mass diffusion of the book, taking education out of the hands of the aristocracy and liberating access to the written word.

Or not quite. In truth, train tickets and mail rates were still organized according to class, and reading remained a leisure activity available primarily to the bourgeoisie, leaving the underclasses illiterate, just as today the Internet remains largely inaccessible to our neighbours in Bangladesh. Side interests can always derail the advance of technology.

So the ALPHA research program, while pursuing cultural development through new forms of endogenous activity, retains its emphasis on trying, on testing and self-questioning, on continually remaining open to diverse possibilities while interrogating the sense which is transmitted in basic education. It has acknowledged, on the one hand, the very real danger of technological reform devaluing and even eradicating existing cultural formations and, on the other hand, the possible destruction of the environment by traditional practices. In short, we need to consider carefully before we allow our horses, iron or otherwise, to run rampant across the landscape.

In the making of this bronze, I have tried to follow UNESCO's ideal of openness to diversity. The sculpture is left open to technology – it embraces the form of a car or carriage – just as it is left open to nature, gaping with holes through which the landscape floods, so that finally it stands apart from no background. The body is built up from such diverse sources that foreground and background collapse into it, and it carries on, flattened by the weight of this contradiction. *Open Carriage* is open to the point where perspective collapses, so that it retains nothing private, so open that its separate identity is resorbed into the environment, so open that it is somehow effaced from the world while remaining in it. I was thinking of calling it 'The Disappearance.'

I have had my own personal experience of this curious kind of public disappearance. In the small village where I live in Quebec, my French-speaking friends tended to mispronounce my name, Lisa, as Liza until I began signing it 'lis ça.' By way of this spelling error, people got the sound right, but my name as sign of identity was effaced and replaced with an exhortation to read. I now sign my sculptures as 'lis.'

UNESCO champions the free passage of language and ideas all the way to the point of civil disobedience when human rights are at stake. This, I believe, is also a direction for art, and it is here that I consider the project of UNESCO to be congenial with certain artistic efforts, equally politicized. Departing from campaigns which would promote civil resistance through access to clear information, these artworks advance something else: acts of resistance in which language and representations do *not* communicate clearly.

What could this mean?

Imagine, for example, a body which appears awkwardly, even unmusically, on stage for an hour of chamber music presented by the Kulturbund Deutschen Juden of Berlin. The institution of the Nuremberg Laws in 1935 has rendered it unlawful for Jews to earn an income from non-Jewish sources, and now the Kulturbund is formed – an organism for the ghettoization of Jewish artists – not yet a transport depot but the beginning of more rigorous controls. Yet still perhaps a place where one could mask uselessness – always a risk in the face of escalating fascism. In this case, a violin has been thrust into the hands of a musical illiterate. Tentative fingers of one hand hold and caress the neck of the instrument, touching a resistant string here or there, while the other hand grips its bow and saws through the air, shuttling in time to the strains of its virtual music.

If we wish to name this body, we might call it 'mosaic' insofar as it is going to pieces, playing a diversity of parts, conducting its own musical airs in measure with the airs, gestures, postures, and self-promotions of all the other bodies on stage. The mosaic takes on the appearance of too many things at once, remains as open to view as the rest, going so far as to deliver itself over to the forces of its own destruction. The mosaic body *hides out in plain view* of its deterrents, counting on a volume of signs so inflated – a message so mixed – that sense disappears into the insensible.

What is important here is not what signifies but that representation proceeds in terms of its own failure to signify simply and directly. We might always count on the idea that language cannot be ordered around, that representation can always exceed the logic of a coherent form, that it can bypass even terrorist demands for pure types, be they genetic, linguistic, or otherwise. We must continue to seek and promote this rare and outlandish *illegibility* which still opens out to share itself, however discreetly, with the world.

lis

Ecological Education in Everyday Life

ALPHA 2000

INTRODUCTION

Ecological Approaches in Basic Education

Jean-Paul Hautecoeur

Ecological Education in Everyday Life is the last publication in the ALPHA series, produced since 1990 at the UNESCO Institute for Education. In this volume, we continue to be interested in what we call non-formal *basic education*, which includes a range of literacy practices in vernacular cultures, knowledge transmission practices in communities, and education practices that prove useful to the needs of life. What is new is the ecological component, the strategic objective of lifelong education directed towards sustainable living.

Traces of Community Education

In our view, ecological education is not a specialized discipline within the field of educational sciences that also studies the environment. On the contrary, it is a lifelong practice of social learning and knowledge transmission that is carried out in all spheres of life. In other words: a *community education* (in French, *éducation populaire*, and in Spanish, *educación popular*), with the addition of 'ecological,' which locates these learning practices in the space of our lives, in the current ideological context of globalization, and in a dramatic perception of the future.

The older concept of *'éducation populaire'* was bathed in socialist optimism (Marxist and Christian) or even in an anthropological vision of authentic cultures. It was held by agents external to communities, lacking democratic scruples despite the progressive discourse of 'interveners' or 'facilitators,' and in fact proved to be a renewed version of rural priests, preachers, and traditional schoolmasters. Above all, educators strongly believed in the transformational virtues of education, an activity quite separate from everyday life, the 'common sense' of which was dismissed as attesting to the alienation, ignorance, and paganism of the 'the masses.' The first ten years (1978–88) of our research and publications in Quebec in the field of literacy were infused with the salutary virtues of *éducation populaire*. The term 'conscientization,' borrowed from Paulo Freire, sums up the broad agenda of this research.[1]

Above all, we have retained three features of *éducation populaire*. Firstly, we have maintained a bond with the everyday existence and world of ordinary poor people, a bond that is rooted in a profound consciousness of our common humanity and sensitivity to the dignity of humankind, in what we might call a feeling of solidarity. Most of the authors in this work share this humanist orientation towards the deprived greater part of humanity. Secondly, we pursue *éducation populaire*'s critical vocation, if not its corrosive undercurrent, in an epistemological sense, but also in ethical and political terms. Whereas the dominant function of adult education consists of adapting to the *new*, our tradition of knowledge starts from disobedience, the recognition of reality as pluralist and conflicting, and the quest for sustainable alternatives to imposed forms of education. Today, the principal object of criticism is the economics of globalization, particularly in its effects of rendering daily life subservient to the capitalist mode of destruction (of the environment, our health, our cultural heritage, our intimacy) and the hegemony of market values applied to 'human capital.' Against the new world economic order, we pursue ways of living that value the renewal of our planet's resources, the preservation of biological and cultural diversity, and human work.

The third legacy of community education consists of its practical objectives, that is, improving local living conditions through various formulas of social economy. Thus, in order to more accurately describe our work, we have replaced the term 'action-research' with the term 'cooperative research.' We have attempted, as part of the ALPHA projects, to practise the useful exchange and networking of our resources, while preserving the greatest possible latitude for intellectual freedom and economic independence. Prior to the concept of sustainable development, which informs this research, our previous work referred extensively to concepts of equitable and endogenous development. Basic education must be exercised through local economic initiatives that call on real needs, available resources, and liberated imagination: on *bricolage*. Above all, basic education carries a use value and a useful function that have currency in the margins of the dominant marketplace.

The Origins of the Ecological Approach to Basic Education

Of course, the origin of our ecological approach to adult education issues lies with the United Nations Conference on Environment and Development. 'The Earth Summit' (Rio, 1992) intrinsically linked environmental protection to the implementation of a new mode of global development that is termed sustainable. Among the urgent actions cited in Agenda 21 to achieve this worldwide goal of sustainable development are the following: the fight against poverty; changes in non-sustainable methods of production and styles of consumption; control of demographic growth; and the improvement of health conditions for the most vulnerable populations. Recommendations on education and training actions trail far behind.[2]

In 1997 the World Conservation Union's Commission on Education and Communication reviewed the educational recommendations in Agenda 21, 'the forgotten priority of Rio.' This commission judged it 'imperative to focus strategic development on adults such as consumer groups, workers, women's groups, etc., whose everyday decisions are crucial.'[3] That is one key to understanding everyday life as the primary focus for ecological education in this book.

After the Earth Summit, the NGOs that had gathered at the Rio Conference in an Alternative International Forum published a series of alternative treaties, one of which discussed 'Environmental Education for Sustainable Societies and Global Responsibility.' This document outlines the principles of environmental education and indicates the broad range of societal issues that an ecological approach to education should address. The following principles share a profound affinity with those that formed the basis of our research project:

- a critical and innovative function that aims at a transformation of social practices and the development of alternative ways of living based on dialogue and cooperation;
- the goal of the local and global development of citizenship based on self-determination and respect for the sovereignty of nations;
- a holistic, interdisciplinary approach in relationships between human beings, nature, and the universe;
- encouragement for solidarity, equity, and respect for human rights that presupposes democratic strategies and an open climate of intercultural exchange;
- recognition of, respect for, and use of vernacular knowledge and skills, and promotion of ecological, cultural, and linguistic diversity;

- democratization of communications, particularly the mass media, which are an essential vehicle for the exchange of information, values, and experience;
- development of ethical sensitivity towards all forms of life on the planet, which sets limits to the exploitation by humanity of the resources of the universe.[4]

The second source of inspiration for our project was the UNESCO Fifth International Conference on Adult Education (CONFINTEA V, Hamburg, 1997), in which several of the authors of this publication participated. This conference sought to specify what lifelong learning means from the point of view of sustainable human development and solidarity. It incorporated concerns for the environment in all educational activities, not as a specialized branch of adult education, but as an 'ecological approach' to lifelong learning, a vision and a practice that should cut across all learning activities.

Specifically, the CONFINTEA V 'Agenda for the Future' recommends:

- ... replacing the narrow vision of literacy by learning that meets social, economic and political needs and gives expression to a new form of citizenship;
- ... integrating literacy ... into all appropriate development projects, particularly those related to health and the environment;
- ... making use of adult education activities in order to increase the capacity of citizens from different sectors of society to take innovative initiatives and to develop programs on ecologically and socially sustainable development;
- integrating indigenous traditional knowledge of the interactions between human beings and nature into adult learning programs, and recognizing that minority and indigenous communities have special authority and competence in protecting their own environment;
- integrating environmental and development issues into all sectors of adult learning and developing an ecological approach to lifelong learning.[5]

The 'Hamburg Declaration on Adult Education' defines literacy 'broadly as the basic knowledge and skills needed by all in a rapidly changing world.'[6] This concept is close to what we call 'basic education' in the ALPHA projects, with this difference: that we attach great importance to the socio-cultural context of these education programs rather than to any universal value imposed upon them by mercantile culture.

But to trace the direct origins of our ecological approach to community-based basic education, we must turn to our previous research.

ALPHA 94, ALPHA 96, and ALPHA 97

ALPHA 94 accounts for the crisis of rural areas in several regions of Europe and America, and explores various local initiatives for cultural development.[7] The key concept of this research is that of loss of literacy or *illiterization,* which for rural populations means the loss of cultural frames of reference and their exclusion from mainstream communication and exchange. Several solutions are then seized upon by rural populations: exile or adaptation to the labour market and training programs ('ticket out'); social assistance or dependent marginalization while remaining in rural areas; but also resistance to acculturation and mobilization of regional resources in local renewal initiatives ('ticket in'). Yet if the term *basic education,* which replaces literacy in the sense of adaptation to a dominant mode of communication, seeks to become rooted in a territory and in a lived history, it paradoxically forgets the natural environment. Having interested ourselves in the cultural environment, we neglected the natural environment, which is nevertheless a traditional frame of rural life.

ALPHA 96 accounts for the crisis of work in our post-industrial societies, focusing particularly on the disqualification of workers and the devaluing of their skills.[8] We call into question the usefulness of literacy for the socio-occupational reintegration of the so-called illiterate (growing exponentially according to official statistics), and we explore the adapted forms of survival used by the excluded. Basic education programs become what people know and know how to do in the contexts of their lives, how they actualize their capabilities in times of crisis 'by putting humanity into the economy.' The key concept of this publication is that of *bricolage:* how the poor invent solutions to penury by drawing on their rich legacy and by recycling their skills. Throughout this project, we enter full force into an ecological approach to educational forms that aim to develop 'alternative networks ... less dependent on the free market and on state programs, in a quest for durable solutions to the crises of work ... to create new local and regional solidarity ... in order to co-ordinate local development and make use of all resources' (344).

ALPHA 97 questions adult education policies in the face of the demands and the needs of communities.[9] Increasingly numerous groups are demanding more rights, decentralization, transparency, and more participatory democracy in relations between the State and its citizens, so that their projects might be recognized and supported. The issue of the participation of all individuals in the decision-making that concerns their lives is central here. To conclude: 'Nor are the privileges taken for granted which the cultural and political elites have established for themselves through a network of institutions given legitimacy by a one-dimensional view of history, conservative science and back-scratching laws ... if the vision of *lifelong education within society* is to be achieved, it will be necessary to give strategic importance to basic education in its social context' (352–3), that is, to the potential of the educating society at its base and no longer merely in its recognized institutions (390). 'There is an attempt to create the mental and ecological preconditions for participation in projects that can improve the quality of life' (365).

In the course of our work, we thus opened the field to encompass a comprehensive concept of cultural, social, economic, and political action that we would call *ecological education.* But it still remained necessary to open the geographical field to worldwide diversity, as our research had up to that time been conducted only in the Western sphere. Indeed, an ecological approach to education presupposes the link between the local and the global, between rich and poor, between North and South. We had to associate ourselves with researchers in other regions to better internationalize our vision of the world and to better discover the hidden face of globalization in the West.

The Research Proposal

A provisional theoretical concept of an ecological approach to basic education was proposed to all the authors of this book, to define the content and the orientations of the research. Excerpts from the original text follow:

- By an *ecological approach* to lifelong education we mean both a conscious attitude towards the interactions that we have with our natural/cultural environment, an ethic of preserving resources and bio-cultural diversity, techniques and methods of applying this ethic, and a proactive policy of moral (legal) change aiming to preserve or restore the quality of our environment.

   The ecological vision has generally been ignored by adult basic education programs. Literacy, for example, has helped to eradicate linguistic and cultural diversity in many regions of the world.[10] The recent campaigns for skilled 'literacy' that meets the needs of the global labour market usually obey the productivist, competitive ethic that is diametrically opposed to sustainable human development and solidarity.[11]

Where and how are ecological approaches to basic education resisted and obstructed? Is there an ecological will in the traditional practices of life? Or, have certain customary practices facilitated the degradation of the natural and cultural environment? What are the socio-political contexts that favour the large-scale application of ecological approaches? What are the obvious results of these? What have been the difficulties and failures?

- By *basic education* we mean above all the cultural heritage or the knowledge and skills capital that every person harbours in his or her experiences, and every community in its history. This inheritance, notably a language and particular modes of communication, embraces techniques of education that are compatible with the everyday practices of life and with the values of the communities. For communities and humanity it represents an inestimable heritage.

This heritage is threatened everywhere, where it has not already been squandered or systematically destroyed. An ecological approach to adult education consists of uncovering vernacular types of education, treating them with respect, and drawing as much as possible from them in endogenous development initiatives.

To what extent is the cultural capital of communities recorded and respected? Are traditional resources sufficient for the effective implementation of development projects? Are they compatible with and favourable to the introduction of new technologies? Are adult educators prepared for intercultural interventions of endogenous development with their local partners? What methodologies have been experimented with successfully?

- *Education for all throughout life* presupposes the creation of communities of greater solidarity and responsibility, as well as the implementation of more democratic relations between citizens.[12] Training in new citizenship skills is an indispensable part of the political ecology of basic education.

An economy of sustainable development presupposes a range of investment in socially useful enterprises, in the education of people, in the valuing of local resources, and in the management of the environment. Such an economy refers to a plural model, involving the cooperation of the private, public, and voluntary sectors, and the combined goals of economic productivity, social solidarity, cultural added value, and ecological viability

What are the ethical, economic, and political values of the various basic education projects in different geopolitical contexts? What changes have been made in traditional relations of authority, in the broad picture of the market economy, and in the relations with public institutions, making it possible to implement ecological projects of local development? What types of social organization have these projects engendered, facilitating the sustainability of innovations and a change in the scale of their application?

All these questions merely serve as the introduction to an interregional discussion of the issue to be undertaken by the research teams.

Work Methodology

The research proposal was sent to researchers both known and unknown by the author. Some had participated in previous ALPHA projects, others were selected from UNESCO networks, and still others were identified through various channels of documentary or institutional research (in universities, national commissions for UNESCO, foundations, etc.).

The selection criteria? All the authors who were called upon had to be qualified researchers *and* interveners in local or regional projects. They had to have experienced what we initially called an 'ecological approach to community-based basic education.' They also had to have institutional support that facilitated their voluntary participation in our research project and, if possible, that contributed in the form of finances or services to various stages of the project's operation.

The authors were therefore not selected on the basis of their previous publications or their affiliation with a given school of thought, as is often the case with academic publications, but, above all, on the basis of their experience. Deliberately, no theoretical reference was cited in the initial research proposal. Only references to UNESCO and the ALPHA series of the UNESCO Institute for Education were mentioned.

Another important criterion was the disciplinary diversity of the research teams. All solicited authors are involved in education, but they are not, for the most part, teachers or professors. Some activists-researchers have training in the social sciences, while others are trained in the pure sciences, in medicine or agronomy, journalism, or in theatre, literature, etc. One of the important requirements of our work is to find a common space and language that can account for the diversity of origins and at the same time assist us in building a collective project, if only for the time allotted for research (two years). We do not always succeed, particularly when it comes to writing. In this venue, professors may be more at ease than physicians or agronomists. And entrepreneurs, recognized people of action in their sphere, may experience difficulty in translating their knowledge into a publishable text.

In the past, the ALPHA projects operated between what was then referred to as Eastern and Western Europe, on the one hand, and North America, on the other. This time, we have chosen to incorporate the Arab world, thanks to the assistance of Laila Iskandar Kamel, who recommended setting up a research team based on an Egyptian community action network. Another region, Southeast Asia, unfortunately had to be abandoned as the result of the withdrawal of a major sponsor in this region.

In the Arab world, we attempted to solicit a majority participation of women. Although this majority existed at the very outset, it faltered in the course of the research proposal selection stage. It continued to be curtailed throughout the subsequent stages, particularly following an initial Egyptian seminar: a number of people did not turn up, and others had to abandon their research. In the end, the Arab team included six men and only one woman, from two countries, Egypt and the Palestinian Territories. This accounts in part for the gender imbalance in this publication.

Three teams were set up: one in Western Europe and North America, one in Central Europe, and one in the Arab nations. Each participant was asked to prepare a research proposal to be presented at an initial regional seminar (one for each region was planned, but only two took place: in Brno in the Czech Republic and in Cairo). The purpose of these seminars was to confirm participation, specify major research guidelines, define expectations and tasks, and organize subsequent stages.[13]

Next, each author composed a research report from a distance, in collaboration with the project director. These reports were sent to all the authors before a summary seminar, to which the authors whose papers had been accepted were invited, as well as the representatives of some institutions that had sponsored the project. It was at this meeting that the final outline of the project was drawn up in terms of its direction, composition, style, and editions (in three languages: French, English, and Arabic). It was also on this occasion that other action plans were devised to disseminate publications in regional areas, but also to collaborate differently and more collectively in actions for ecological education over a broader territory.

The purpose of our cooperative research is to share different experiences and knowledge; to study and compare them; thereby to improve our concepts and strategies of intervention; and to produce a common work that we will attempt to disseminate in each of the regions and the networks of UNESCO. We also seek to constitute other networks of cooperation for regional, inter-regional, and international actions.

The conclusion of the book reflects our work method. The title and the composition of the book, its major ideological orientations, and the meaning of its principal concepts have only been developed at the end, on the only occasion that was afforded us to work together. This conclusion is the only written trace of our collective work. There exist other traces that are not dealt with in this work: for instance, the constitution of a network for ecological education based in Egypt, and the creation of research-action network addressing the same theme in the Czech Republic.

The Outline

The book is divided into three sections: the first deals with our paradigm of ecological education; the second covers social strategies guided by an ecological vision of social change; and the third discusses sustainable local economy. Each section is composed of local research reports that were submitted for assessment by all the other authors. Unfortunately, a section dealing with art has been left out, as is recalled in the conclusion (art would have been the next ALPHA theme). At the beginning of this volume, however, L. Zucker presents the sculpture depicted in the cover photograph, a work of art that comprises an integral part of ALPHA 2000.

What does this *paradigm of ecological education* mean for us? It is 'popular,' consisting of the learning, discovery, and teaching that occur in the active life of communities, which may include teaching institutions, as attested to by Gurova and Orefice. Such education draws its knowledge and know-how from the community's popular culture and heritage, and it is transmitted in the spoken language of people (Kamel, Wagner, El-Geretly). It is active, cutting across various day-to-day activities that affect the economy, health, social relations, and cultural creation (Kamel, Wagner, El-Geretly). All generations may participate, which means that we speak more readily of community education than of adult education (Fasheh, El-Geretly, Kamel).

Basic means above all survival and the quest for better living conditions, which presupposes work, employment, wages, literacy, hygiene, a sustainable environment, dignity, equity, and legal equality, particularly between women and men. Many of these minimally decent living conditions do not exist in environments of poverty and segregation. They have yet to be built in collaboration with individuals and external NGOs, one of whose tasks will be to assist in the development of local NGOs.

An ecological vision of community education stresses the capital importance of a living natural and cultural environment, generous, and renewable. Life, abundance (Fasheh), fair sharing, and potential for renewal are the dramatic issues at stake, which cut across generational, gender, ethnic, social, and ideological conflicts. An ecological education sets itself the task of sensitizing individuals and communities to these global issues as well as of seeking the resources for dealing with them effectively and sustainably in everyday life. This is what Gurova calls the initiation of a new ecological culture, one including a vernacular cultural heritage but also requiring a critical attitude in the face of imposed 'truths,' as well as experimentation with new ways of doing things in the face of the world's crises.

The second section is entitled 'Stimulating Participation through Social Action.' Changing ways of thinking and persuing education is inadequate if education remains an activity apart, separate from collective life and the stakes of power. Almost all the authors broach political criticism of traditional forms of education as they operate in various socio-political contexts. An ecological approach to education is practised through demands for more democracy in daily life. Learning of this kind occurs in the most minor endeavours undertaken to protect citizens' rights in the local sphere (Barton, Abu-Zahra), as well as in national and even international offensives for information, mobilization, and civil disobedience in the face of globalization's grand manoeuvring (Keller, Bartos, Sarwer-Foner).

Violations of our vital environment constitute a major crisis in contemporary societies that calls for effective strategies of information and the testing of more democratic forms of social organization. Here, literacy or basic education means access to information, the learning of communication according to participatory strategies (friendship clubs, resident associations, the Internet, networks, public demonstrations), and the adjustment of the means of expression and of pressure so that they can genuinely change the dominant order (Sarwer-Foner, Abu Zahra). What is valued is not so much a rare or special technique as creativity that draws on ordinary tools and existing resources (Barton, Keller). What is to be recognized are the possible and surprising links between people and the things already in place. What is to be done is to discover the existing resources, create bonds, open up networks, facilitate them, and share one's knowledge; that is, to arrange an interactive learning environment with the responsibility of building more cooperative, creative, and independent communities.

The third section addresses ecological education in several regional sustainable development projects in rural settings. An ecological approach to regional development is rooted in a feeling of belonging to the region and in local social organizations, in the will of the inhabitants to preserve and enrich their natural and cultural legacy, and in the creation of economic added value in traditional local productions. It is a vision that is diametrically opposed to an exogenous, productivist approach to development that promotes the dislocation of inhabitants and economic activities, seeks maximum exploitation of natural resources, and values mass cultural production and an intensive investment in new technologies and external skills (Flaccavento, Arafa, Daiq and Sarsour).

The major issues that guide development strategies vary throughout the four contributions to this section. For Flaccavento in the United States, the vital need is to change ways of living, by drawing on how people actually exist, and on the natural legacy of their region that needs to be regenerated. For Arafa in Egypt, community education intervention seeks to fight – through social participation, technical training, and innovation – endemic illiteracy, over-population, and poverty. For Mihaly and Nagy Czanka in Hungary, technical education in the new occupations of ecotourism is part of an overall educational process that seeks to mobilize the population in projects that begin with the traditions and resources of a region in decline. For Daiq and Sarsour in the Palestinian Territories, agricultural education consists of revitalizing indigenous knowledge and skills by improving them, while consolidating local social solidarity, particularly in women's organizations, to better resist the occupation and to improve living conditions.

As stated in the Foreword, our work in its entirety must address three major issues that affect the practices of ecological education in everyday life: the fight against poverty, the fight against resource depletion, and the building of a type of intercultural learning that respects difference. I believe that we have chiefly cleared the ground on the first two issues, through an inductive approach that starts from the experience of each and everyone to attempt to constitute a common knowledge base as well as to deepen the links of cooperation and solidarity. Following the Nuweiba seminar, we felt certain of having come together to build a work that would be useful in pursuing our common quest for more sustainable, renewable ways of living, as well as for the reinforcement of local projects.

But the third issue, the learning of intercultural ways of living, remains to be fully addressed. Of course, we have acquired rich and often successful experience in cooperative work among the researchers of the different regions. The book's conclusion attests to this. Yet our concepts of relatively homogeneous communities and of an education chiefly founded upon their cultural heritages leaves unexplored the building of mixed communities and therefore the important issue of learning the art of such mixes: not in the mould of existing institutions (school, church, village, family, homeland ...), but in experimenting with forms that are malleable to the experience of cultural diversity, the movement of people, and a variety of projects.

We have mainly focused on rural regions rather urban centres, on traditional communities rather than citizens' groups. Where the latter have been observed – for instance, in Alexandria and in Lancaster (Abu Zahra, Barton) – literacy no longer carries the meaning of a single language for the purpose of standardized communications; rather, it means the quest for information, the demanding of human rights, experimenting with original and cooperative means of expression, and the creation of collectives with the skills appropriate for the requirements of new situations. The anthropogenic quest for a singular identity in a familiar environment would not be the goal of the intercultural ecological education to which Orefice would lay claim. Rather, we might seek this goal in the acquisition, by individuals working in association, of versatile, inventive capabilities that could take into account changes in communities, cultures, and environments. I believe that that is a fertile avenue for the pursuit of our work on ecological basic education.

Notes

1 Jean-Paul Hautecoeur, 'The Story of ALPHA – in Three Parts.' *International Review of Education* (forthcoming).
2 M. Grubb, M. Koch, A. Munson, F. Sullivan, and K. Thomson, *The Earth Summit Agreement: A Guide and Assessment* (London: Earthcan Publications, 1993); Michael Keating, *Agenda for Change: A Plain Language Version of Agenda 21 and the Other Rio Agreements* (Geneva: The Centre for Our Common Future, 1993).
3 IUCN Commission on Education and Communication, *Education: The Forgotten Priority of Rio? Statement on Rio + 5 on Chapter 36 Agenda 21* (Gland, Switzerland: CEC, 1997).
4 International NGO Forum (INGOF), *The NGO Alternative Treaties and the NGO Treaty Process: A Complete Edition of the Alternative Treaties from the International NGO Forum, Rio de Janeiro, Brazil, June 1–14, 1992* (published by INGOF with assistance from the Canadian Council for International Co-operation and Robert Pollard, International Synergy Institute, 1994).
5 Fifth International Conference on Adult Education, Hamburg, 14–18 July 1997, *Final Report* (Paris: UNESCO; Hamburg: UNESCO Institute for Education, 1997).
6 Ibid., p. 23.
7 Jean-Paul Hautecoeur, ed., *ALPHA 94 – Literacy and Cultural Development Strategies in Rural Areas* (Hamburg: UNESCO Institute for Education; Toronto: Culture Concepts, 1994).
8 Jean-Paul Hautecoeur, ed., *ALPHA 96 – Basic Education and Work* (Hamburg: UNESCO Institute for Education; Toronto: Culture Concepts, 1996), p. 344.
9 Jean-Paul Hautecoeur, ed., *ALPHA 97 – Basic Education and Institutional Environments* (Hamburg: UNESCO Institute for Education; Toronto: Culture Concepts, 1997), pp. 352–3, 365.
10 Ad Hoc Forum of Reflection to the Executive Board, 'Report of the Forum of Reflexion,' UNESCO Executive Board, 142 EX/37, 1993. The 'Summary of Discussions' says in paragraph 20: 'Literacy education refers implicitly to a hierarchy in the forms of Knowledge transmission. It supposes that societies with an oral tradition are "inferior" or "backward" compared with those that favor the written word. Yet, everyone is aware of the

disillusions that are associated with literacy education. In many countries, populations which have been newly educated lose other forms of knowledge or wisdom and are incapable of producing or working; they have lost their capacities for sharp observation and accuracy in the perception and expression of the world, they have lost a culture of tolerance and social interaction ... they have lost the sense of global ecological balance, and the place of the human being in this global balance – thereby putting numerous countries in a situation of "paradoxical backwardness"' (11).

11 Jean-Paul Hautecoeur, ed., 'Literacy in the Age of Information – Knowledge, Power or Domination? An Assessment of the International Adult Literacy Survey,' *International Review of Education* 46, no 5 (2000).
12 International Commission on Education for the Twenty-First Century, *Learning: The Treasure Within* (Paris: UNESCO; London: HMSO Books, 1996).
13 The seminar reports are available upon request at the UNESCO Institute for Education, Hamburg.

Part One

Shifting the Education Paradigm ...

... by observing the wisdom of the poor
— *Laila Iskandar Kamel, Egypt*

... simply, in reaping the abundance of experience
— *Munir Fasheh, Palestinian Territories*

... reversing recent colonial practices
— *Serge Wagner, Canada*

... through creative language that stimulates dialogue and raises doubts
— *Hassan El-Geretly, Egypt*

... so that the environment reactivates the art of reading and interpretation
— *Paolo Orefice, Italy*

... within the school, in provocation
— *Viara Gurova, Bulgaria*

Ecological Education in the Living Environment

Laila Iskandar Kamel

The word 'ecological' means different things to different people. What does it mean in the Egyptian context? How are the main environmental and educational issues expressed and understood by local populations whom we describe as marginalized, disenfranchised, dispossessed? Do these communities possess any knowledge? If so, what is it? How do they perceive their environmental contexts? How do they learn within them? Have they constructed any models that we can describe as sustainable, viable, and replicable models of development? Was there any kind of learning embedded in these models? If so, how was this community and individual learning conceptualized, designed, and institutionalized? This paper examines these concepts and explores ways of investing in the future of developing nations using lessons learned from grassroots communities. It proposes a new strategy for development practitioners: one that uses popular knowledge to construct a new way of learning, a new way of living.

Years of work in developing countries have led many development practitioners to the conviction that development has become an activity which breeds and perpetuates the dependence of recipient countries on donors. The overarching principle of empowerment and enablement which true development calls for seems lacking in the bilateral and multilateral aid scene. Development projects appear to be governed more by a 'terms of reference' imperative than by true change and transformed lives. Donors seem more preoccupied with the input-output considerations than by lasting change in communities brought about by a transformed way of viewing and doing things.

Concomitantly, the growing trend towards globalization has led to a growth of patterns in consumption, production, and trade that seem to be slowly eroding respect for popular knowledge and valuing instead mega trends led by a few powerful giants in the global economy. These giants, by and large, have thus far demonstrated little respect for local knowledge, for nature, or for indigenous patterns of consumption, production, and learning. Thus, while learning in the formal economy is transferred across boundaries through governments and private-sector conglomerates, vital popular knowledge survives in local communities, and struggles to transfer its riches via a vast network of NGOs in the developing world.

This paper will discuss learning in the non-formal sector of education within the context of grass-roots development. It will explore the rich world of transformative learning in which adults engage. It will critically assess the predominant paradigm adopted by governments and policy-makers in the field of development and seek alternatives to that paradigm.

What Does an Ecological Approach to Education Mean?

In Egypt, ecology is equated with the natural environment. But in our view, an ecological approach to education implies adopting an approach that is cognizant of both the physical and natural environment, as well as the social and cultural environments.

For instance, if we were to focus on rural communities in Upper Egypt (the South), we would have to look at both the agricultural environment of the land and its related activities, as well as the social structures which predominate in that region, and link both of these environments to the historical patterns of rural productive activities: animal husbandry, community organizing, housing construction, parenting, pooling family incomes, gender roles, health interventions, going to market, dealing with local structures, expressing oneself in music and dance, rites of passage, death and mourning, etc. In short, an ecological approach to education would have to include all these variables as parameters to guide the teaching/learning process and to assist the designers of curricula in producing an ecological learning experience.

To give a concrete example: rural women bake traditional bread in mud ovens using cow dung for fuel to produce a huge crepe-like bread consisting of wheat, maize, and fenugreek. This last seed is a natural preservative and therefore 'ecologically' sound. Cow-dung cakes are a source of renewable energy in a country which lacks forests and firewood, and where kerosene and gas are prohibitively expensive for the poorest of the poor. But both mud ovens and cow-dung cakes are perceived by development planners to be 'ecologically' unsound technologies: the first because it allows billowing smoke to be vented into the faces of the bakers and thus affect their eyes negatively; the second because it is perceived to be full of bacteria harmful to the women who have to handle it – that is, shape it, dry it, and store it on rooftops before using it for fuel. Consequently, major development efforts have supplanted this technology and this bread with modern bakeries, state or privately owned, that produce white bread from wheat received by Egypt as aid from donor countries.

This bread has no natural preservative, rots after a few hours, and is produced using technologies that are not connected to previous generations' know-how or to the local ecology. Consequently, an ancient traditional 'craft' is lost and younger generations are unwilling to learn it or use it. Additionally, a new national dependence on wheat received as 'aid' from foreign donors is entrenched. Dependence, disempowerment, and lack of proactivity are fostered on a national strategy level.

An ecological approach to learning within the context of food processing and production in this instance would involve a very different approach than summarily dismissing a way of life rooted in the natural, social, and cultural contexts of bread-baking in this region. An 'ecological' approach would seek to:

- uphold the use of natural preservatives;
- maintain practices of using renewable energy;
- elevate and remunerate the labour of women spending hours in front of a hot oven.

But an ecological approach would also:

- seek ways to slightly modify the technology to offset its negative health effects (e.g., vent pipe, test cow dung for authoritative data on its danger to human health, invent newer, safer ways to dry and store it);
- market these 'ecologically' produced food items and draw young girls into the trade to protect the craft;
- seek alternative renewable energy sources by mixing animal and human waste to produce bio-gas to fuel the modified mud oven, etc.

How Are the Main Environmental Issues Expressed and Understood in Our Contexts?

The urban context of development in Egypt presents further insights into the disconnectedness which exists between how people learn to change the environment at the community level, and how official policy either remains aloof from that valuable learning, or insists on using ready-made formulas from other cultural contexts. The result is a dysfunctional national development as each trend pulls the country in a different direction – one drawing from the experiential base of inherited models of living, and the other a predominantly global paradigm which is not referenced to the vernacular model.

An ecological assessment of the world's solid waste situation draws our attention to the escalating magnitude of the volume of man-made waste. This is a result of increased consumption levels and wasteful patterns of use of the earth's non-renewable resources.

Garbage is perceived as a nuisance by Egypt's affluent and formally educated. Not so by the garbage collectors of Cairo. This socially excluded group has learned – and has taught us – to radically alter our perceptions of garbage and perceive it as a tremendous resource. Through their indomitable strength, hard work, perseverance, and ingenuity, they have shown a megalopolis of 15 million how to recover and recycle 80 per cent of the waste they collect. Their methods are based on culturally intrinsic ways of dealing with solid waste. These go back to:

- the natural environments of rural communities (raising animals on food remains);
- their social inclination of conservation and hatred of wasting;
- a cultural heritage of returning every discarded element to its original state;
- production patterns that use total, closed systems that do not 'leak' any waste into the environment.

> *... but no one thinks of a poor man as wise or pays any attention to what he says. It is better to listen to the quiet words of a wise man than to the shouts of a ruler at a council of fools.*
>
> Ecclesiastes 9:16–17

Unfortunately, this is perceived by the educated elite as 'dirty,' low-level technology and fit only for those who are forced by poverty to eke out a living from dirt heaps. Such a perception is coloured by the unhygienic way in which the garbage collectors perform their recovery and recycling trade, and because garbage is of necessity an unhygienic material to handle manually.

It would seem more 'ecologically' sound to perceive the enormous benefits gained by such 'lowly' activities, namely:

- creation of unlimited employment opportunities for youth
- recovery of 80 per cent to 90 per cent of the materials that the rich use and discard in their consumption patterns
- production of new materials from existing ones
- protection of the earth's non-renewable resources
- protection of land from being used as sanitary landfill
- protection of the air from the uncontrolled burning of garbage
- saving of energy by using basic technology rather than hi-tech energy-consuming technologies
- creation of learning environments in which youth learn to operate, maintain, and repair machines
- application of science in informal learning settings
- generation of income
- preservation of family-style, family-owned businesses
- creation of economically thriving communities
- creation of supporting industries
- fostering of an inventive, innovative spirit
- transfer of technology between and among communities
- creation of an entrepreneurial class that has business and management skills
- contribution to personal family and community welfare as a result of increased income, productivity, and higher living standards
- spillover effect in improved housing construction
- increased enrolment of children, especially girls, in primary education
- contribution to national development

The Environment of Our Life and Work – Where Our Lives Flourish or Are Diminished

The physical space where the garbage collectors live and work is made up of a series of excluded enclaves surrounding Cairo. They constitute five neighbourhoods: Mokattam, Tora, Ezbet el Nakhl, el Moetamadeyya, and el Baragiil.[1] There the garbage collectors maintain ties with their rural origins by hanging on to their animal breeding trade. They preserve community organization by intermarrying and living in extended family situations, and kinship ties predominate both in terms of solidarity and rivalry. The latest generation, though, represents a new breed. Their parents came to Cairo in the late 1940s and early 1950s, but they were born in the capital itself.

Garbage villages in Egypt are an urban phenomenon which dates back to the late 1940s. They are informal settlements inhabited by people who migrated from the rural south of Egypt to the outskirts of Cairo, specifically from the province of Assiut, 400 kilometres south of the capital. They formed an agreement with the *waahis* (from the oases of Egypt) to take over the collection and transport trade of household waste. The *waahis* had been organized in collecting paper from the homes of Cairenes, as there was a market for this paper in public baths of Cairo and among traditional *foul medammes* (Egyptian fava beans) merchants. The understanding was that the garbage collectors (*zabbaleen*) would continue to deliver the paper to the *waahis*, while keeping the food and any other components for their benefit. They ingeniously saw profit in using the organic component to raise animals and to trade metals and plastics which had begun appearing in household waste in the 1950s.[2]

Up until 1990, garbage collectors used to set out in donkey-pulled carts to individual residences in Cairo. From 1990 they began converting to mechanized trucks. They were thus responsible, in large measure, for the improved technical expertise of the city's solid waste system. Although the decision to convert to motorized trucks was made by the authorities, minimal assistance was extended to the *zabbaleen* in the conversion to the new system. No credit was extended to them to purchase their own trucks, and no driving lessons or literacy in road signs or basic Arabic were offered. Yet they made the strategic decision to comply with the new system and came up with adaptive strategies to function within it.

Learning Content

The Mokattam recyclers improve environmental strategies and decision-making

Some of the strategies the *zabbaleen* employed revolved around market information, which dictated renting a truck from outside the neighbourhood for only a few hours. This meant having to change environmental strategies for collecting solid waste. Thus they adopted the habit of using bigger cloth containers, which allowed them to collect garbage from several buildings and store it at the corners of streets, in anticipation of the rented truck and hired driver. This meant that they did not need to rent the truck and driver for the full six hours that the collection task required. Instead the truck could roll through the assigned route and quickly pick up the large containers which had been 'planted.' The activity lasted two hours instead of six.

A further strategic decision was based on an investment and credit acquisition initiative. This was to acquire the capital to purchase trucks. The *zabbaleen* did this by selling any gold belonging to their wives or daughters; by pooling cash savings among brothers; by selling any remaining small plot of land or house in their ancestral village; or by getting credit from loan sharks in the neighbourhood.

A third decision was in the social field: the *zabbaleen* decided to teach their sons to drive and to give them an education. In later years, this was to prove to have been a critical decision in increasing their social mobility and their acceptance by Cairenes at large. Some learned to drive themselves.

The Mokattam recyclers improve the implementation of environmental strategies

The *zabbaleen* collectively upgraded the technical capability of the city of Cairo to manage its solid waste. Today, they have established a daily door-to-door pick-up of an estimated three thousand tons of household waste. This is about one-third of the garbage that Cairo, one of the world's megacities (estimated population 15 million) produces.[3] In addition to the three thousand tons managed daily by the informal-sector *zabbaleen* system, another third of the waste generated is collected by municipalities. It is transported to large, open, unmanaged dumps outside the city limits. The remaining 30 per cent is left uncollected on the streets of Cairo. It is subject to uncontrolled burning by residents, driven by frustration into taking survival initiatives to offset the negative health impacts of rodents and various disease vectors.

The *zabbaleen* take the garbage back to their neighbourhoods and sort it into separate recyclable components: paper, cardboard, plastic, cloth, glass, tin, aluminum, food, animal bones, etc. The food is fed to pigs, and the other items sold to recycling centres in the neighbourhood.

Of all the collection systems which service the city of Cairo, the garbage collectors' system has proved to be the most regular. The reason for this regularity springs from the survival strategy of making a living from the garbage, since the fee for such a service traditionally went to the *waahi*. This sense of survival is so deeply rooted in the *zabbaleen*, as individuals and as a community, that they have never given up on the city of Cairo and expressed their anger at it when it does not seem to learn from them. Indeed, at times the city shifts them about, moving them from one neighbourhood to the next without thought for how this will affect collection routes or the efficacy of service. Other groups in Egypt have reacted to similar poorly designed environment and development initiatives with violence and criminal activities. In contrast, the *zabbaleen* have responded, each and every time, by coming up with amazingly creative strategies to make the most of the new situation with the city and to improve its implementation of environmental strategies.

The Mokattam recyclers improve environmental information and technical expertise

A total of about forty thousand people are engaged – either directly or indirectly – in the collection, transport, recovery, and recycling aspects of managing the solid waste of one-third of the city's household waste.

Most of these people live in the garbage neighbourhoods. Many young men from other neighbourhoods seek and find employment in the small- and medium-sized recycling workshops owned and operated by the *zabbaleen*. In 1996, at least two hundred of these workshops existed in Mokattam alone. They employed an estimated 1022 youth, and had invested a total of U.S. $287,045 in start-up capital investments, mainly in plastic granulators, paper compactors, cloth grinders, aluminum smelters, and tin processors. Supporting industries to these main industries spread throughout the neighbourhood.[4]

The *zabbaleen*, therefore, improved the city's knowledge of how to handle man-made municipal solid waste. They demonstrated to Cairo how this waste could be recovered and reprocessed to create new wealth, employment, and economic opportunity, while at the same time protecting the environment from incineration and landfilling, and the need to extract new materials from its non-renewable resources. They have provided information about their ability to recover and recycle household waste (80% to 85%), and their performance exceeds that of many industrialized countries, such as Germany and Denmark.[5] They have also improved the city's employment generation potential – 40,000 jobs to handle 3000 tons of garbage daily *at no cost to the government*. And they have created a sustainable model of cleaner cities revolving around employed youth.

In short, they have created *a city that learns*. And learning cities are sustainable cities.

The Mokattam recyclers institutionalize environmental planning and management

> *I will destroy the wisdom of the wise and set aside the understanding of scholars. So then, where does that leave the wise? Or the scholars? Or the skillful debaters of this world?*
>
> 1 Corinthians 1:19–20

It would have therefore been extremely disconcerting if the official trend in solid waste management had neutralized the practical, experiential knowledge of these local communities. The rootedness of the practice of the garbage collectors in Egyptian history and culture has scientific and technological value from the environmental point of view. Its immense contribution to the education of entire communities at the local level cannot be denied.

In Cairo, the credibility of the *zabbaleen* would have been lost but for the partnerships they forged with Egyptian professionals who combined their competencies with the popular knowledge in the community to create new situations and new measures for change.

Association of Garbage Collectors for Community Development (AGCCD)

Two non-profit organizations institutionalized the know-how of the *zabbaleen* and channelled more innovative and creative interventions in the area of solid waste management. These were to change the face of environmental planning and management in Egypt. The first was the Association of Garbage Collectors, through which the credit program for small- and medium-sized development was implemented. Additionally, this NGO implemented the first experiment in Grameen-style lending in Egypt and planted the seeds of the Primary Health Program in the neighbourhood. It experimented with new institutional arrangements for waste companies to service the city[6] and also established a veterinary clinic in the heart of the neighbourhood. AGCCD was registered in 1976. The board consisted mainly of garbage collectors from the community, the neighbourhood religious leaders, and entrepreneurs from the recycling industries of Cairo.

Other community groups sprang up in the neighbourhood. Various attempts were made to coordinate efforts among them and to create linkages that would magnify individually implemented interventions. Some succeeded; others failed.[7]

Association for the Protection of the Environment (APE)

Of the forty thousand adults that handle Cairo's solid waste in all five neighbourhoods, one-half are women. They are almost exclusively responsible for the manual sorting of household waste into its recoverable components. Only 15 per cent to 20 per cent is not recovered. This is transported to Cairo's main municipal open dump, where it is left without any sanitary treatment. While the collection of garbage is the domain mainly of men and children, the task of manually sorting the garbage into separate piles of recyclables belongs to the women and adolescent girls. These girls can no longer accompany their fathers on the garbage routes as Upper Egyptian cultural norms dictate that they stay home in order not to jeopardize family honour.

Registered in 1984, APE started operating its first project – a composting plant – in 1987. The rag recycling centre was launched in 1988, followed by a paper recycling project, a children's club and nursery for infants, a mother and child health project, and an adolescent girls health project in 1996. The NGO is governed by a nine-member all-volunteer board, which played an active role in project implementation for the first seven years of its life. It has now trained a staff of forty-five people from the neighbourhood to manage projects, but still plays an active role in strategic planning, fund-raising, advocacy, monitoring, and evaluation.

A pilot project testing at-source separation of garbage in two neighbourhoods in Cairo (Manial and Deir el Malak) constituted a major intervention in the area of providing information for the development of new environmental strategies for the city and improving decision-making about how to produce a cleaner city while ensuring a more efficient use of resources for change.[8] The pilot project findings were that 65 per cent of residents in the two sample neighbourhoods continued to separate their garbage at source into two components – organic and non-organic – for two years.

This pilot project was critical in proposing a new environmental strategy that would affect all environmental planning and management strategies for cities in Egypt. It primarily concerned the role of women since it precluded the need for them to sort rotting garbage manually ever again. As residents were to separate their garbage into food and non-food components, the plan was to deliver the organic waste to composting plants around Cairo while keeping the non-organic waste in Mokattam to sort and separate for processing and remanufacturing in the micro-enterprise workshops run by the men. The driving concern behind it was women's exposure to health hazards while sorting. This pilot project indicated that:

- sorting time was reduced by 50 per cent (two instead of four hours per day);
- women would have more time to work, learn, and earn in other productive activities in the neighbourhood revolving around 'clean' recycling industries, namely in the rag recycling and paper recycling projects run by the Association for the Protection of the Environment (APE);
- women and children would be spared the health hazards that they were exposed to while sorting garbage manually;
- no animals would be raised in any of the garbage neighbourhoods in Cairo;
- a more sanitary situation would prevail in the homes and neighbourhoods of the garbage collectors, who manage one-third of the city's household waste;
- there would be potentially more non-organic waste to recover as it would be unsoiled;
- more income would be generated from recycling industries;
- the loss of income from raising animals would be compensated for by the increased income from recycling more recovered, unsoiled, non-organic waste;
- Cairo would thus become a cleaner city as more garbage would be processed in a sanitary way and fewer animals would be raised in the urban context

Other studies implemented in the Delta (Dakahleya) and Upper Egypt (Sohag) indicated that Egyptians traditionally sort organic from non-organic household waste. The habit dies out among residents who have for a long time adopted more urbanized patterns of living, and achieved higher income levels.[9]

In 1998, APE began to transfer its institutional know-how from Mokattam to another garbage collectors' neighbourhood in Cairo, Tora, and the affluent neighbourhood it services – Maadi. Hand in hand, two communities were learning from each other how to adapt the new system and fine-tune it to accommodate the technical, cultural, and social contexts of both. This was truly adult education at its best.

The Mokattam recyclers make more efficient use of resources for effective change

Born in Cairo, the young garbage collectors have little or no roots in the villages from which their parents came. They are a new urbanized generation who grew up in the context of the oppression and exclusion of their parents, but who have experienced opportunity through limited education – formal and non-formal. Their formal education did not equip them with jobs, but their non-formal education at the recycling machines afforded them employment, income, social standing, and empowerment. However, without their encounter with the formal school system, their socialization into mainstream Cairo would not perhaps have been as complete. For that portion of their education did equip them to deal with society at large, and with local municipalities, government offices, and trading partners from outside of their neighbourhood.

Having come from a family and rural tradition of recovery and recycling, they preserved their culture well in urbanized patterns of living. They further maintained kinship and solidarity ties with their community and did not leave it when they gained social and economic mobility. The majority stayed behind. Some did leave – those who had deep traces of oppression and wanted to break away from their painful childhood memories. Others simply left the neighbourhood because they married men from other neighbourhoods who had housing available elsewhere.

The ones who led this experiment in urban living fought for their survival with a resilience that allowed them to live through several official evictions and resettlement plans around the fast-growing city of Cairo. When they finally settled in the 'belly' of the Mokattam hills in 1974, as they put it, it was a calculated decision designed to make it harder for an official eviction to occur once again. Two generations therefore lived through the experience of being rejected by the city they were serving. Each time they carved out a niche for themselves in a new spot on the fringes of the city – on the fringes of existence.

To their great credit, they did even more. They enlarged that niche, expanded their penetration into Cairo, and upgraded their trade. In 1986 they introduced the small- and medium-sized recycling projects. In 1988 they trained their first team of thirty primary health-care visitors. In 1987 they started their first rag-recycling project. In 1990 they began converting from donkey-pulled carts to motorized trucks. In 1992 they formally launched their paper-recycling project. They never stopped learning. They flowered in knowledge even while surrounded by rotting garbage, animal manure from their pig pens, burst sewage pipes from poorly implemented infrastructure projects, and rats amongst the uncollected garbage outside their homes and on their streets remaining from their sorting activities. And the major sources of institutional learning about life were the 'projects' implemented by NGOs.

How Is Community Basic Education Connected to the Environment?

At the Mokattam rag recycling centre, a deliberate and conscious decision to link the natural, social, and cultural environments to basic education was made from the very beginning.

The *natural* environment was one of garbage – a dirty environment of man-made waste in which people had survived by their ability to recover as much as was humanly possible, to process, remanufacture, and trade it. This had exposed them to a *social* environment of untold health hazards and unspeakable human indignity. It had made them one of the most severely excluded groups in society and had deprived them of basic human rights of education, health, and civic participation. It had made them incredibly stoic, resourceful, and determined to survive. But it had also left them with a deeper experience of injustice and oppression than any other group in Egypt. The *cultural* environment was one of building on ancient models of production, conservation, and materials-use. These realities all went into the design of a basic education program revolving around the collection, transport, recovery, recycling, and trading of man-made waste. The design of this experiment followed the following arguments.

Argument 1: The natural environment had to consist of clean man-made waste. The educational program could not revolve around an undignified learning setting or learning situation. However, the curriculum would be based upon the very essence of that aspect of their activities and their lives: sorting garbage. Therefore the physical environment of clean rags would elevate the sorting expertise to a learning setting that would lead to the highest level of aesthetic and cultural expression: handmade crafts from organic fibers of the world's most-renowned cotton – Egyptian cotton – made by the world's most unique and renowned people – the garbage collectors of Cairo, and with the same hands that had suffered unspeakable indignity by having to sort rotting filth manually 365 days out of every year.

Argument 2: The social environment not only would be one that protected the learners' health from hazards of man-made waste, but also one that taught people about how to protect themselves from the health hazards of handling Cairo's garbage at home. Thus the health education component became of paramount importance at the rag recycling centre. Indeed, learning about health was celebrated by de-licing hair together in a party mood, receiving prizes (towels, soap) at the event, and learning new things about health at the Monday noon-time 'parties.'

Argument 3: The non-formal school used *culture* and *theatre* to learn about health. The girls and women produced puppets from rags, made up their own plays, presented socio-dramas, and composed songs and poems around health themes.

Argument 4: The *social* context of oppression and exclusion dictated that the admission policy specifically target those who were illiterate, those who had never gone to school, and those who were utterly poor. Children who went out on the garbage route therefore got first priority. They were extracted from a situation of oppression and placed in a healthy, dignified situation of 'learning and earning.' Observers from the West, from formally schooled economies and contexts, called this 'child labour'!

Argument 5: The design deliberately planned to transfer learning to the home and ensure the 'school's' holding power over students by altering the perception of the school/centre's walls and enlarging the area of the 'school' or 'learning place' to include the home, the street, and the community at large. Thus the students continued producing at home, came to school for their 'homework assignments / production orders,' and back for 'grading homework / quality control.'

Argument 6: Justice issues were further incorporated into the design by ensuring equal access to education. The better producers did not get more work assigned to them, but 'pay/grades' were based upon merit.

Thus the concept of excellence in education was upheld as the producers did not compete among themselves. Instead, they competed against a 'standard,' i.e., quality.

Argument 7: The *cultural* imperative of conserving the earth's non-renewable resources meant that the design had to make use of every scrap of rag received, and that rags would not be purchased to make quilts. Only what the textile and garment industry discarded would be *recycled*.

Argument 8: Further, *cultural* tools were preserved by using a handloom to weave rag rugs. This ancient Egyptian piece of technology was not supplanted by more modern technology imports. Cultural production models of collaboration rather than competition were the rule. Weavers who had no room in their homes for a loom could weave at a cousin's or girlfriend's if her parents approved.

Argument 9: Cultural patterns of women's mobility were observed. The school – i.e., the NGO – sent a truck to collect and transport the rags from the formal sector textile industry to the centre. The centre was located in the heart of the neighbourhood. Women and girls would go out to local sales events always accompanied by a volunteer from the educated classes. Men would not be allowed at the training centre – i.e., the school – so that husbands and parents would not fear sending their wives or daughters to socially 'dangerous' situations.

Argument 10: Publicity about the school encouraged, indeed urged, people to visit the centre. Shuttle buses would facilitate and assure a steady stream of admirers and shoppers. Self-awareness, pride, and new self-perceptions and valuation would result. Not to mention increased sales and full pockets!

The elements of this design rested upon finding new solutions to the learning and development dilemma by finding a direct relationship between local indigenous knowledge and formal scientific knowledge. Why erase and replace the old with the new? What parts of the old could contribute towards the new in a dynamic, innovative way? Where were the linkages between the two? How were they to be connected?[10]

The following lessons were learned from the production process of the *zabbaleen*:

1. Collecting man-made waste efficiently made sense – the NGO collected clean rags directly from the textile factories around Cairo just as the *zabbaleen* collected household waste directly from the homes of Cairenes.
2. Maintaining gender differentiated roles of the trade were necessary

for the respectful and sustained implementation of the project – women and adolescent girls were never sent to collect the rags, but only men and children in the NGO truck.
3. Upholding the specificities of old social and cultural norms increased acceptance of the new model of learning and working. Men were not allowed on the premises of the women's development building. Women and girls would not go to sales events unchaperoned by people from the educated elites. This practice gave the men assurance that their women were in good hands. The centre was physically placed right in the heart of the community – girls and women would not have to brave the traffic of Cairo or leave their safe and 'allowable' space. The invisible walls of the neighbourhood always surrounded them. They were always close to home and so could care for their siblings and aging parents.
4. Trading with outside partners was essential and inevitable, as the *zabbaleen* had shown. The NGO used all of its formal learning to market the new crafts intelligently and aggressively. Having a formal address, telephone number, fax, web-site, catalogue, bank account, etc., were ways that the 'new' linked up to the 'old,' the 'formal' to the 'informal.'

After six years, five hundred girls and women were trained. They had been selected on the basis of need (economic) and dispersion from different homes, so that a target of five hundred graduates would be placed as development 'seeds' in five hundred homes out of the seven hundred in the neighbourhood, over a six-year period.

- Of the five hundred, 250 continued to be regular producers, earning from a low of EGP 80 per month to a high of EGP 350 (U.S. $1 = EGP 3.34 in 1996).
- This income was spent on nutrition for children, health care, education, clothing for feast occasions, and household appliances, in that order.
- Sixty-four per cent (64%) of the women were practising family planning.
- Fifty-six per cent (56%) said they would not circumcise their daughters who had still not been circumcized.
- Seventy per cent (70%) of the single girls said they would not circumcise their daughters when they got married.
- Over 250 girls had achieved functional literacy in 1996 (measured

by tests administered by the centre and not by the national literacy examination).
• The people – girls, women, men – and their institutions (NGOs) had begun teaching others their trade. APE established a training department in 1997 and began instructing trainers to spread the 'gospel' of recycling to Egypt and, indeed, to the whole world. Partnerships with other NGOs in North Africa (Tunis and Morocco), the Middle East (Gaza), Africa (Senegal), and Latin America (Colombia) served as conduits for the exchange of learning. A South-South dialogue had begun.

Development projects, therefore, provide invaluable non-formal learning settings where individuals who participate learn new problem-solving techniques, new work methods, and new ideas. These individuals then go on to change the face of their community. The rag-recycling centre was designed as an alternative educational delivery system which offered learning in out-of-school settings, as well as earnings outside both the formal sector and 'sweat-shop' settings. It is doubtful that the interdisciplinary nature of the development curriculum at the rag-recycling school could have met with donors' approval from inception to implementation. Quantitative data could not have been offered from the outset since the experiment had to be allowed to flow freely in response to learners' needs and community preferences.

These preferences covered economic, environmental, social, financial, and political sectors. The experiment indicated that multi-disciplinary approaches to education and multi-sectoral approaches to development were complementary. They belonged to the world of 'ecological' adult learning. Education and development were therefore inextricably intertwined to produce change. How therefore could development planners view that activity in 'terms of reference,' or 'input-output' terms? Did people's learning to live intelligent, productive, environmentally responsible lives start and stop so rigidly as donor-driven development project documents seem to imply? Do we not need a rethinking of the established, predominant paradigm governing development, learning, and the environment?

What does literacy mean?

For too long we have defined literacy as the mastery of the written word. National plans for development have focused major efforts on the 'eradication of illiteracy' as if it were a disease. Even though nobody contests that a nation's ability to progress depends in large measure upon its educated, literate population, the time has come to critically examine our understanding of what 'literacy' means.

Years of action research and field-based practice have led some to propose a new definition of literacy – one that is linked to the environment of poverty. In 1992, a rag-recycling project at Mokattam garbage village expanded from a weaving project (established in 1987) to a patchwork-quilting one. While the rag recyclers in the first stage were weavers at a hand loom, and mostly young girls, the patchwork quilters were married women who could not take the back-breaking work of weaving at the loom for three hours a day.

The weavers had become engaged in literacy classes as a result of carefully designed strategies to generate their desire to acquire literacy, but the production in the patchwork process involved more numeracy than literacy. Thus the patchwork project succeeded in generating a desire for numeracy only. Furthermore, the weavers were young girls who did not have to rush back home to care for families and so could attend literacy classes. The patchwork quilters, on the other hand, had time constraints which made it impossible to offer learning in a classroom setting and at set times.

The teaching methods employed were therefore extremely flexible, individualized, and personalized. Teachers were trained to deliver this learning as part of the 'production' and 'work order distribution' function. Thus they were unaware of the full pedagogical/andragogical implications of what they were doing.

Adult women were self-directed to learn only as much as was relevant. The work orders involved geometric designs and patterns in which the rags had to be stitched together and delivered. The women were therefore interested in learning how much of each pattern (square, rectangle, triangle, octagon, etc.) needed to be sewn together to produce the final pattern.

Each month, a different geometric configuration would be requested of each woman producer. The scale of the patterns differed with the differing availability of rags in quantity and colour. These rags were delivered to the non-formal 'school' as a donation from the textile and ready-made garment industry. The teachers therefore had no idea what 'lessons' they would be 'teaching' to their students, that is, what 'orders' they would be 'placing' with their 'producers.' They therefore had to be prepared with 'lesson plans' or 'work orders' that could be tailored to:

- learners' needs = producers' needs;
- learners' readiness = producers' competence;
- availability of raw material = content matter;
- market demands based on:
    - inventory to satisfy daily and weekly sales
    - seasonal sales
    - export orders
    - customized orders.

This meant that for both the 'teacher' (project officer) and the 'student' (producer) learning had to be completely fluid, flexible, and dynamic.

As a result of this repetitive, but non-monotonous, acquisition of learning content, after a few months into the teaching/learning cycle, both 'teachers' and 'students' had acquired an aptitude for learning which far surpassed that of a student in a classroom devoted to basic literacy, in the sense that term is traditionally defined.

For one, it taught students to anticipate the unknown, the unfamiliar, and unexpected. Nobody could predict the quantity of rags that were to be received as donations, their colour, or their size. Nobody could actually predict the trend of sales in a given week or the customized orders that were to be received. This uncertainty about the next 'units' of learning gave both 'teachers' and 'students' a remarkable capacity for adaptability, ingenuity, and proactiveness.

Women transferred this learning by demonstrating an increased ability to face unforeseen circumstances in their personal lives. The physical environment in which they lived – twelve hundred tons of garbage arriving in the neighbourhood every day, to be sorted by them, their daughters, or neighbours – made it an environment fraught with health hazards, crises, and emergencies.

Women now knew where to take a child who had accidentally been burned by an open fire, how to find a husband who had been thrown in jail for illegally going out on the garbage route in a donkey-pulled cart instead of a truck, how to procure an identity card, how to open a savings account at the post office, etc.

Was that literacy? Or wasn't it?

Our research contends that while they may not have acquired a competence to read and write the written *word*, they had acquired a competence to read the *world*.

A Fundamental Cultural Factor and a Justice Issue

This local initiative by the garbage collectors of Cairo demonstrates how a small, disenfranchized community hung on to a national culture of preservation of the environment that was not valued or understood by national policy-makers because it was perceived to be backward and technologically incompetent. This knowledge was rooted in popular knowledge, transmitted by practice through generations, and provided the framework for some of the most dynamic learning in the field of non-formal education. This learning involved the environment (managing solid waste); technology (recycling industries); literacy and numeracy; business; health (community-based primary health care); community organizing (NGOs); and technology transfer (through networks of NGOs).

But while non-profit organizations were institutionalizing the know-how of the *zabbaleen* and transferring it, there was still a big learning gap on the part of the municipalities, the public, and the media. This meant that new strategies for information and education had to be designed so that the city of Cairo could learn more. New partnerships needed to be cemented and new processes of decision-making explored. New institutional set-ups as well as a new vision for Egypt's development were also needed. It was for these reasons that Community and Institutional Development (CID) came into being.[11]

In 1997, CID implemented a technology-transfer intervention targeting at-source separation and recycling in the South Sinai (Dahab and Nuweiba).[12] CID and APE Mokattam taught two other NGOs, Hemaya NGO in Nuweiba and Hope Village Society (HVS) in the 10th of Ramadan, 50 kilometres from Cairo, as well as two other towns, how to adopt this technology and adapt it to the peculiarities of a region blessed with some of nature's more amazing wonders – coral reefs in the Red Sea and mountains in the South Sinai.

Recently national development plans in Egypt have called for a major thrust towards the promotion of tourism in the Sinai Peninsula and the Red Sea coast. Tourism represents one of Egypt's main sources of GDP, employment opportunities, and foreign currency reserves. The Sinai, known for its magnificent mountains, beautiful sand beaches, unpolluted waters, and rare corals, is also home to an exquisitely unique fauna and flora – a veritable treasure for both Egypt and the world.

Slowly but surely, that priceless treasure is being destroyed by unchecked development of tourist towns and resorts. It is being destroyed by the conscious and deliberate decisions of politicians and private-sector opinion leaders – a lethal partnership between adults educated in, and graduated from, formal schools and the global economy. By contrast, local populations and NGOs have responded by instituting a model of solid waste recovery and recycling that is rooted in indigenous popular knowledge and characterized by an abhorrence of wastefulness, promotion of sustainable consumption patterns, and the protection of the earth's non-renewable resources.

These recent developments in Egypt have caused many to ponder critically the current learning delivered by the formal system. How can it produce adults who wilfully and knowingly destroy natural and cultural environments? How can they perceive their actions to be constructive? What are their true motives for making decisions which, in the long run, will ultimately lead to ruin? Are they driven by concern for national welfare or are ethical issues waived in the face of greed, self-preservation, and a global trend towards exploitation – of nature, of man, and of dignity?

Be it in urban contexts like Cairo, or rural ones like Upper Egypt, the 'learners' in question are not just the poor, the marginalized. With very little resources and with the help of external partners, they are attempting to effect a change in their situation, a transformation of their realities from one of neglect and need to one of dynamism and productivity. They use age-old approaches in interfacing with their cultural environment. Many of the issues they face have to do with their natural environment.

But the striking feature of today's national development plans is that none of the systems or solutions proposed for these communities is in touch with the people's inherited way of doing things, nor do any of them attempt to understand it. Instead, top-down, blue-print initiatives are administered to local development issues without consulting the local populations. Official solutions have more to do with donor-driven aid, private sector commercial interests, or an emulation of whatever seems Western or modern. Such an orientation fails to validate popular experience based on local practice, and denies populations the chance to learn new ways, to 'invent' and construct their realities by building incrementally on tried and true culturally indigenous patterns of living.

There seems to be an urgent need for the well-fed and the well-read to learn from the less fortunate and to create dynamic links between the two communities with the aim of re-imagining a single world and rebuilding it in a regenerative way that reflects our rich diversities.[13]

Notes

1. Community and Institutional Development (CID), 'Study on Brand Name Fraud' (June 1998), commissioned by Chemonics / Ahmed Gaber Associates.
2. Laila R. Iskandar Kamel, *Mokattam Garbage Village, Cairo, Egypt* (Cairo: Stallion Graphics, 1994).
3. Arab Republic of Egypt, *Environmental Action Plan* (Cairo, 1992).
4. Survey Conducted by Romani Badir Zikry; Commissioned by Community and Institutional Development (CID), 1996.
5. Albert Adriaanse et al., *Resource Flows: The Material Basis of Industrial Economies* (Washington, DC: World Resources Institute, 1997), p. 28. See also Danish Environmental Protection Agency, Ministry of Environment and Energy, *Waste Managemement in Denmark* (1997).
6. Extensive documentation about the Mokattam *zabbaleen* experiment has been compiled by Environmental Quality International (EQI), 3B Bahgat Ali St, Zamalek, Cairo.
7. Elena Volpi and Doaa Abdel Motaal, 'The Zabbalin Community of Muqattam,' *Cairo Papers in Social Science* [American University in Cairo, Social Research Centre] 19, no. 4 (1996).
8. Marie Assaad and Ayman Moharram, 'Final Report on the Separation-at-Source Scheme As Implemented by the Association for the Protection of the Environment' (Jan. 1995); submitted to the Ford Foundation.
9. Community and Institutional Development (CID), 'The Social Development Aspects of Solid Waste Management in Sohag and Dakahleya' (May and August 1996); two studies conducted by CID commissioned by ENTEC Consultants to the Technical Cooperation Office (TCOE) of the Egyptian Environmental Affairs Agency (EEAA).
10. Paolo Orefice, discussion at Alpha Seminar, Nuweiba, South Sinai, Egypt, 18–23 March 1999.
11. Community and Institutional Development (CID) was founded in November 1996 by three people from the private sector and one from the NGO sector. It was specifically created to address the need to search for new formulas for Egypt's economic, social, and cultural development, based on its past history and a recognition of a tremendous untapped reservoir of wealth in its human resource base – its people, the Egyptians. The underlying philosophy of CID is the need for a dialogic approach to development, that is, a respectful partnership between the different segments of

society (the haves and the have-nots); between the different contexts of learning (the formal and scientific, on the one hand, the local and indigenous, on the other); and between the different sectors of the economy (the formal and the informal).

12 CID seeks to create networks among NGOs to strengthen ties and at the same time to connect them to an invigorated private sector in new public/private partnerships which do not rely on donor-driven assistance for development. The author of this paper is a member of APE, CID, and AGCCD, and has been involved with the Mokattam recyclers since 1982.

13. Anthony Flaccavento, 'Sustainable Development Literacy in Central Appalachia' (11 Jan. 1999), draft article presented at the Alpha seminar held in Nuweiba, South Sinai, Egypt, March 1999.

References

Adriaanse, Albert et al. 1997. *Resource Flows: The Material Basis of Industrial Economies*. Washington, DC: World Resources Institute.

Assaad, Marie, and Ayman Moharram, January 1995. 'Final Report on the Separation-at-Source Scheme As Implemented by the Association for the Protection of the Environment.' Submitted to the Ford Foundation.

Assaad, Ragui, and Malak Rouchdy January 1998. 'Poverty and Poverty Alleviation Strategies in Egypt.' Report submitted to the Ford Foundation, Cairo.

Community and Institutional Development (CID). May and August 1996. 'The Social Development Aspects of Solid Waste Management in Sohag and Dakahleya.' Two studies conducted by the CID commissioned by ENTEC Consultants to the Technical Cooperation Office (TCOE) of the Egyptian Environmental Affairs Agency (EEAA).

Freire, Paolo. 1987. *Pedagogy of the Oppressed*. New York: Continuum.

International Development Research Centre (IDRC). 1986. *With Our Own Hands*. Ottawa.

Kamel, Laila R. 1990. 'Innovation and Change in Non-formal Education: Two Experiments in the Cross-Cultural Transfer of Technology [from Mokattam to Sharmoukh and Back].' Ed.D. Dissertation, Teachers College, Columbia University.

– 1994. *Mokattam Garbage Village, Cairo, Egypt*. Cairo: Stallion Graphics.

UNEP and HABITAT. 1997. *Implementing the Urban Environment Agenda: Environmental Planning and Management (EMP) Source Book*. Vol. 1. UNCHS (Habitat)/UNEP, Kenya.

Volpi, Elena, and Doaa Abdel Motaal, 1996. 'The Zabbalin Community of Muqattam.' *Cairo Papers in Social Science* 19, no. 4.

Abundance As a Central Idea in Ecological Approaches in Education

Munir Fasheh

The most transforming single experience in the life of Munir Fasheh was the discovery of his illiterate mother's mathematical ability more than twenty years ago. That experience forced him to reconstruct his perception and conception of reality and knowledge, and altered the direction of his research.

Ecological approaches are linked to the conviction that people living in a certain community are the basic actors in the solution of the collective problems faced by that community. However, they are the solution only if they take their lives and experiences, and what they do, seriously. They do this by reflecting on what they do, expressing it, and communicating it to others so that it becomes part of the basis for building collective understanding and thought. Ecological approaches require a shift of mind that brings current daily activities to the centre of life and learning; they are built on what people have naturally and in abundance.

I started my career as a math and physics teacher. Then, the 1967 Israeli-Arab war broke out. It raised the first doubts in my mind about formal education. One question that became dominant in my mind was how could we make education more relevant, meaningful, and effective? More specifically, in my case, the question was how could I make the teaching of math more relevant to Palestinian society, where I was teaching?

While I was looking – as an educated person faithful to tradition – for answers in books and magazines, I realized that I was living with a very inspiring example at home. I was made blind to it exactly by the rigidity of the ideology I had absorbed and internalized through my school and university education. I started realizing, in the mid-1970s, that my illiterate mother was much better at math than I could ever be! At the time, I was teaching in two universities (Birzeit and Bethlehem), was in charge of math instruction in the West Bank schools, and was training teachers how to teach math![1]

That discovery made me realize several things which, with time, became strong convictions in my life, and which I believe are relevant in thinking about ecological approaches in education.

The *first aspect* is the importance of looking at what people do, how they think, and the tremendous wisdom that they usually embody – all of which are generally invisible to the minds formed by the dominant ideologies in today's world. Thus, the first aspect in ecological approaches is to dig into that hidden treasure and make it visible through some form of cultural expression. That expression could take the form of a dress, as in my mother's case, or the form of an article, a song, a drawing, or a new way of perceiving a phenomenon, defining a word, or articulating a problem. The basis of all learning, I believe, is for people to take their experiences seriously, and as worthy of expression as part of the basis for constructing meaning and understanding. In this sense, each one of us is potentially a creator and a constructor. This is linked to the conviction that what makes every person a distinctive human being, and thus the basis of one's value, is his/her experience. Experience is an abundant commodity in every society: every person has it. Therefore, reflecting on each person's experience and on what the person does, and expressing it, is the most important process in education. The 'secret formula' in using this abundant commodity of experience is to acquire the habit and ability to link our words and ideas with our actions and the context in which we live. Most of the answers are there: people and history have them. Innovation does not mean ignoring people and history, but rather taking into consideration what is there, our place in it, and the direction we want to go; such an innovation improves human paths.

The *second aspect* is that, unlike the type of education I received and disseminated, my mother's knowledge was embedded in life. It was impossible to separate it from context, action, and values. In addition to naturally integrating thinking, practice, and expression, her work was beautiful and useful. In contrast, my type of math was directed mainly towards producing equipment such as tanks and warplanes. Ecological approaches in education have to embody this linkage of thought to context and action, as well as to the aesthetic and the human – in their design and practice, and not only in their rhetoric and intentions.

The *third aspect* is the breakdown of dominant categories. For example, instead of seeing people as either literate or illiterate, I started seeing them as those who connect their words and thoughts with practice and life as opposed to those who do not. For instance, I never heard my mother use a word that was not connected to action or to some concrete aspect in life. By contrast, my teaching was mostly related to ideology; that is, my words and meanings were detached from my life and the context in which I was living. This means we have to make sure that ecological approaches in education do not become an ideology. And we do this by constantly reflecting on life as we experience it, our place in it, and the direction in which we are going.

This leads to the *fourth aspect*, simplicity. The answers to the big problems or issues in today's world are simple; otherwise, we would be sucked into the maze of inhumane solutions. Reading, walking, playing, conversing, listening, expressing, doing, and being generous are traits that are available everywhere, and almost to everybody, and they take care of a lot of the needs related to human existence. It is difficult for me to imagine ecological approaches in education without friendship and generosity being at the heart of that education. Generosity here refers to generosity of the spirit, generosity with time and compassion, and the generosity of listening to other human beings and to nature. Generosity is probably the most distinctive value of the Arab culture. It is about time to include it as a central value in our education. It could be one important aspect that we, as Arabs, could contribute to the world of education.

A basic idea in ecological approaches is respecting both physical and human natures. If there is an 'absolute truth' or an 'eternal truth,' it is that we have to protect the planet we all share from anything that destroys it. This is the cardinal measure. Put differently, the cardinal value in any ecological approach in education is a sense of responsibility towards nature, self, others, and future generations. Most of all, we have to protect the planet from the concepts of development and progress as they are currently perceived and practised. This is the responsibility we share as educators, teachers, health workers, artists, workers, students, farmers, etc.

We have acquired a lot of experience and knowledge during the past three hundred years. We know that science without wisdom cannot sustain life. It can bring control and profit in the short run, but neither happiness nor a healthy relationship with nature or with other people. When Robert Boyle, the famous scientist, declared his intentions to rid American Native Peoples of their ridiculous notions about nature, he probably meant well. Now we have learned to listen to what the Native Peoples of America were trying to tell Boyle and other Europeans: 'The earth does not belong to man; man belongs to the earth.' In contrast to Bacon, Boyle, and others, respect for nature and living in harmony with it is central to the beliefs of the American Native Peoples, as expressed in the proverbial saying 'caring for the seventh generation,' and in the words of the Canadian Cree:

When the last tree is cut down,
the last river poisoned,
the last fish caught,
then only will man discover
that he cannot eat money.

The crucial question then becomes: What does all this mean to education? How is it translated in our conceptions, perceptions, and practices in education? And how can we practise responsibility and act as creators, rather than as consumers?

The answer lies in what I tried to outline above. It lies in acquiring certain simple and abundant abilities and habits. Reading is essential. It is only through reading freely that one can know that a single daily edition of the *New York Times* consumes what is equivalent to 150 acres of trees! You don't expect, of course, to read this in the *New York Times*. The second essential habit is reflecting on what we do and experience, and expressing that and communicating it to others. Other essential habits include dialogue, working in small groups, and building one's own meanings and understanding. These habits are very important if we want to avoid being imitators and consumers.

For at least the past ten years, I have been involved in working at both the local level (Tamer Institute for Community Education in Palestine) and at the pan-Arab level (through the Arab Resource Collective, the *Qalb el-Umour Magazine*, and the Arab Education Forum). All these projects embody learning as the pivotal idea, with a clear commitment to the value of responsibility, and the common theme in all of them is linking words and ideas to context and action. The centrality of vision is also crucial. By vision I mean trying to understand the world as it is, our place in it, and the direction in which we want to go.

There is a special relationship between Arabs and reading and expression. Arabs are known for their hospitality and generosity. Reading is a form of hospitality: it is inviting the ideas, perspectives, and experiences of others into your innermost home – yourself. At the same time, reflecting on and expressing one's experiences is a form of generosity: it is giving the most valuable thing you have – your innermost self. Reading and self-expression are at the heart of Arab culture. The Holy Quran itself opens with the emphasis on reading and learning through the pen.

The habit of reading and the capacity for self-expression are indispensable for learning, for personal and community growth. Both the habit and the capacity are important. One without the other is like walking on one leg; one's growth suffers. Without the habit of reading and the capacity for self-expression, whatever we build will eventually fall apart. Just as food and water are crucial for growth at the physical level, reading and self-reflection and expression are crucial for growth at the intellectual, social, and spiritual levels. In addition, expressing and reading bring out the presence and difference of each person, as well as the diversity in human existence.

One of the most distinctive characteristics of a society is the extent to which it gives value to reading and self-expression. The experience of Córdoba in Spain in the ninth century is revealing. Córdoba, then, had seventy public libraries! Not seventy public schools that lack spirit and life, and that lack habits of reading, expression, and dialogue, but seventy public libraries free of the tyranny of textbooks and grades. Think of this as an inspiring fact, which suggests many possibilities and ideas for change for formal education. Without reading, reflection, and expression, at best, technology allows things to grow around individuals, but not inside them. Replacing reading and self-expression, with television and the computer is like replacing water with cola. The cost is detrimental to the healthy growth of human societies. The television and the computer are tools that can enhance learning, reading, and reflective writing, but they cannot replace them.

Through reading, one can travel around the world, wander into the future, but especially travel into the past. Without knowing history, especially one's own, a person lacks an important part of the basis for developing meaning and understanding.

All of the above form, in my opinion, crucial aspects of ecological approaches in education. Accounts of the approach we took at the Tamer Institute, and which was manifested in its work, have been published mostly in Arabic, though also in English.[2] More recently, I have been involved in the *Qalb el-Umour* youth magazine and the Arab Education Forum. The magazine is to be a forum by and for youth to express and build their own understanding and vision of the world they live in. The editorial collective is formed of about twenty young people from several countries. It is still in its formative stage. The Arab Education Forum tries to do the same at the level of those involved or interested in education in Arab countries. Both projects look at people as springs or streams. Both ask people to articulate what they are doing and why. The idea is to enrich each stream and to help it join other streams in order to form a 'river'; in other words, to help streams avoid becoming isolated and eventually drying up, but instead to join together to form a river that irrigates lands and gives life to communities.

I will choose one example to illustrate. A young man at the Huson refugee camp in Jordan was engaged with some friends in trying to secure funds to address some needs in the refugee camp. Their efforts mostly failed. One of them had an idea: to collect information from inhabitants of the camp about how much the camp spends on cigarettes. They came out with a very troubling, but revealing, answer: at least $2 million a year was spent on cigarettes! The number of inhabitants in the camp is 35,000. Through that simple approach (which I would refer to as an ecological approach), they first of all changed the perception of the problem and, thus, its solution. Second, they used 'research' in a very meaningful and useful way. Third, they put people back in position of actors, not watchers and demanders. Fourth, they loosened the locks in our imaginations that constrain how we perceive the world and what options for action we entertain and take. Opening the imagination to new ways of perception and to new options is the essence of being free. Fifth, the example illustrates how ecological approaches often combine the local and the specific with the global. This example is in fact one of the examples of what we look for for *Qalb el-Umour Magazine.*

The vision of the Arab Education Forum reflects the other main dimension of ecological approaches in education: culture. The central example is the Arabic language. It is inconceivable for me to talk about ecological approaches in education in the Arab world without the Arabic language being the backbone of it.

In the Nuweiba meeting in Sinai, Egypt, I felt each participant came with her/his own stream.[3] The challenge which I see facing ALPHA is how to help form a river out of these various and diverse streams. One way I see to start to do that (and which we have not yet done) is for each of us to reflect on that common experience and express it. Otherwise we will remain isolated and parallel, and never join one another to create the momentum needed for forming a river in ecological approaches in education. This is what I see as practising what I tried to outline in this paper. A river, of course, is not formed out of practising this only once, but every time people meet to discuss the issue of ecological approaches in education (or any other topic, for that matter). I suggest that we practise reflection and expression at the end of every meeting and every seminar. We can reserve fifteen to thirty minutes at the end of every day to reflect on what went on that day and to express it in any form and give it the dimensions we choose. It could be one word, one sentence, one page, one drawing, a small sketch. By doing this, we can build a small 'dam' which collects the few 'streams' that we have in the particular gathering. Hopefully, others will be inspired to build 'dams' in their own places. These streams and dams could slowly pour together and form the needed river/s.

Notes

1 For more details about the 'discovery' of my mother's mathematical ability and what it meant to me, and how it impacted not only my perception of education and of knowledge but also my life and my thinking in general, see my article 'Community Education Is to Reclaim and Develop What Has Been Made Invisible,' *Harvard Educational Review* 60, no. 1 (February 1990).
2 In particular, in two articles in the *Harvard Educational Review*. One is cited in note 1, above. The other is 'The Reading Campaign Experience within Palestinian Society: Innovative Strategies for Learning and Building Community,' *Harvard Educational Review* 65, no. 1 (Spring 1995).
3 In March 1999 Arab and European teams met for the first time at the final seminar of the ALPHA 2000 Project. The seminar report is available at the UNESCO Institute for Education.

Ecology and Basic Education among the Indigenous Peoples of Canada

Serge Wagner

The text explores the relationship between ecology and education, arguing that adult basic education systems often pay little regard to the populations concerned and that they sometimes even contribute to the degradation of their environments. The hypothesis is based on the situation of indigenous peoples in Canada. The solutions that had previously been found to the problem of their relationship with the environment, and the place given to education, are described. The series of shocks caused by contact with European culture is then discussed, as is the role of education in the destruction of endogenous cultures. Two positive cases which are far from typical of general practice are used to illustrate the issue: the Metis and the Inuit. These demonstrate the opportunities for basic education to be part of an ecological perspective. The marginal nature of the two projects reveals a number of obstacles to the adoption of ecological approaches to basic education.

> *The problem of literacy also arises in the industrialized countries. These have had to recognize that despite the positive results of a whole series of new literacy and basic education programmes, deprivation of access to basic education on grounds of race, gender and social origin is still very widespread. Participatory approaches, recognition of cultural diversity, network building, work in partnership and flexibility are ... major requirements. A young Canadian Inuit put it thus: 'Everyone, whether in Canada or elsewhere in the world, can help me to keep my culture and my language.'*
> Report, Fifth International Conference on Adult Education

Background[1]

This text explores the frequently forgotten relationship between education and ecology. The author considers that systems of adult basic education pay too little attention to the populations concerned and sometimes even contribute to the degradation of their environments.

Of the two poles, ecology and education, the more important is the former. In the conventional sense, ecology studies the interactions between people and their environments, natural, interpersonal, social, and cultural. While ecology appears to focus on relationships with the natural environment, the notion of *human ecology* is explicitly interested in interactions between people (individuals and groups) and their environments (Quinn 1971). It shows which values it regards as most important by placing the autonomy and creativity of human beings at the heart of environments and demonstrating concern for preserving humanity's diversified heritage, both natural and cultural.

The dominant contemporary forces, the worldwide mechanisms of globalization and neo-liberalism, reveal themselves to be anti-ecological when they plunder the environment and weaken or dehumanize the relationship between humans and their environment. Worse, they inhibit the expression and creativity of a large number of people, producing exclusion and marginality. The destabilization and disintegration of numerous environments are causing intolerable stress and leading to serious dysfunctions among individuals, communities, and even whole cultures.

Such situations, however, are not inevitable or inexorable. Humanity is in no way condemned to such a fate. Institutions, education being chief among them, have the aim of ensuring the autonomy and self-realization of individuals and societies, and of bringing about the establishment of harmonious relations with the environment. But education systems are themselves enslaved by the dominant forces (whose grip they help to spread) and subservient to goals contrary to the well-being of the people whose culture these forces despise or scorn. In some cases, they even accentuate dependency and dysfunction.

One element of the institution of education interests us here: literacy and adult basic education systems, which are addressed to people whose interactions with part or all of their environment are frequently disrupted. Inadequate basic education can result from various causes: in some cases, breaks that have occurred in the environment; in others, deficiencies even in initial education. Whatever the causes, education systems must face up to a challenge that is above all ecological and ethical by equipping these individuals and groups to (re)gain their dignity and independence and to achieve a more functional and human interaction with their environments.

In the light of the complexity of interactions with different ecosystems, an ecological perspective forces us to refocus education by reconsidering its purpose and methods.

Ecological and Anti-Ecological Approaches among Indigenous Peoples[2]

Indigenous peoples number around 800,000 persons (almost 3% of the Canadian population) and are spread across the territory of Canada. They are subdivided into three main groups: the Indians (624,000 persons), the Metis or half-castes (152,000), and the Inuit (42,000).

Successive waves of indigenous peoples entered America from Asia across the Bering Strait some 12,000 years before our era, and they consolidated their settlement in the two Americas around 5,000 to 8,000 years ago. Indigenous ways of life were particularly influenced by the physical environment, but were nonetheless very diverse: some peoples lived largely as gatherers, others from hunting and fishing, and yet others from agriculture; some were nomads, and some, sedentary. Each was closely dependent on surrounding nature, a dependency that was manifested in 'religions' largely based on a particular cosmogonic vision of the world. Most seemed to coalesce around an enlarged family structure (clan or tribe), a structure that was both simple and complex, in which a high degree of independence and equality was generally manifest.

The lives of the indigenous peoples were remarkably ecological, the natural, interpersonal, social, and cultural environments being linked in an extraordinary symbiosis. In the original indigenous society, everything was culture: 'religion' and art did not exist outside other utilitarian or political activities, but were intricately interwoven with them. There were usually neither social classes nor specialized spheres separating political, economic, religious, or cultural activities. The indigenous peoples accumulated essential, extensive, varied, and precise knowledge of a territory with a difficult topography and climate: dress, means of transport, botany, geography, etc. There was no need of separate educational institutions: the culture, which was transmitted orally and by imitation, was largely created within the extended family and was governed by a set of norms (according to gender, age, season, etc.), in which the oldest members played a predominant role.

This organic indigenous culture was essentially different from an already rationalist European culture, to which it cannot be said to have been inferior (or superior). It was animated by a different paradigm and found its realization according to different perspectives. It was perfectly capable of inventing languages, producing thought, and even representing thought by signs. No fewer than eleven families of languages and a far greater number of dialects could be distinguished at one time.[3] Each of these reflected the experience, way of life, and culture of the people using it. The Inuit, for example, had twenty distinct words to describe different sorts of snowfall.

The 'discovery' of America and Canada by the Europeans profoundly disrupted the lives and cultures of the indigenous peoples, since radical differences separated the societies that were henceforward in contact with one another. The relationships between indigenous and non-indigenous people have evolved over several centuries and are still evolving today. And contrary to the Hollywood cliché of the cruel, primitive 'savage' and the intrepid, intelligent white man, the relations between the societies were for a long time generally harmonious. It was thus often thanks to the indigenous people that the newcomers succeeded in familiarizing themselves with their new environment. Human, commercial, and even military relations were regularly marked by tolerance and respect. In some places and at some times, cooperation even led to a fusion between the two societies by giving rise to a new people, the Metis.

But the dominant model, particularly from the nineteenth century onward, was that of the 'civilizing' offensive of a non-indigenous society that set out to domesticate the indigenous peoples. The aggression, which sometimes took the form of armed struggle, was largely carried out 'peacefully' with the help of the institutions of the dominant society. Education (often supported by the Christian religion) was a favoured tool of linguistic and cultural assimilation and the subjugation of indigenous people. Schools (of inferior quality to those for Whites) were created, responsibility for them being entrusted to religious communities.[4] In them, Christianity and a morality based on Western values were taught; literacy was generally provided in English, and the use of indigenous languages was often forbidden. The natural environment was generally despoiled by colonization and urbanization. Furthermore, the majority of indigenous people were dispossessed of their lands by unequal laws and 'treaties,' and relocated in reserves.

The effects of this huge campaign of acculturation, amplified by the phenomenal and invasive expansion of 'modern' culture and new cultural media, were deadly both to individuals and peoples. These transformations led to the collapse of organic, age-old ways of life and value systems. The indigenous environments (micro-systems) disintegrated as a result of the activities of the dominant macro-system. Most indigenous people became a sub-proletariat subordinated to the non-indigenous society. A number of languages and nations died out or disappeared. Many individuals were drawn into inhibiting and self-destructive behaviour, largely manifested in the interpersonal environment: individual traumatism, alcoholism, drug-dependency, family and community violence, family breakdown, suicide, etc.

Nonetheless, resistance to the oppression was manifested, at first sporadically and then more widely. Many indigenous people, for example, refused the literacy of the oppressors that was forced on them: through large-scale drop-out from school or even, in some cases, by setting schools on fire. Since the second half of the twentieth century, indigenous people have begun working together across Canada: a number of court rulings have been in their favour, and a significant proportion of Canadian and world public opinion has expressed interest in their fate. The phase of domination has slowly started giving way to a phase of negotiation, with a few advances and many retreats.

The education system not only faces accusations,[5] but is also called on to repair past damage and to make a real contribution to the self-realization of the peoples and cultures concerned. In particular, given the scandalously high rates of illiteracy among indigenous people, their massive unemployment, and their linguistic and cultural assimilation, adult basic education systems have an urgent duty to institute self-reform.

The Metis

Unions between Whites and indigenous people have generally been an individual experience. On occasion, however, they have given rise to new cultures and new peoples. The most significant phenomenon was that of the Western Metis Nation, the fruit of an original fusion, rather than a mingling, of the cultures of indigenous nations (in practice, their women) in the Prairies and Euro-Canadians (French- and English-speaking) in the first half of the nineteenth century. These Metis (also contemptuously called half-breeds) adopted a distinct ecological way of life, out of which grew a feeling of separate collective identity. As semi-nomads, they entered upon economic activities associated with wildlife (trapping and hunting), wild plants (gathering of fruits, berries, and roots), and subsistence agriculture. Their semi-nomadism called for movable forms of artistic expression (song, dance, fiddle music, decorated clothing, etc.). As a general rule, relationships among Indians, Metis, and Whites were harmonious. Indians and Metis thus coexisted in this immense territory, and the few Whites were usually sequestered in trading posts.

But the situation changed radically when, following the establishment of the Confederation of Canada in 1867, the Canadian government obtained control of the West and decided to transform the economy and to people it with Whites, thereby subjugating the Indians and Metis, whom they forced into enclaves. When, in 1869, the federal surveyors started to record and draw up boundaries for the lands they were occupying,[6] the Red River Metis took them prisoner, demanded negotiations over joining Confederation and set up their own provisional government modelled on their usual arrangements for the annual buffalo-hunting season. The Federal Government had to back down and accept Metis demands: in 1870 the bilingual province of Manitoba was created, recognizing Metis territorial rights. But the promised rights were not delivered, and after harassment and exploitation, approximately two-thirds of the 10,000 Metis in Manitoba went into exile further west, where 'civilization' caught up with them in the shape of the surveyors in 1885. This time, the balance of forces played out in favour of the armed Federal Government. The Metis Rebellion, which was joined by indigenous peoples, was crushed, and the Metis leader and eight Indians were hanged.

Thereafter, to be a Metis was a term of abuse. Deprived of their lands and ways of life, with their leaders regarded as pariahs or criminals, poor, without rights, and suffering discrimination, the Metis sought to merge into the dominant culture or established themselves outside conventional economic and political life. Moreover, after the abolition of the rights accorded to the French language, French-speaking Metis had also to fight against anglicization.

Oppression and Resistance in Saint-Laurent

The main focal point for the survival of the culture of the French-speaking Metis was the village of Saint-Laurent in Manitoba, on the banks of Lake Manitoba, about 80 kilometres from the provincial capital, Winnipeg.

Settlement by the Metis in Saint-Laurent went back to the first half of the nineteenth century. The place was a seasonal campsite and meeting place for a number of semi-nomadic extended families who lived from fishing, hunting, and trapping, and the land was divided in the Metis manner into long narrow strips, unlike the surrounding homesteads. These Metis found it difficult to adapt to the new economy following the creation of Manitoba and the colonization of the West. The Catholic Church, which set up a mission there in the middle of the century, and then a French school, encouraged them to settle and to integrate into the new economy, which was based on agriculture. There followed decades of confrontation between the two cohabiting cultures.

A considerable proportion of the Metis retained their traditional way of life, their close relationship with nature, their dress, language, customary amusements, and their contempt for institutions, including the Church and schools. In the light of this resistance, the Church encouraged immigration by French-speaking Catholic Whites: *canadiens* (that is, French-speakers) from Quebec, and Bretons from France. A peculiar social and racial hierarchy thus came into being. At the bottom of the ladder were the Indians and the Metis (of whom a couple of missionaries wrote that they were 'a race accursed by God' and 'a band of degenerates and sensualists' [quoted by St-Onge 1990]); next came French Canadians, and the Bretons were at the top. The major study on the Metis by the ethnologist Marcel Giraud, published in Paris in 1945, also refers to the social and racial hierarchy that prevailed in Saint-Laurent, which was exacerbated in the case of mixed marriages:

> It is logical that this fragmentation [of the Metis] should be reflected in the effective isolation of a large part of Metis society in the Western provinces. Groups reduced to this level of decline could not be expected to gain ... right of access to White society. And, when intermarriages occur, they are likely to take place between groups of similar level ... In Saint-Laurent, French and Canadians join in equal contempt for the coloured group. Their hostility is expressed in malicious, almost malevolent, terms, especially by the French families ...: the latter's behaviour, the product of work and self-denial, could not sit in harmony with the habits of the Metis. (Giraud 1945, 1271)

In Saint-Laurent, as elsewhere, to be a Metis became a disgrace. Furthermore, the term Metis no longer referred to an ethnic identity but rather socio-cultural behaviour that was regarded as inferior. In 1887, for example, the parish priest of Saint-Laurent decided to baptize as 'White' the children of 'good Metis families' (St-Onge 1990).

The systematic devaluing of Metis culture carried on for most of the twentieth century. Marriages between Metis, Canadians, and Bretons nonetheless occurred. Over the decades, integration into the dominant society increased, but a large part of the group still retained their cultural heritage and continued, for example, to fish (commercially or for amusement) on Lake Manitoba, especially on the ice in winter.

An important marker of identity was 'Mitchif.' This dialect variant of French, still spoken by a few French-speaking groups of Metis in the West, differs from all other French dialects in America 'in numerous phonological, morphological, syntactic and lexicographical aspects' (Papen 1993, 25). Although largely French, its vocabulary includes some Indian words: for example, from the Cree and Saulteux languages. *Mitchif* was looked down on socially and was passed on within the family and the community, but its use was forbidden through punishment by the two great institutions of assimilation: the Church and schools.

Reassessment and Theatre of Action

Throughout the twentieth century, a significant core group of Metis continued to affirm their identity; this pride became stronger during the 1960s, and the Metis at last gained recognition in 1982 as an indigenous people under the Canadian Constitution. But after more than a century of discredit, the reverse process of reassessment will not easily be achieved within a society that is as much White as Metis.

Today, Saint-Laurent is a small community of around 1,100 inhabitants, almost half of whom say that they are of Metis origin, while it is estimated that between 70 and 80 per cent of individuals really have Metis ancestry (Roy-Sole 1996) – which clearly illustrates the persistent effects of the devaluing of Metis identity. Interracial and intercultural relations are becoming more harmonious. The Catholic Church no longer condemns the Metis and mixed marriages: the French primary school, which no longer punishes the use of *Mitchif* dialect, is even trying to restore the value of the Metis inheritance. The community also organizes the annual festival of 'Metis Days.' Obviously, the reassessment of the Metis people is not without its tensions.[7] The growing anglicization of French-speakers (non-indigenous and Metis) is complicating the situation.

This was the background against which an abortive initiative to teach French literacy transformed itself into the collective creation of theatre. Since the early 1990s, minority French-speaking communities have been trying to promote French literacy among adults with poor literacy or who are becoming anglicized. In Manitoba, the community organization 'Pluri-Elles' provides such activities (focusing largely on academic education) in a number of French-speaking localities. The French-speaking Metis villages (such as Saint-Pierre and Saint-Laurent) were approached, but the individuals targeted (in quite large numbers, according to the figures) showed little interest. This may reflect Metis cultural resistance to the institution of school. At all events, the non-indigenous facilitator brought together the people concerned and, after some discussion, the teaching project was transformed into a project to write a play.

The topic of the play (suggested by a Metis) relates to the first relations between Bretons and Metis in Saint-Laurent, an event that was, as we have seen, significant and dramatic. Entitled *Love and Passion in Saint-Laurent*, the piece dramatizes the tensions resulting from the love and marriage between a Metis and a Breton girl. The play is acted in French, but the Metis speak *Mitchif*. Although the action takes place at the beginning of the century, the tensions addressed are still current: the status of the Metis, relations between Metis and Whites, the relationship between *Mitchif* and French, etc. These topics are treated with humour, but still address the fundamental factors affecting the life and identity of the community, Metis self-esteem, and relationships between individuals. The Metis way of life and language are rehabilitated *a posteriori*, and the legitimacy of different cultures and identities is recognized. Furthermore, surprisingly, past history has been substantially altered. The tensions with the Metis are seen, for example, to result more from misunderstandings and prejudices than from (White) racism. As for the Catholic Church, it is seen to have been neutral between the two communities, having even encouraged the marriage of the two young people.[8] The form taken by the activity is far removed from the usual teaching of French in the province and from the hierarchical relationships to which it generally leads. The subject matter has been agreed upon creatively and cooperatively by the group. Moreover, the scenario is part of the cultural tradition of the Metis and French Canadians, incorporating song, dance, and music.

In retrospect, this theatrical basic education activity has been a cathartic step towards healing deep and inhibiting wounds. It symbolizes and recreates history and the present by calling for values that are inherent to balanced relations between individuals and cultures, such as respect for identities and recognition of the merits of cooperation between individuals and groups. It has been an experiment in 'learning to live together' based on the tolerance and respect for differences promoted by the Delors Commission (UNESCO 1996).

Lastly, this cultural and socio-educational activity has not only affected its immediate participants; it has led to a public performance for the community of Saint-Laurent. The partners were anxious about the reactions to the delicate issues they were addressing. The audience's enthusiastic reception appears to have shown that the community as a whole joined in this vision of its history, present situation, and values. Organizers thus felt legitimated in performing the play for the French-speaking leaders of Saint-Boniface, and then at the Winnipeg indigenous festival, where it was the only event in French and *Mitchif* – which nonetheless demonstrates the continuing fragility of a French-speaking indigenous presence in the Canadian West.

The Inuit

In addition to their being designated indigenous, several other factors align the Inuit more closely with the Metis and the Indians. Their way of life is based on the land as in the (past, present, and symbolic) case of the Indians and Metis. Similarly, the norms and values governing their cultures and social relationships are influenced by unified ways of life that are close to the soil.

The Inuit belong to a circumpolar people of around 130,000 persons spread across Canada, Alaska, Greenland, and Siberia. They speak variants of a common language, *Inuktitut*, which enables them to communicate among themselves (though not without difficulty). The Canadian Inuit (numbering around 42,000) are the last indigenous people to have immigrated into America. Their ancestors, the Thuleans, settled in the Far North approximately 1,000 years before the common era. The Inuit population is currently divided into eight major families dispersed over a vast territory of some 4,000 kilometres (the distance from London to Cairo).

A unique culture has enabled them to survive in one of the most hostile environments on Earth, in the northern tundra at the limit of the tree line. The Inuit adapted to the natural features of the various territories which they inhabited. Most of them lived as nomads, and followed a traditional way of life centred on hunting, fishing, and trapping. Cooperation for survival and the sharing of goods were basic features of their culture. The most important decisions were taken by the elders, in cooperation with the group; should conflicts arise, the main aim was to resolve them harmoniously rather than to condemn a guilty party. As in the traditional culture of other indigenous peoples, Inuit education was informal and non-formal: it was integrated into everyday life and manifested in certain key stages of life. Moreover, the elders were the ultimate repositories of knowledge and skills.

The Inuit have been able to preserve the essential elements of their language and culture. They were indeed protected from 'civilization' until recently by their geographical remoteness, the rigour of the climate, and the lack of interest shown by the non-indigenous society of the South. Religious and educational institutions, which had nonetheless been present for a considerable time, did not take such an aggressive stance as that pursued among the Indians and Metis. It was not even possible to anglicize the Inuit, as most of them communicate with each other in Inuktitut.

The collision with modern Western culture occurred about forty or fifty years ago. The Inuit were then settled in villages by the Federal Government, and the mass media penetrated every home. The Inuit have nonetheless preserved a large part of their culture intact. Their integration into 'modern life' is incomplete because a large number of them (especially the older generation) still pursue the traditional way of life, at least for part of the time: hunting, gathering and fishing, traditional foodstuffs, etc. One of the ways of compensating economically for the decline in the sales of natural products has been the introduction of an international trade in Inuit sculpture. Sculpture has been practised for a long time by the Inuit as part of the traditional way of life. Since the 1950s, sculpture as an art form or for the tourist trade has been encouraged, with varying results.

Overall, however, as happened in the South in previous centuries, the culture shock has been violent. Among the major institutions that have been set up, schools experience serious difficulties in training young people who could take on the new tasks of greater integration into modern society while maintaining the essential features of traditional culture. As a whole, English is the dominant language in schools, while the school drop-out rate is among the highest in Canada.

Upheavals in Nunavut

In the central and eastern portion of the Far North, an unprecedented experiment is currently occurring. On 1 April 1999, a third Canadian Territory came into being, covering a sixth of Canada: Nunavut. A government has been elected with responsibilities for education, language and culture, social affairs, and justice, among other matters. Since the Inuit are by far in the majority (five out of six inhabitants), it is *de facto* an indigenous government. The Inuit of Nunavut thus face the unprecedented challenge of creating an administration that suits their cultural model.

Sanaguavik

The capital of Nunavut is Iqaluit (formerly called Frobisher Bay), situated on Baffin Island. Its population of more than 4,000 persons is growing rapidly, attracting non-indigenous civil servants from the South and Inuit from other villages in Nunavut. Iqaluit is 62 per cent Inuit and 38 per cent non-Inuit, unlike other communities in the Territory in which the percentage of Inuit is close to or above 90 per cent. The pressure of 'modern' culture is probably one of the causes of a certain cultural and linguistic dislocation: massive school drop-out among young people; rapid anglicization of public, social, and even domestic communications; problematic social behaviour, etc. Many young people are rootless, on the fringes both of the dominant invading culture and of the traditional culture of their parents and grandparents.

It is in this context that the Sanaguavik project (meaning 'the place where we sculpt') was devised in summer 1998 for marginalized young adults, and particularly those who had been failed by the education system. The project sets out to achieve a set of complementary objectives: training in sculpture and improvement in the quality and marketing of works produced; socio-cultural and socio-economic integration of young people with problems; and personal, cultural, and community revival. The project lasts six weeks and was offered three times in 1998 to groups of a dozen young adults each, initially only to men, and then to mixed groups.

The approach adopted differs radically from the academic model, such as that of the jewellery course at Nunavut Arctic College, where structured training with courses and credits, according to the prospectus, is offered (largely in English) to 'motivated, responsible and reliable' students. At Sanaguavik, the training is largely given by Inuit master sculptors by way of unstructured learning. Demonstration-discussions are also given by the teachers (elders); more formal courses (for example, in computing or carpentry) are then given. The language of instruction and communication is Inuktitut. The project site is a huge industrial building near the airport, comprising an outside courtyard, a large open warehouse, and a heated room where meals are taken, sculptures are polished and set out, and where the lecture-discussions are held. Most of the participants set themselves up in the courtyard or the warehouse, sometimes going into the closed room to warm up and talk. Tools are available for everyone. Each trainee (and each teacher) selects a material (a piece of stone, a bone, an antler) which he or she starts sculpting, consulting when it seems necessary one of the three master sculptors to whom he or she is attached. Everyone receives a subsistence allowance and pockets half the sale price of his or her work.

The code of conduct is simple: to be punctual and sober, to respect others, and – to sculpt. Any problems in the running of the project are discussed collectively. Breaches of the code are treated in the customary manner: after deliberation by the elders, the solutions reached are entrusted to the group for discussion and execution. Cooperation and collaboration (rather than competition) are the principal ways of working. Moreover, food is traditional: at mid-day every day, participants kneel in the heated room around a plank of plywood, under the direction of the elders, before a raw piece of whale, fish, seal, or caribou. Finally, at the end of every session, the works produced are put on sale at an open evening for the rest of the community, and the event draws on average about two hundred people. Certificates are also given to each participant.

Differences and Similarities

These two projects are obviously different: popular education among the Metis addresses an entire community (which is marginal in several ways), whereas community development among the Inuit addresses marginal young adults in a group which is itself marginal. Above all perhaps, the first project only seems to have taken on its global, ecological direction as a result of suggestions from members of the community, whereas the activity carried out among the Inuit was the outcome of systematic planning. In fact, the second project has been more thoroughly documented and evaluated than the first. However, despite the differences and the 2,200 kilometres that separate them (the distance from Lisbon to Prague), the two activities have a number of common features:

- Both projects started on the fringe of dominant models of basic education in which the learning of subject matter or techniques predominates: formal literacy in French in Saint-Laurent, and an English-dominated academic program in Iqaluit.
- Each project is in effect integrated into a larger project: socio-cultural activities in the first case, and re-entry into society in the second.
- Both adopt an approach based on equity for adults who were poorly served by initial education. Concern for equality, and a desire to respect and make people independent, apparently inspires both projects; the Inuit case is part of an authentic attempt to provide 'second chance' education.
- The projects are marked by their organizational flexibility: both use a minimal framework for intervention, and are evolutionary and iterative in nature.
- The projects focus on learners and their needs rather than on rigid or predetermined programs of study: the education proposed suits the context and is linked to learners' knowledge, skills, and competencies.
- Since both deal with indigenous people, it is crucial that they take into account and foster linguistic and cultural identity. Each project aims to protect and restore value to a fragile culture, the language of which it respects. Each seeks to facilitate the recovery of an identity that is rooted in the present by trying to regenerate individual and collective life.
- A similar atmosphere in relationships inspires both projects: an easy-going relationship between project workers and participants; a spirit of co-operation, mutual respect, and tolerance; and creativity and pleasure.
- The openness and flexibility of both projects does not imply, however, that they demonstrate less professional competence than rigidly structured programs. Although in different ways, both activities make use of real expertise that is shared and effective.
- In its own way, each project includes an ethical dimension: respect for people and sensitivity to their situations and needs; the estab-

lishment of new social relations based on tolerance, devolved responsibility, and solidarity; and an effort to make individuals and the surrounding community independent.
- Each activity also includes an inseparable aesthetic aspect that exploits each person's creativity and artistic sense through theatre or sculpture.
- The ecological dimension, which derives from the foregoing characteristics, is visible particularly in the harmonious links that the projects aim to restore between individuals and their human, natural, and cultural environments.

Lastly, each project includes an 'added value' leading to 'added being,' 'better being,' and 'well-being.'[9]

Obstacles to an Ecological Approach

Both projects are exceptional in relation to the dominant practices of literacy and adult basic education. Numerous writers (and our experience) show that basic education systems often have little sense of their environment, in which they are transplanted rather than rooted. However, some of the performance indicators of these systems are symptomatic of major problems: the difficulty of recruiting adults (people still write that illiterates have 'lost their way'), so that provision exceeds demand; considerable drop-out rates; inadequate evaluation; lack of quality control, etc. It is thus pertinent to identify the factors that, in contrast to the two projects discussed here, make it difficult to adopt more ecological approaches.

1. One of the major obstacles appears to be the *traditional insistence on independence* in (basic) education systems. In the field of education, this leads to behaviour and ways of doing things that are contrary to the needs of people and communities. For example, many educational activities concentrate on a narrow conception of pedagogy or andragogy (Fullan 1993) that is monopolized by a panoply of techniques for teaching and intervention, and by methods of 'class and group management,' conflict solving, and educational planning ('educational engineering'). Particularly in literacy work, disproportionate importance is given to the teaching of the written code to the detriment of other needs, including that of learning and using written communication (rather than the mere techniques of encoding and decoding). All

too frequently, basic education is translated into predetermined, centralized formal programs of teaching 'basic subject matter' that reuses the curriculum of primary and secondary education.

2. Moreover, many education systems are marked by a narrow *functionalism*: funding related to circumscribed numbers of entrants and leavers (enrolments, drop-outs, and those gaining certificates); and (pedagogical) evaluation focusing on individual formal learning and performance rather than on the impact of learning on participants' real lives, on their circumstances and conditions in the community. Although initiatives are limited in some cases by constraining factors, dominant models are merely reproduced in other cases with little awareness that this is what is happening.

In contexts in which school traditions and culture weigh heavily, the staff usually prove to be in sympathy with tradition: defining themselves above all as clinicians or technicians, they frequently adopt one-sided, authoritarian, or paternalistic relationships between 'the teachers and the taught.' Such attitudes and behaviour, which assume that teachers are technicians and are typical of a certain type of professionalization, often predominate in those teachers' educational programs (Wagner and Turgeon 1998).

3. Moral, cultural, and social problems are transformed into practical, technical, pedagogical, and individual problems especially when educational activities and institutions are *isolated from the environment* in which teaching occurs. Basic education systems then become impermeable to the human, cultural, and natural environment. And they prove particularly insensitive towards minority languages and cultures.

What is required is to see education systems as part of a wider purpose than mere pedagogical functionality. Education is more than a technique; it is a fundamental vehicle of social justice. What are its aims, and how will it promote and improve the lives of the individuals and groups concerned?

What is lacking in many cases is the relationship between education systems and their environments, their learners' needs, and their ethno-cultural and socio-cultural contexts. Civic and ethical preoccupations are too often glossed over or relegated to the background (Goodlad 1990). In adult basic education, they should be in the foreground since the individuals concerned have often experienced failure at school during their childhood, and their self-esteem and integration into society are frequently problematic.

In Conclusion

Our description of the situation of basic education sheds light on a number of fundamental educational and ecological factors. Without falling into the trap of reductionism, it has to be admitted that the ecological challenge, which is at the heart of the aims of education systems, has often been neglected or glossed over, especially in the (basic) education of indigenous peoples. The very treatment of the notion of ecology in education is a reflection of academic reductionism. By attempting to apply ecology to education, the academic world has created interesting concepts – *school ecology, pedagogical ecology, educational ecology*, even *school pollution* – but these are often narrowly defined in terms of the attainment of 'academic goals' and 'specific learning objectives' (Legendre 1988). In education, ecology is still imprisoned in academic dross.

If it is well founded, this analysis calls for pause and radical reconsideration of the links binding educational projects to their environments and to democracy. That said, it would be wrong to go to extremes in particularizing or to wish to define educational programs purely on the basis of their relationships with their immediate environments. Basic education programs must ensure that all learn the same basic skills that are required by every member of society. All the same, appropriate education need not be 'on the cheap,' and, in a democratic society, what an individual learns (especially as an adult) must be socially recognized and agreed.

The problem that is too often encountered is that basic education programs are not sufficiently open to the wider, more demanding perspectives of democracy and democratization. The relationship between (basic) education and the community is an important link in an educative, democratic society. It requires a genuine relationship of partnership between educational institutions and the community.

The appeal made to all participants at the Hamburg Conference by an Inuit from Iqaluit (quoted at the head of this chapter) calls into question each and every policy and practice.

Notes
1 The Metis and Inuit communities involved in the two projects agreed to share their experiences, but the author nonetheless accepts full responsibil-

ity for the presentation of their views: in Saint-Laurent, Manitoba, a certain number of Metis and project workers, including Michelle Fortier and Guy Dumond; in Iqaluit, Nunavut, the project worker Fedos Panyi, the administrator Jimmy Markusie, and the master sculptors and trainees. Marie-France Duranceau, of the Research Laboratory on Adult Literacy and Education at UQAM, contributed to documentary research. Moreover, some of the issues had already been addressed with Professor Marc Turgeon of UQAM.

2 The main sources for the data are *The Report of the Royal Commission on Indigenous Peoples* (Canada 1996), Dikason (1992), and research carried out over recent years.

3 The term 'dialect' should not be understood in a belittling or pejorative sense. To counteract this prejudice, some people regard the dialects as languages, stating that there are currently fifty indigenous languages in Canada.

4 Any assessment of the work of the churches should be made with care since their paternalism was often accompanied by a genuine desire to do good.

5 In 1992, the majority of the churches apologized (with reservations, it is true) for the mistakes made in the school education of indigenous people. In 1998, the Government of Canada also admitted its mistakes in establishing residential schools for Indians.

6 The Metis had measured out the lands of their meeting place in narrow strips starting from a water course, after the 'French' strip model employed in Quebec, while the 'English' divided them into equal squares, forming 'homesteads.' The conflict thus not only related to the ownership of land, but also to its configuration.

7 The pupils and teachers of the French school, for example, organized an annual pilgrimage to Batoche, Saskatchewan, the focal point of the crushed Rebellion of 1885. It was the custom when they set out to hoist the Metis flag on the flagpole of the school building shared by the French and English schools, but the English management, which owned the building, demanded that the flag be removed.

8 The participants in the project seem not all to have been equally aware of the retrospective process of rehabilitation of the Metis and their culture. The tensions between Metis and Whites, which have been attested by research studies, as has been seen, are often glossed over in public nowadays, but they are still discussed in private.

9 This list may appear idyllic and uncritical. Only in-depth evaluations could indeed allow the impact of projects to be assessed in the long term. There are, however, effects that can be observed on the ground among the work-

ers and participants in these two projects. That being the case, failure is an integral part of such projects. One of the participants in the Inuit project, for example, committed suicide.

References

Alain, L., ed. 1998. *La communauté Mitchif de Saint-Laurent*. Saint-Laurent: Aurèle-Lemoine Community School.

Canada, Royal Commission on Indigenous Peoples. 1996. *Report of the Royal Commission of Inquiry on Indigenous Peoples*. Ottawa: Communication Group Canada.

Dikason, O.P. 1992. *The Myth of the Savage and the Beginnings of French Colonialism in the Americas*. Edmonton: University of Alberta Press.

Fullan, M. 1993. *Change Forces: Probing the Depths of Educational Reform*. London: Falmer Press.

Giraud, M. 1945. *Le Métis Canadien*. Paris: Institut d'Ethnologie.

Goodlad, J.I. 1990. 'The Occupation of Teaching in Schools.' In *The Moral Dimensions of Teaching*, ed. J.I. Goodlad, 20–7. San Francisco: Jossey-Bass.

Hessel, I. 1998. *Inuit Art*. Vancouver: Douglas and McIntyre.

Legendre, R. 1988. *Dictionnaire actuel de l'éducation*. Montréal, Paris, Guérin: Éditions ESKA.

Nunavut Arctic College. 1997. *Calendar of Courses, 1997–1998; 1998–1999*. Iqaluit: Nunavut Arctic College, Policy and Programs.

Papen, R.A. 1993. 'La variation dialectale dans le parler français des Métis de l'Ouest canadien.' *Francophones d'Amérique* 3: 25–38.

Quinn, J.A. 1971. *Human Ecology*. Hamden, CT: Archon Books.

Roy-Sole, M. 1996. 'Histoire de la résistance tranquille.' *L'Actualité* 21(5): 36–48.

St-Onge, N. 1990. 'Race, Class and Marginality. A Metis Settlement in the Manitoba Interlake, 1850–1914.' PhD diss., University of Manitoba.

UNESCO. 1996. *Learning: The Treasure Within*. Report of the International Commission on Education for the 21st Century. Paris: UNESCO; London: HMSO Books.

– 1997. *Fifth International Conference on Adult Education, Hamburg, Germany. Final Report*. Paris: UNESCO.

Wagner, S. 1997. 'Literacy, the Institutional Environment and Democracy.' In *ALPHA 97 – Basic Education and Institutional Environments*, ed. J.P. Hautecoeur, 297–322. Hamburg: UNESCO Institute for Education; Ottawa: Culture Concepts.

Wagner, S., and M. Turgeon. 1998. *La scolarisation de l'éducation des adultes au Québec et son impact sur les formateurs d'adultes.* Montréal: Laboratoire de recherche en éducation et alphabétisation des adultes.

Wotherson, T., and B. Schissel. 1998. *Marginalisation, décolonisation et voix: les perspectives de l'éducation des Autochtones du Canada.* Discussion paper of the Pan-Canadian Educational Research Program. Toronto: Council of Ministers of Education (Canada).

From Reaching In to Reaching Out: El-Warsha 1987–1999

Hassan El-Geretly

The re-examination of Western forms of theatre, the dominant reference in Egypt since the early nineteenth century, led the El-Warsha Theatre Company to turn to Egypt's popular cultures as a wellspring for the crafting of original works. In addition to creating new, original works and training actors, El-Warsha has reached out to its audience, to amateurs and professionals from other fields wishing to make use of drama, and to children within the school system, as well as to the socially and economically marginalized. El-Warsha is now experimenting with an interdisciplinary approach by collaborating with those who intervene in social action. In this context, El-Warsha is learning to play a specific role – without collision and, more importantly, without collusion – within the institutional frameworks of its partners, whose agendas may be quite different from that of the troupe.

> *The theory of photography can be learnt in an hour, a basic grasp of the practice in a day. What cannot be learnt ... is the feeling of light ... it is the artistic appreciation of the effects produced by different daylights, separately and in combination ... it is the application of one or the other of these effects in accordance with the type of physiognomy, which you as an artist must seek to reproduce. What can be learnt even less is the moral intelligence of your subject ... it is that fleeting touch that puts you in communion with the model, lets you judge him and gives you an insight into his habits, ideas, and character, and allows you to create not some haphazard, banal, and indifferent plastic reproduction that would be within the reach of the humblest laboratory servant, but the most familiar and favourable resemblance, an intimate resemblance.*
>
> Félix Nadar (1857)

El-Warsha in the Beginning

El-Warsha is an independent theatre troupe which had its beginnings in a working group that gradually came to be sustained by a shared language. Its work evolved out of the process of evaluating the Western model predominant in Egyptian theatre. This re-evaluation neutralized for us the role of foreign theatre as a single pivot and defined it instead as one of several important resources for our theatre.

> El-Warsha represents a group of people who have come together through a shared attitude and sensibility. Its members, whether amateurs, professionals, or aspiring professionals, work together united by the quest for horizons of wonder.
> While *Waking Up*, by Dario Fo and Franca Rame, performed in 1987 and 1988, was to us an exploration of the roots of folk performance and of a socially relevant theatre free of slogans, in *The Ward Wishes to Become a Guardian*, by Peter Handke, performed at the same time, we attempted, through this silent show, to highlight the discrepancy between the messages transmitted by movement, rhythm, and scenography and the messages of the spoken work, and to show that a text is alive inasmuch as it leaves space for all the other components of performance.
> In performing Pinter's *The Lover* and *The Dumb Waiter* in 1988 in colloquial Egyptian Arabic, we aspired to a succinct language that would generate dramatic tension through verbal economy, and which would imply the depth and violence of the feelings the characters hide behind the mask of everyday mundane behaviour. Then came Kafka's *The Penal Colony*, a rich and painful parable related to our reality, where institutions prefer to die of stagnation than live the adventure of growth and development. ('El Warsha's Progress 1987–1999')

After this neutralization, the troupe found itself at a new equilibrium, rich with potential possibilities. The performance arts in folk Egyptian culture started suggesting themselves to us as sources. A theatre that included folk material (*Dayer Maydour*) was introduced; then a theatre whose creativity was triggered by the folk spirit (*Dayeren Dayer*), since material without spirit runs the risk of turning into commercial or tourist folklore. Subsequently, the troupe directed its attention to the construction and architecture of the theatrical work itself to incorporate our own particular vision of the world, without which both material and spirit are lost, resulting in the feeling of dual cultural vision that has haunted us since the dawn of modern history.

When, in 1989, we egyptianized Alfred Jarry's Ubu-plays into *Dayer Maydour* more freely than in any previous attempt, we were not unlike people building their own temple in another's holy land.

The show contained much material from popular culture, which made for intimacy with the audience and which was in keeping with Jarry's rebellious spirit. It also marked the beginning of our association with the traditional shadow-players; the play was later reworked to reflect the spirit of the shadow-play, making use of its aesthetics. In this form, *Dayeren Dayer* was performed at the Cairo Opera House, and at theatre festivals in Zurich, Carthage, and Cairo.

The changes that *Dayeren Dayer* underwent, over the two years of performance, showed us that linear logic, whether common or 'absurd,' limits the scope of the imagination in the structuring of plays to reflect alternative perceptions of the world. So the fragments of *Ghazir el-Leil* (Tides of Night), first performed in 1993, started emerging after a long period of practice in storytelling, with its multiple perspectives and its interaction with the audience. The revealing of encounter points with our audience in the popular material, its different voices and rhythms, and the freedom inherent in the logic of fantasy, led to the reshaping of the space shared between performance and spectators and to the birth of a theatrical form that could embrace the rhythm of human emotions. ('El Warsha's Progress 1987–1999')

Al-Darwish (or the Man Who Walks with the Love of God): A Story from the Nile Delta

Pray to the Prophet!

Once there was a poor wretched man who walked along holding a rider's crop in his hand. He would crack it in the air and shout: 'Our Lord is able to create the world in a nutshell.' A man came up to him and said: 'You're saying our Lord can create the world in a nutshell?' And he got hold of the poor wretched man and gave him a thrashing. Then the man who beat the poor man went into the mosque to pray.

Inside the mosque there is an enormous well – they call it the dipping pool – where people perform their ablutions. The man took off his clothes and hung them up and got into the well. Suddenly he found he had turned ... into a woman!

She was standing in the middle of a vast endless sea. A fisherman came up and said: 'Hey you, Lady!'

'Yes,' she answered.

'What are you doing in there?' he asked.

'I was washing my clothes and they fell into the water ...'

'I'll take off my galabiyya and give it to you and I'll stand clear until you put it on. Then we'll leave together.'

'All right,' she replied.

The fisherman took off his galabiyya and threw it over to the woman and stood clear. The woman put on the galabiyya and got out of the water and went off with him. The fisherman said to his wife: 'Keep this woman here with you.'

The fisherman's wife agreed to keep the woman with her for one year. Then the fisherman's wife died. On the advice of the villagers, the fisherman married the woman who was staying with him. She was soon pregnant. First she gave birth to a boy, then to another boy, and then she gave birth to a girl. Then what happened?

The woman went to wash her clothes. At the shore, she said to herself: 'Why don't I go for a swim?' She slipped into the water and found herself changed ... into a man. He got out of the well, and found his clothes hanging up. He put them on and went in to pray and found the poor wretched man sitting, still cracking his rider's crop and saying: 'Our Lord can create the world in a nutshell.'

The man said to him: 'You're right. By God, you're right!'

The poor man answered: 'Did it have to take you two boys and a girl to at last believe?'

> *Ghasir el-Leil* was first performed in a theatre and subsequently in a tent that can be remodelled according to the needs of each new production, which allows us to tour. We also presented the play in Zurich, Rabat, Casablanca, Beirut, Amman, Menia, Paris, Gothenburg, Rotterdam, London, and Washington.
>
> We simultaneously continued to perform *Layaly El-Warsha* (Nights of El Warsha), which had started in 1992 with popular stories – in Cairo, then in Alexandria, Menya, Port-Said, Beirut, Amman, Paris, Gothenburg, London, and Washington. These evenings now contain shadow plays, glove puppet sketches, stick duels, and popular music, which are the arts that our actors are learning from the popular masters.
>
> In 1994, we finished a documentary film about Mouled El Sayyeda Aisha (The Birth-Feast of Holy Aisha) in collaboration with the people of the Sayyeda Aisha neighbourhood, who organize a carnival-like procession different from those of other saints' feasts in that it parades carts with satirical tableaux of everyday life.
>
> In the same year, we started to collect the oral versions *of Al-Sira al-Hilaliyya*, the epic of the Beni Hilal tribe, from its last great bards. We

trained to recite and sing it and presented excerpts during *Layaly El-Warsha* in anticipation of a play that opened in Cairo in January 1998: *Ghazl el-Ammar* (Spinning Lives). ('El Warsha's Progress 1987–1999')

After five years of getting acquainted with the Egyptian folk heritage in its various forms, and the production of several theatrical shows in relation to this heritage, El-Warsha is starting to interact with the reality of contemporary life in Egypt and its new arts, in both the city and the village. Over the last five years, we have perhaps managed to discover the perspective that will permit us to deal with all this, while avoiding the traps of realism and the shallow treatment of reality characteristic of the mass media, which takes into account neither the depth of history and its various shadows, nor the specificity of our cultural character.

> Playwright Karen Malpede, who was a guest of the festival, wrote in the *New York Times* (October 18): 'El Warsha extracted from an Egyptian epic an intensity akin to ancient Greek drama.' According to her, El Warsha works in an epic ritual theatre tradition akin to that of Ariane Mnouchkine and Peter Brook in Paris. But this is not the only aspect of El Warsha's work, and Karen will be surprised when she hears that this wonderful group, who have a dread of classification and stagnation and an amazing ability to renew and develop themselves and branch out in new directions, are currently involved in developing 'an epic of modern daily life,' as El-Geretly calls it, based on their personal and social experiences. Meanwhile, work on the Hilaliya epic continues side by side with the company's touring and its many valuable para-theatrical activities, particularly in Upper Egypt, which has always suffered a chronic and scandalous lack of cultural and other developmental services. (Nehad Selaiha, 'Taking Stock,' *Al-Ahram Weekly*, 31 December 1998)

Touring within Egypt

We aim to extend the scope of our audience geographically, culturally, and socially, to avoid as far as possible the atmosphere of 'ghetto theatre' in Cairo, and to meet with the rich fabric of humanity in Egypt. This richness is reflected in the troupe, whose members are actors and teachers of the folk arts, members of the urban and rural populations, amateurs and professionals, young and old, men and women, Moslems and Christians, and Egyptians of varied ethnic origins.

The audience has become a cornerstone in our present experience, and its members are no longer merely spectators – be they active or passive. We have to return to them and, together with them, build that intimate theatre for which we are looking within ourselves.

This priority embodies a return to the sources which have inspired our works since 1992, with the contemporary productions that emerged from our interaction with these sources. We propose a renewed dialogue, one whose vocabulary is made up of feelings, with an audience that is aware of a shared artistic heritage, so that the movement of the traditional material is not restricted to one direction – from the country to the city, or from its original producers to others – but rather creates a new dynamic whose substance is the imagination in which people have stored their emotional and moral experiences through the ages.

We understand that our continuity requires a healthy environment for us to live in and by, and that this necessitates the existence of strong links with effective partners. We have found them in a number of NGOs, with whom our links have become stronger through the conviction that our need of each other is shared, and through the fact that these NGOs believe that art's contribution to the process of development also permits a broadening of the concepts relating to vital issues about their work in society. For this reason, we are working towards planning our own touring in collaboration with these NGOs during the upcoming period, so that this cooperative civil effort underscores the specific role of art as an expression of the space occupied by imagination and the emotions in our lives. We would then negotiate a role for our artistic work in society, which necessarily transcends the limits imposed by the utilitarian view of art as a learning aid for the conventional developmental agendas (birth control, literacy, etc.).

Outreach, Education, and Training

In 1995, the El-Warsha troupe embarked on a new phase. The members felt the need to make the group's maturity and experience available to those who sought it. Such a process implied a test of this experience, an essential condition for the group's growth in subsequent years.

This was the context in which our cooperation with the Jesuit and Brothers' Association in Menia took root three years ago. We worked with the children of the Association to help them acquire various artistic skills reflecting areas of their experience that are otherwise muted in conventional means of expression. They also learned theatrical exercises that reveal – in a secure space – the idea of difference and conflict, one that paves the way for change and development and, combined with the power of the imagination, opens the door to envisaging an alternative relationship with reality, one that opposes the violence that is engendered by the perpetuation of the status quo in our society.

> We have started a long-term collaboration with the Jesuit and Brothers' Association. After a pilot five-day workshop in the summer of 1995, we decided to launch an eighteen-month project ...
> We worked intensively through July and August of this year with a group of children on making shadow theatre playets and on acquiring other arts of our heritage (storytelling, dance, music, singing).
> This first stage of the project ended successfully with the performance of three shadow playets invented entirely by the children, under the guidance of three of our group and a number of the traditional masters.
> It was an emotional moment for me to watch scores of shadow puppets come in and out of the light during this performance, dedicated to the last puppet-maker of Egypt's millennial tradition, Hassan El Farran, who had just passed away and who for the last few years had been a generous member of El Warsha ...
> It was marvelous to behold the openness and enthusiasm with which this aged artist reworked his material with others, without ever feeling that change is betrayal of the tradition, not that the old is better than the new, nor that a beginner is not an artist or even a potential master ...
> The Jesuit and Brothers' Association has decided to consider our collaboration as being the beginning of a Children's Centre for the Performing Arts. ('1996 Progress Report')

In 1997, our children's theatre team learned the techniques for making cartoons with video from their inventor, Erling Ericsson, and from Ninni Rydsjo, in the small town of Abu Qurqas of Middle Egypt. The outcome was a wonderful eleven-minute film, *Balawi El Souk*, the story of the revolt of vegetables and animals against man. A documentary about this experience has just been edited.

With the beginning of the summer 1997, the group of children in Menia who started to work with shadow puppetry in the summer of 1996 now moved on to an apprenticeship of the 'cartoon school' techniques, based on cut-outs moving on a flat surface. The organic links between the shadow theatre techniques they had learnt and those they were using to make cartoons fascinated them and brought up the questions about the dialogue between the past and the future that have always preoccupied us in El Warsha. ('1997 Progress Report')

Our group, with its long process and its productions, is not so much reviving the popular traditions as making sure that the dialogue between the future and the past is kept alive. ('1996 Progress Report')

This experience indicated the need for training teachers who are concerned with this area of development. We wished to widen our circle of trainers and engage with the educational and practical experience of teachers, which is necessary for us.

A new group of children, working along lines we had traced with the first group, started simultaneously and was run by the three teachers who had actively followed the first year's work. Hesitant at the start, they gradually became confident, to the point of making a critique of the first year's 'curriculum,' and sometimes proposing better solutions. ('1997 Progress Report')

In the autumn of 1998, a workshop for 'animateurs' was held in the village of Abu-Qurqas in collaboration with the Menia-based Association of Upper Egypt for Education and Development. In the last two years, we collaborated with the Salama Moussa Association on preparing the artistic component of a program designed for children aged nine to thirteen who had dropped out of school. We subsequently collaborated with this NGO on training their 'coordinators.'

This inspiring side of El-Warsha's work, which started three years ago in close cooperation with the Jesuit and Frères Association in Menia and other non-governmental organizations, needs to be extensively aired and discussed as a possible model for using theatre in development. It involves workshops and training sessions, in schools and community centres, geared to help both children and adults acquire various artistic skills (making-up plays, story-telling, making shadow plays and creating video cartoon films with the help of a simple technique devised in Sweden by Erling Ericsson, a TV producer and animator at the Swedish Educational Broadcasting Company. These and other activities, the philosophy that informs them, and their effect on the community deserve a separate article which I hope to write soon. (Nehad Selaiha, 'Taking Stock,' *Al Ahram Weekly*, 31 December 1998)

Professional Training

In Cairo we train actors, from both El-Warsha and elsewhere, in the folk arts and in those techniques which we have developed for the kind of theatre that we are seeking. We also train them in other techniques with which we became familiar through artists who are moving in different directions than ours, such as the American Joe Goode Performance Group (April 1997 and May 1998) and ALIS from France, which creates a theatre of objects (October 1997). We have also worked with folk artists in launching a number of projects in the provinces. This approach allows the amateurs and the new artists to learn these arts in the environment which produced them. It enables the masters to preserve their cultural and social balance by staying in close contact with their sources, which counters the process of emptying the country of its energy in the direction of the overpopulated capital. Such an approach also implies, perhaps, a re-evaluation of the role of the professional artist in the social fabric of this traditional setting, where terrorism is rife. These masters now derive part of their income by teaching, a profession which they are now practising for the first time as they pass on the heritage of the past to future generations.

The first of these projects was El-Warsha's Centre for Stick-Fighting and Dancing in Mallawy, in which fifty people (masters, young men, and children) work on 'tahteeb' (stick-fighting) and the accompanying dance and music. The roots of these arts go back to the Pharaonic age, as can be seen on the walls of the Bani Hassan tombs near Mallawy. This work is being done at the same time as young people all over Egypt are absorbed in learning the Asian martial arts in the style of Bruce Lee and Jacky Chan. Researchers from Korea have come all the way to Egypt to study this ancient art.

We also collaborated with the choir of the Association of Upper Egypt for Education and Development. The Association established centres for singing, and its programs incorporate the skills that we discovered while working on the various folk arts. Thus the choir can replace the young people who leave the choir to work after getting their diplomas (the boys) or for early marriage (the girls). Two young men from the choir have been appointed as trainees in El-Warsha while continuing to attend the choir practices in Menia. We expect that they will someday work in their original group as assistants to the teachers in singing and music. Trainers also come from our stick centre in Mallawy to participate in training children and young people in 'tahteeb,' mizmar, and drums. This creates work opportunities that are rare in this region and in this field.

We also organized two courses over a whole season, one of which was for a group of adults (1995–6) wishing to enter our profession, to fully exploit a personal hobby, or to use theatrical techniques in other fields, such as working with the disabled, outreach, etc. Three of them subsequently joined the troupe (two actresses and one assistant director), while another went into the field of looking after 'working children' in the 'Geel Centre.'

The following year (1996–7), we trained a group of adolescents from Al-Nossour Al-Saghira (The Young Eagles' Association) who had attended our shows regularly and had asked to learn our arts. So we taught them story-telling, singing, puppet theatre, and drums, and today three of them are training to be educators in our centre for children's theatre in Menia and one of them has joined the troupe as a trainee actress.

Conclusion

Theatre, which is a craft that brings in many other crafts, must help the children perceive life holistically and escape the truncated narrow perspective that they obtain from our educational system.

We have acquired expertise in outreach over the years, which has developed for us a view of art and the creative process as an epistemological system, capable of achieving what the conventional educational process fails to achieve, with its distrust of dealing with intuition and emotion.

However, as our system became more defined/refined, our 'animateurs' became more specialized and the children slipped out of touch with the artistic potential and activities of El-Warsha, which had been the original source. Ties have to be restored between the creative process and the outreach activities. Otherwise they lose their *raison d'être*, which is to espouse change and movement. Both we and the teachers also need to master new artistic skills to teach the children and to raise our level in the skills we already have.

A large number of NGOs started asking us to work with them. This is difficult to achieve since we are essentially an artistic troupe that depends for its outreach work on 'reaching in' through the creative process. We do not want to repeat the same experiences twice, while we are still feeling our way towards developing a system that is viable for our environment. We thought of founding a centre for trainers, which would include a number of young people from various NGOs, in addition to hosting in El-Warsha artists and educators from the provinces, the Arab world, and beyond to work with us over periods ranging from two months to a year.

We need to adopt an interdisciplinary approach, as we have always tried to do in our artistic work, not only in our process, but also in our monitoring and evaluation. We – but also the teachers – need to acquire a higher level of expertise in child psychology and also in the design of curricula based on more interactive theories of learning. We must also remain in touch with other vital experiences in Egypt, the Arab world, and further afield.

In our conservative society, there is a danger of art being considered as a mere safety-valve: the results we have achieved might then turn into an end in themselves, the steps by which we reached them becoming curricula, and even eventually compulsory, to be repeated every year, so that the principle becomes duplication instead of expression, experimentation, and discovery.

Because we are not here to heal but to raise doubts, our work creates a delicate balance with the Establishment. That balance must be protected from the temptations of fusion or co-optation because it is out of this tension that we hope to gain more knowledge.

Our society is hierarchical in structure, its sectors separated from each other. And our Egyptian theatre, whose perspectives are distorted, is inspired by theatre and not life and is caught in a vicious circle like an animal chasing its shadow. This is why we know that we will need much time to reach a satisfactory balance in our relationships with the various local communities with which we work now and will work in the future. We have not yet perceived the richness of the complex realities that surround us, and this understanding is essential if we are to succeed in developing appropriate instruments for our work. The first such instrument is a language that calls for equality, respects the specificity of people, and allows us to receive and transmit at the same time so that we can counter preconceptions and prejudices

The Creation of Knowledge through Environmental Education

Paolo Orefice

Environmental problems occupy a primary place in adult education. They concern the natural environment of communities, which cannot be understood without knowledge of the historical contribution of humankind to its construction, its habitat, and its interpretation. The author calls this the 'anthropologizing of the natural environment.' One of the major goals of adult education is the reconstruction of personal and collective identity, particularly for marginalized individuals and groups, and adult education must begin with a renewed reading of the environment. The article defines the methodological criteria of a contemporary environmental pedagogy that enables adults to appropriate their identity and to participate in community life. It then summarizes the operational modes of a constructivist, participatory pedagogy that are useful to educators.

The A to Z of Natural, Social, and Cultural Environments[1]

Adult education has to meet the needs of the contemporary world. It cannot evade that task for to do so would result in abandoning the role of innovation and transformation that is typical of educational activities, and to be reduced to the status of a tool for the maintenance of the huge contrasts and inequalities that mark the end of this century.

The key issues of development are the stuff of adult education, which engages with the social actors involved. Adult education can thus make a crucial contribution in addressing these issues, thereby helping to build, in the creative sense of the term, people's personal and collective identities.

At the European and world level, the issue of the environment – in both its natural and its man-made dimensions – is among the most significant development issues. It is to be henceforward recognized that one of the major threats of the current phase in the development of world society is the progressive degradation of natural and man-made environments. Given their frequent occurrence and profound impact, problems such as the widespread pollution that is altering the balance of ecosystems, and the deterioration in urban frameworks that is giving rise to the breakdown of social norms and marginalization among ever wider sections of the population, amply demonstrate the need to protect and cherish the natural and cultural environment.

The social, economic, and cultural conflicts that still persist today at national and local levels are beginning to have world-wide repercussions, and they reflect the difficulties experienced by different societies and cultures in living side by side over vast areas of the planet. The construction of personal and collective identity, and the building of world citizenship, come up against forms of social, economic, and cultural integration that have preserved undiluted the relationships of subservience and dependency that affect the social classes at greatest risk, the weakest cultural communities, and the economically least favoured regions of the South and East.

The whole territory of the European continent, like those of the other continents, can be seen as home to many different cultures and societies which, over time, have adapted their diverse natural environments to human ends. They have built their group identity on these environments and have given expression to their supremacy in agreement – though more often in disagreement – with the societies and cultures of the neighbouring territories, and also with those of the same territory.

This attachment to local roots, and the patchwork of societies and cultures within one and the same territory, have led to the formation of particularly complex natural, social, and cultural environments. The modifications to nature and the stratification of human intervention have proved exceptionally severe and far-reaching. In any given territory, they provide characteristic evidence of the way in which humanity and nature have lived together over the years. Such evidence can be seen in the dynamic organization of life that is characteristic of the human groups that still inhabit a particular territory, whether the macro-region of a national society or the micro-region of a local society, the expression of one or more cultural aggregations.

The people of the new millennium seem more than ever willing to feel once again that they belong to the world that surrounds them. It is not just a matter of saving the natural and cultural heritage passed down from preceding generations but, above all, of saving 'self,' that is, of rebuilding personal identities and the larger human identity.

The improvement in global conditions has not gone hand in hand with increased security in community life, either in terms of a consolidation of a feeling of self and of the overall well-being of the individual, or in terms of the cohesion and solidarity of the group or groups. The continual, growing, and often alarming depersonalization of the individual and the group is affecting a wide range of people and is marginalizing them economically, socially, and culturally.

The key issues of development on this continent and around the world therefore demand that a crucial role be given to the building of the personal and collective identity of the population, in particular among the groups that are experiencing the worst disruption to their marginal position in society. This implies that people should be given the chance both to acquire a feeling of collective belonging, and to enlarge and express their own originality: two necessary prerequisites for any development project.

In this respect, adult education can play an important part by addressing both the natural and the man-made aspects of the issue of the environment as a learning priority, both in formal and in non-formal education. The key issues of the development of the local and regional community and its environment are the subject matter and the goal of education and training. In this sense, *the complexity of the environment becomes a text to be continually reread and interpreted, constantly helping people to build and rebuild themselves,* by seeking to go beyond the limits and contradictions that they gradually uncover in themselves and in the environment in which these are reflected.

Through the educational act of discovering and rediscovering the environmental heritage of the territory and its inhabitants, the individual and the local community are engaged in a task of cultural self-knowledge and hence of the enlargement of their own personal and collective identity, and are called on to play an active and original part in the development of the area and in the well-being of the collective itself. To this end, it is important that adult education programs should take into account not only the most elevated and highly esteemed manifestations of culture in the environment, but also those that are less far-sighted and are usually less well known because they are thought less significant. It is not unusual for the forces of creative renewal to work through the silences and the least audible and least heard voices in the environment, which, like their marginalized owners, are lost if no light is shed on them and no regard is paid to them.

The key issues of local development which a reading of the natural and man-made environment raises and interprets are thus the objective of education and training, in accordance with the theory and practice of 'environmental education.' If approached from this angle, the dilemma of building either a personal or a collective identity can be resolved by finding out, firstly, whether people end up losing their own room for freedom and creativity by adopting the values of the group, with all the dangers of authoritarian denial of will attendant on such a development, or, secondly, whether the collective dimension is having to bend to the requirements of the individual by legitimizing the most extreme individualism. This dichotomy is generally overcome if the individual and the community accept each other in the project of global environmental development, which naturally sheds light on, rather than obscuring, the contradictions and interests of the parties, while showing up directions for solidarity and bringing together the forces of renewal.

If adult education does in fact pay attention to the nature, culture, and the developmental problems of the rediscovered territory, it engages individuals, groups of adults, and the entire local community in the task of getting to know and appropriating their own culture and the other cultures present in the territory. This involves overcoming all preconceived discrimination and seizing the opportunity to recognize the most significant human meanings among the cultural evidence that had been overlooked. If individuals, especially those most exposed to marginality and anonymity, enter into communication with these meanings, they more easily find reasons for making contact with and rooting themselves in reality. Adult education thus makes a specific contribution to adults: it assists them in building and enriching a stronger, more open personal and collective identity based on broadened knowledge and a recognition of – and allegiance to – the natural environment and its varied cultures.

Through environmental education, adult education can achieve a further aim that is closely linked to what has gone before. Adults, especially those occupying weaker or more subservient positions in society, are called on to 'reactivate' themselves, to become actors because their reality of life is recognized and because it is they themselves who will, by decoding the signs of the environment and cultural self-knowledge, seek and produce the most original human meanings.

This 'reactivation' finds expression not merely in the discovery and creation of the new knowledge that education about natural and cultural environmental phenomena sets in train: it also allows people to regain a position of true creative participation in the development activities of the territory. Through commitment to protecting the right to difference and the coexistence of differences, people develop greater solidarity, which makes them more creative.

Thus adult education is an integral part of the recent trend to the rediscovery of the environment, which enables individuals to free themselves from immoderate consumption, and which counters the strengthening of discrimination and the mass treatment of people at both the local and the global levels.

Methodological Criteria of Environmental Education

Environmental education does not merely formulate general principles on the 'A to Z' of the environment, but tries to translate these into educational activities for adults. We shall here look at a number of methodological criteria that may be used by educators to facilitate the creation of knowledge among adults by using the A to Z of the environment. The educators – teachers, facilitators, advisers – who use this A to Z of phenomena are concerned both with the evidence of the natural, social, and cultural environment to be found throughout a given territory, and with the public whose attention they call to this evidence. In each case, the education will be conducted differently.

In the case of the evidence (whether an archaeological site, items in a museum, a monument, a square or buildings, a river or a marsh), the approach is not enumerative, effect-seeking, and undifferentiated, but constructive, lively, and targeted. It is not enumerative in the sense that the educational activity has nothing in common with the arid, stereotyped enumeration of information that is proper to what is known as a guided tour. That is a very inadequate way of introducing the public to the environmental heritage of a place: it falsifies the perspective since it empties it of meaning and generally only provides superficial information.

The presentation of the evidence must make reconstruction possible: it must make explicit the complex meanings hidden behind its signs, and shed as much light as possible on the real dimension that it had in the past or that is revealed through a composite reading of its elements. This composite reading emphasizes the evidence in its multiple facets, and therefore different points of view.

This type of approach does not aim to produce 'effects' at any price, the superficial awe or admiration that is generated by unusual, extravagant information. We must stress again that we are a long way from the quick visit for well-behaved tourists. Rather, our 'vital' approach attempts to emphasize the 'personality,' the essence and the specific characteristics, of the object examined. Awe and admiration are not the aims of the presentation; should they occur, they do so as part of the personal reaction of an individual who grasps the evidence's hidden cultural or natural breadth.

We can therefore see why a standard approach is not suitable, since it lumps information together haphazardly. A targeted presentation, by contrast, stresses the most enlightening information, the structural data that reveal the soul of the object studied. In this way, an internal order is created and an intelligent choice of information is made from among what is available. As a result, the public does not become distracted but finds its way through the information given, being enabled thereby to enter into better communication with the cultural or environmental heritage. Finally, the task of the educator must consist in making the message of this evidence as clear as possible.

As for the public, educators must be careful to develop a sense of search and discovery, not merely restricting themselves to recording information. That means that the public must not simply take note of the subject matter that is presented to it; the information must not be revealed all at once, but gradually brought out at the instigation of the educator. The educator supports the learner as he or she learns, individually and as part of the group, following a path of exploration in time and space, and awakens the learners' interest so as to bring them to discover the information in question.

Such an approach elicits personal attachment and participation, as opposed to an attitude of withdrawal from and indifference towards the heritage sites visited. The educator must elicit and foster attachment and participation – mental and emotional involvement on the part of the public. Relationships with monuments, archaeological sites, and more generally with the natural and cultural environment must be approached through perception and emotions: visitors are invited to remap space in their minds and to travel in time, so as to understand the people who lived in the age being studied. Particular importance must be accorded to aspects of everyday life, to customs, and to the difficulties encountered by society in a given location and period. The more the visitors encounter problems similar to those that concern them in everyday life, the more they will be able to understand the culture being presented, even if the problems have been resolved differently. That is how understanding and openness towards other cultures is fostered.

A third element of the approach is the creative and expressive nature which public participation in this 'journey into the environment' must adopt. The public does not undertake the 'journey' in order to learn news items, like the fragmented information provided by mass communications which is then buried in people's memories. The 'journey' should unleash something else, so that people can 'translate' the evidence with which they come into contact into familiar forms. It is important here to stress that the ways in which learners express themselves – through colour, sound, images, words, or movement – are both personal access routes to creativity, and equally personal 'bridges' to communication with the Other across time and space.

In sum, the approach of search and discovery, personal adhesion and participation, creativity and self-expression, treats the people undertaking the journey through nature and the given culture as global learners who are involved in a fully integrated journey, in which everything must be mobilized: their intelligence, their perception, their emotional capacities, and their imagination. In the same way, the lively, targeted constructivist approach regards and treats environmental evidence as relating to living, dynamic realities that are complex and full of meaning.

'Journeys into the environment' that follow these two types of educational and methodological criteria aim to establish direct and immediate communication between the natural and cultural environment and the public, by creating a symbiotic relationship that will certainly help to strengthen, expand, and enrich the citizen's personal and, ultimately, European identity.

Operational Procedures of Environmental Education

The pedagogical and methodological principles set out above need to be translated into operational procedures in order to produce specific educational activities. The constructivist approach is based on the educational principle according to which the individual builds his or her own education. Through his or her experience of learning, the individual elaborates the knowledge which he or she already has and arrives at new cognitive and non-cognitive syntheses that may be transferred to other contexts of experience. Hence we have adopted a 'building' methodology and teaching approach, which are based on four reference criteria.

The first can be defined as a reference to the learners' knowledge. Each learner brings his or her baggage to every stage of teaching, corresponding in this case to different points in the development of the 'journey into the environment.' Obviously the educator's activities must take this factor into account during the various stages of teaching. The educator must refer to it systematically in order to avoid the danger of losing touch with the knowledge possessed by his or her public. In this way, the educator ensures that the learners feel involved at a cognitive and non-cognitive level and actively participate in the intended journey.

This criterion is especially important in the initial stage of teaching. If cognitive and non-cognitive communication with learners is not established from the inception of teaching, they will not be motivated to follow the path. They will also experience difficulties in learning because the information given and the way in which it is presented – particularly the language used – will not resonate with their way of seeing and perceiving things.

It is therefore imperative to refer to learners' knowledge – to their patterns of thought, their fields of perception and emotions, their familiar worlds and language – in order to implement the pedagogy of discovery, participation, and creativity, centred essentially on the learner and his or her process of educational growth.

The second reference criterion relates to the support of new knowledge. It goes without saying that any educational activity brings about new knowledge. To say that no teaching takes place unless there is something to teach is to state the obvious, but it is important to stress it in relation to the teaching of environmental and cultural phenomena. Culture is a subject that is taught in its own right; the teaching is of a slightly different type from that of traditional subjects, but aims in the same way to provide new content. We have already spoken about environmental evidence as a heritage of knowledge, the meanings of which have to be spelled out – that is, the 'unknown' messages of the unfamiliar. These messages are the new subject matter to be learned. As educational activities unfold, in non-formal education but even more in formal education, the treatment of new knowledge, to which the public must have access, is an indispensable pillar of the edifice, not a secondary factor. Particular attention must therefore be paid to the selection and organization of the subject matter to be transmitted. The information to be provided must be evaluated for its meaning in terms of the evidence, but also in terms of the subject matter taught. In the first case, we have to ask ourselves about the value that a piece of information may have for the understanding of the environmental evidence in question. Some knowledge does not help to define the object; other information reveals its fundamental messages. In the second case, we need to evaluate the information in terms of the perspective we adopt to examine the object. The information may be elementary, but it may also have a structural function in the analytical framework, as in the case of basic concepts of a historical, economic, artistic, or biological nature, or relating to any other teaching subject. These two requirements naturally have to be combined and adapted to the knowledge system of the learner. Thus the educator is simply extending and enriching that system through the communication which the learner succeeds in establishing with the new information on the environmental evidence of the 'journey.'

The third reference criterion can be defined as a structuring of new knowledge on the part of the learner: the learner integrates pre-existing knowledge and added knowledge, which leads him or her to a new cognitive and non-cognitive synthesis. Learners must not be content with the mere acquisition of new knowledge; they must succeed in internalizing new points of view.

In other words, learners enter into the reasoning of the discipline that decodes the evidence. They internalize it gradually, progressively, and in proportion to the depth of detail that the educational program offers; they acquire the basic structural aspects of the analysis, and they reorganize their previous points of view. Learners thus restructure their cognitive field. The structural aspects of the subject and the structuring effects of the learning combine to cause change in the learner. The process of internalizing knowledge contributes to the development of the participation and the creativity fostered by this pedagogy, because it encourages learners to produce new knowledge.

The fourth and last reference criterion is that of the transfer of learning. The structuring of new knowledge in the learner through this type of educational journey must be verified, consolidated, and expanded. The process of internalization of knowledge has its own internal development. Learners will not succeed in mastering the use of knowledge in an immediate and definitive manner. They will reach that point gradually, and as the process advances, the presence of new knowledge in the learner will improve and take firmer root. It is appropriate to accompany learners through the internal dynamics of this process so that they internalize it. If new knowledge is merely juxtaposed with previous knowledge, learners will be unable to use it and will eventually abandon it.

It is therefore important for the educator, having provided new knowledge about the environmental evidence, to elicit responses from the learner which show the extent of assimilation and internalization. Genuine transfer of learning occurs when learners who have acquired knowledge of a specific subject, situation, or event are able to 'read' and interpret other similar objects, situations, and events. Only then can it be said that the process of internalization is taking effect.

The teacher must allocate well-defined times for 'personal return' by the learner to the evidence being studied, and must also provide opportunities for learners to test themselves. The educator invites the learners to examine other aspects of the evidence (of the building, the monument, or the nature park, for instance) and to formulate a point of view. Together, teacher and learner discuss the nature of this point of view, and the ability to transfer knowledge is evaluated. Where gaps or uncertainties appear, the educator will be able to take action for subsequent cognitive reinforcement and assessment of learning.

The pedagogy of research, participation, and self-expression finds its realization in the transfer of learning. For each of the criteria mentioned below, it is possible to find a series of technical operations that derive from it and make it possible to move from theory to practice.

A variety of technical solutions can be adopted for assessing learners' knowledge before they begin a program of environmental education: these may range from a rigidly constructed procedure to a more participatory approach; the former will make it possible to collect quantitative information, and the latter, qualitative information. We indicate a number of these procedures:

- distribute questionnaires on the environmental sites that will be visited and studied;
- hold a group discussion based on a well-defined grid of points to be covered;
- hold a group discussion based on the observations and interventions of the participants, and record the emerging knowledge in writing or by using a sound or video recorder;
- have participants write reports on their experience and knowledge of the environmental subject to be explored;
- request that learners gather documents that discuss the subject,

which the educator can use to channel participants' interest in the treatment of topics related to the evidence.

New knowledge can be supported through various channels that refer both to the content to be conveyed and to the learners who are to appropriate it. The first channel is naturally the phenomenon itself, which might find expression, for example, through a monument or a green space: the visitor's first contact with it through the senses (sight, touch, hearing any sound it makes, and perceiving any smell) provides the initial subjective, personal knowledge of it. But, as is well known, this is not sufficient to decode the evidence. The transmission of knowledge relating to these phenomena may be made orally or in writing, using words or pictures, depending on whether an explanation of the environmental or cultural phenomenon is given orally by an expert, or particular teaching aids or multimedia tools are used.

In order to structure the new knowledge, learners must patiently decode the environmental phenomenon through learning activities allowing them to grasp the 'architecture,' the fundamental aspects, of the phenomenon under study. They must move from a superficial and indistinct knowledge of the environmental or cultural phenomenon to a specific, enriched knowledge through their own interpretation and reflection. They must not be content merely to acquire information that is stored in their 'system' of reading reality.

The mental operations to be carried out will vary according to the problem of interpretation of the environmental phenomenon, the discipline that is used to explore the problem, and the degree of learning reached by the learners. Some of the most common mental operations, present in most disciplines, are listed below:

- separating more important from less important information;
- arranging the most revealing information in a logical order;
- describing the object examined by using the information received;
- analysing the object from the point of view of the type of information received;
- finding and classifying the various aspects presented by the object;
- bringing out similarities and differences within the object;
- organizing the information according to a map of concepts in order to read the object;
- using a map of concepts to interpret the object;
- comparing the characteristics of the object with those of another object examined during the journey into the environment.

The transfer of learning can in the final analysis be seen in the teaching exercises which enable the learner to use the new knowledge.

It is true that in actual teaching practice it is not possible to clearly detach the operations relating to the structuring of new knowledge from those that aim at the transfer of knowledge. The last few mental operations given as examples above in relation to the structuring of the new knowledge also involve the reinforcement of the transfer. Nor must it be forgotten that, aside from the definition and adoption of specific, distinct teaching criteria by the educator, educational experience is global, as is the process of learning that takes place in the learner during the 'journey.' The learning of knowledge is not something mechanical, but follows the learner's internal rhythms and dynamics.

After these few clarifications, we should like to conclude by listing a number of operations to be carried out to see whether the transfer has been established and consolidated:

- exercises to synthesize the knowledge acquired;
- exercises to apply that knowledge to the object studied;
- exercises to use that knowledge to 'read' other objects encountered in the environment;
- exercises to 'restock' the knowledge, that is, to work around the object in order to generate additional knowledge.

Note

1 This text is based on the author's studies and experience in the field; in particular, his contribution to Group IV (The Creativity of Actors and New Social Issues) of the European Adult Education Conference (Barcelona, 12–14 December 1996). It draws also on the Socrates Project of the Commission of the European Communities, *Mediterranean Itineraries for the Environmental and Cultural Education of the European Citizen: Didactic Pathways through Lleida (Catalonia)*, Montalbano-Mediovaldarno (Tuscany) and Nauplia (Argolis), of which he was the academic director. The project produced a pedagogical guide and teaching sheets, which were published in 1998 in four languages (French, Italian, Catalan, and Greek) by Pacini, in Italy.

An Ecological Culture for Teachers

Viara Gurova

This paper argues in favour of an ecological culture to be passed on to future generations, who will provide for the future of Bulgaria and the construction of a democratic society. The author describes ecological culture as a global approach to solving the problems associated with the socio-economic, cultural, and environmental context.

According to the author, we must now ensure that basic education has an ecological perspective, and introduce all aspects of this approach into university courses and continuing education and training. Having examined the programs and courses offered by faculties of education and institutes of continuing education, she indicates the directions to be taken in order to improve the training of future teachers, who will contribute to the adoption and generalization of responsible behaviour in the difficult relationship with the environment.

To Begin with a Story

Let us imagine a blue sea, a young man who looks like a Greek god, and a baby dolphin. The young man goes up to the dolphin and holds out his hand to touch it. His blue eyes are full of goodness, tenderness, and love. They seem to say, 'Don't be afraid, I am a friend.' The baby dolphin responds with a trusting look: 'I'm not afraid. Do you want to play?' 'Let's play,' answers the young god. The baby dolphin happily approaches him and kisses him on the cheek. The young man returns the kiss and embraces the dolphin tenderly. The two friends plunge beneath the waves, free and happy, and quite without fear. They swear eternal friendship in a sort of sacred dance, taking turns touching each other and moving away. The corals witness the carefree frolics. The mother dolphin swims calmly around them, knowing instinctively that there is no threat to her child.

This is a true story (an episode during the ALPHA 2000 seminar held in March 1999 in Nuweiba, Egypt). There were three participants – two men who decided to dive for the last time into the realm of the corals with their cameras, and a free baby dolphin that was as trusting, affectionate, and charming as a child.

How could such an extraordinary meeting come about? Nature? Goodness, perhaps? The baby dolphin is a little god plunging into the blue waters of the Red Sea without understanding the wonder of what is happening to him. He has only been in the world for a short time, but already he loves life and feels free and happy. The young man still has in his heart the enthusiasm of the child. He feels free and happy in the water, in this world of beauty and quietness. When he joins in this fantastic dance, full of joy, it is the child in him which predominates. The dance is a game played by two children who are free and equal.

We are all equal before the mystery of nature. If we carry goodness, humanism, and love of the beauty that surrounds us in our hearts, wonders can come true. A Bulgarian proverb says: 'It is not beauty that one wears on one's brow. It is goodness.' People come into the world free, sincere, pure, and trusting. But how do we become oppressed over the years and cease to feel godlike? What pushes us to reinforce those very mechanisms that oppress us? The history of humanity shows that we are ever more constrained by our own laws and ever more dependent on a technology that lulls our instincts to sleep and leaves us completely at a loss when it can no longer deliver. People are living increasingly anti-ecologically in our perfect world. We are prisoners of this infernal circle and ask ourselves complex questions: How can I free myself? How can I escape from the labyrinth of dependency? How can I change myself? How can I become closer to nature once again?

Is this indeed possible? Can human beings live as their ancestors did, dwelling in a more real and natural world? Could they give up all modern commodities? How long would they survive without restaurants, automobiles, watches, and machines?

Most would not hold out for long. The freedom of nature would be another prison, an alien world, and they would long to go back to noise, dust, machines, and 'junk food.' For a moment, they would feel like gods, but a short while later they would resent the quiet, the greenness, and the peace. They would nonetheless seek to go back to them, just for a while, and every second would make them happy, changing them into children freed from the cares of everyday life.

A flower, a bird, or a butterfly can awaken in someone the spirit of childhood and the desire to live, just as did the baby dolphin's kiss. Then the hands reach out of their own accord to caress, the eyes sparkle with tenderness, and the heart overflows with love and solicitude.

How Can This Story Be Made to Come True?

In this troubled world of constant change, can people keep the child within them and at the same time live in harmony with their surroundings? What can help them to overcome the stress of everyday life, and to evolve? Usually, when people have serious problems, they turn to education, schools, and teachers to help and guide them. They look for the miracle that will turn children and adults into educated human beings who can adapt to sudden changes, can cope and develop in a way that will contribute to the well-being of society.

In all the international forums of the last decade of the twentieth century, there has been an emphasis on the role of basic education in the development of the individual and that of society. At the International Conference on Adult Education held in Hamburg in 1997 (CONFINTEA V), our attention was called to a new dimension of education, namely education for sustainable development, which consists of learning throughout life to solve the ecological problems associated with the socio-economic, political, and economic context. It will be impossible to guarantee a stable future if we do not take into consideration the close relationship between the environment and development.[1]

Given that rapid changes are taking place in all areas of life, the problems facing human beings and the environment are complex and interrelated. Whether we are aware of it or not, the solving of any problem calls for a global approach to the difficult relationship between human beings and the environment (natural surroundings, society, and culture in their historical context). This holistic approach to the environment requires a particular kind of preparation: a new awareness, and the adoption of new attitudes to the professional and civic responsibilities which men and women bear today.

In Bulgaria, teachers are playing a very important role in this period of transition from totalitarianism to democracy. They must educate the next generation, who will live in the twenty-first century and will have to build a democratic society. They must help the adults (parents and young people) to acquire a new perception of themselves and of how Bulgaria can survive in the new world order. For them to achieve this, a new ecological culture has to be introduced into university and continuing education. This culture rests on an understanding and implementation of better relations between humanity, nature, and the environment.

An ecological approach to education is at the heart of this culture. According to Jean-Paul Hautecoeur, this approach presupposes 'both an awareness of the ways in which we interact with our natural/cultural environment, an ethic of conserving resources and biocultural diversity, techniques and methods of applying this ethic, and a proactive policy of changing customs (laws) with the aim of preserving or restoring the quality of our environment.'[2] That means, in the case of teacher training, that specific knowledge has to be brought into line with universal knowledge.

An ecological approach comprises the following three aims:

1. *The professional and personal development of teachers*, through the acquisition of the most recent knowledge of how to teach their particular subjects; and through the acquisition, use, and creation of successful teaching methods and tools.
2. *The improvement of educational systems and processes*, through the encouragement of an interdisciplinary approach and teamwork; through support for innovation; through the development of skills for problem-solving and prioritizing of educational objectives; and through the development of the capacity to manage interpersonal relations.
3. *The acquisition of an understanding of the social milieu and the environment*, through the encouragement of the development of a closer relationship between the education system and the economic system; through the establishment of relationships between schools and businesses; through support for research into the influence of economic factors on young people's behaviour; and through the encouragement of teachers and students to adapt to economic and cultural changes.[3]

One of the priorities of education, as proclaimed at CONFINTEA V, is the development of the human factor. University courses are only one stage in continuing education. They have to complement the knowledge acquired at school by taking the four major parameters of education as their basis:

1. *Learning to know*, or acquiring a broad general culture and specific skills. This process is linked to the objective of 'learning to learn in order to profit from the opportunities offered by continuing education.'
2. *Learning to do*, that is, not only acquiring vocational training but also learning about social experience, working as part of a team, and how to cope as an individual.
3. *Learning to live with others*, or acquiring a culture of communication and tolerance in order to benefit from pluralism, to develop joint projects, and to promote peace.
4. *Learning to be*, that is, forging one's own 'survival' skills in the present context of rapid changes, by assessing each situation and taking personal responsibility in the search for solutions and in decision-making.[4]

Taken together, the knowledge and skills acquired have the effect of transmitting values to men and women, who will thus be able to carry out their occupations in an efficient and responsible way. These are the elements of teachers' new ecological culture. This culture includes everything that is closely or even remotely connected with the environment: norms, laws and regulations, institutions, and individual awareness and behaviour. Ecological culture rests on the secular values of the relationships among human beings, nature, society, and culture. It involves knowledge of the environment, and ecological attitudes and values.

In the way in which they are organized and conducted, and in their content, university courses must provide training in ecological culture, whatever the subject area studied for a degree. Teachers' professional activities will contribute to the sustainable development of the economy, and of relationships and culture within a given society, in all spheres of human activities, from the least to the most specific.

The Ecological Dimensions of Teacher Training

Traditionally, ecological culture has been taken to mean the knowledge, values, and behaviours governing the relationship between humanity and nature. In a wider sense, ecology is 'a science that studies the conditions of existence of a living being and the relationships which are established between this being and its environment.'[5] The ecological dimensions of teacher training embrace all the elements of contemporary ecological culture. They presuppose teaching that will develop positive values and attitudes in students, not only towards themselves (by stimulating self-knowledge and self-esteem), but also towards others, towards nature, towards culture in all its manifestations, and towards society. A better society is the intended outcome of education for human rights and citizenship.

In the last few years there have been a number of initiatives in Bulgaria to strengthen and modernize teacher training, although these have not included aspects of ecological culture. A brief review of the syllabuses of a range of pedagogical subjects taught at the University of Sofia illustrates the changes undertaken in this direction. An examination of the content and the outcomes of the educational process reveals the presence of elements of a contemporary ecological culture: knowledge of the environment, adoption of ecological values and attitudes, and the formation and development of an awareness of responsible behaviour towards the environment.

Teachers are educated by the introduction of topics specific to ecological culture into the content of the basic disciplines of pedagogy, but also into other disciplines such as aesthetic education, sexual education, ethnology, etc. Given the university's autonomy, it is the faculties and their teaching heads who decide whether to include new topics in syllabuses, or to adopt new approaches. These decisions are often taken in the wake of national or international conferences, round tables or discussions, or of the reading of documents circulating in the Ministry of Education and Science.

The vice rector of the University of Sofia, Dr Dimitar Pavlov, summarizes the new postulates of university education thus: creativity, dynamism, a forward-looking orientation, awareness of the future, openness to learning acquired independently, and adaptation to the needs of students and society. Given the conservatism of some professors, and especially their traditional attitude of dominance over students, the direction being taken by the rectorate can be said to be innovative.

Research activity accounts for a significant part of the preparation of future teachers. In the course of their studies, they visit various social and academic institutions, and carry out research into family problems and the environmental activities of non-governmental organizations. Most students pursue their research in projects that extend beyond the university context. They thus have the opportunity of acquiring and exercising ecological behaviour. They meet with ethnic minorities, hold discussions with parents and teachers, and investigate the links between social problems, culture, and the way of life of these communities. One tangible result of the practical work done by students is the adoption of new values and attitudes in their relationship with the environment.

Voluntary social action is an important aspect of their studies. One example is that of members of a young people's organization, most of whom are students, cleaning historical monuments. Through this activity, they learn about their history and culture, and how to discuss historical facts; as well, they enrich their ecological culture by drawing directly on the experience of foreign organizations which are tackling environmental problems.

More and more students are taking part in activities involving street children, poor children, children who take drugs or are involved in prostitution, etc. The organization Aid to Bulgaria–Lily Schmid provides significant support for these measures. Three areas of activity are shared between this organization and the Faculty of Education:

- learning about the specific problems of children;
- strategies for running individual resocialization projects;
- research and collaborative work with pupils, teachers, parents, police, the prosecution service, and volunteers.

Students who took part in a seminar on the problems of street children have stated that working with disadvantaged children was a real lesson in humanism and a good field in which to apply theoretical knowledge to real life. These projects are one of the best ways of acquiring the awareness without which ecological behaviour is impossible.

Strengthening Teachers' Ecological Culture through Continuing Education

Qualified teachers have the opportunity to complement and update their knowledge of ecological culture in short courses provided by the Liberal Arts Faculty and the Institute of Continuing Education. Some of these courses relate to the field of applied ecology: environmental evaluation and protection, ecological expertise, protection of the vegetable world, mountain tourism, industrial ecology, etc.

The Technical University of Gabrovo offers students a one-year course on 'the economy of the educational environment.' This course deals with the problems of pedagogical ergonomics in the educational process. Most students taking the course are teachers in secondary technical schools who have no teaching certificate.

Some of the other continuing education courses are more open to various aspects of ecological culture. For example, the University of National and World Economics and its Institute of Continuing Education offer the following courses: ecology and environmental protection; ecological protection in the context of small enterprises; and special courses on public administration and the management of European integration. The syllabuses of these in-service courses cover environmental policies, sustainable development, public relations, regional economics, the European Union and its institutions, etc. The courses vary in length from thirty hours to eighteen months.

The University of Sofia also provides training courses that help to expand the ecological culture of final-year students, regardless of their specialization. Teachers can choose any course. The accompanying table shows some of the options.

The list of courses changes according to needs. Teachers can specialize in groups or as individuals and can obtain training in communication. Courses are regularly provided for those with higher education qualifications who wish to gain a teaching certificate. These optional courses enable them to familiarize themselves with the issues of ecological culture. Some stress the relationships between humanity, nature, society, and culture. For example: communication and education, family and education, religion and education, comparative education, youth sub-cultures, educational ethnography, etc.

Courses at the Institute of Continuing Education also enable students and administrative staff to enlarge their scientific knowledge relating to ecology.

Holders of higher education qualifications can also take part in non-formal continuing education. The Federation of Societies for the Propagation of Knowledge offers a range of specialist courses in ecology, notably for experts who analyse and evaluate the influence of human activities on the environment. Some public institutions and private companies also train their staffs in ecological issues.

Faculty	Subjects	Duration of course
Biology	New school syllabus for years 4, 5, and 9 Teaching of life and earth sciences	20 days
Chemistry	Problems relating to the teaching of chemistry	20 days
Mathematics	Teaching of ecology in vocational secondary schools Pedagogical communication and group work Alternative methods of education Conflict management	36 hours
History	Ethnology of Bulgaria	3 months + one year of specialization
Pedagogy of pre-schools and primary schools	Pedagogy of the arts Acquisition of technical skills for out-of-school teaching	12 to 18 month
General pedagogy	Modern communication and group work techniques Specialization as educational counsellors Certificate of education	1 to 3 days 6 to 12 months 12 months
Institute of Continuing Education of the University of Sofia	Health education Civic education Knowledge of economics for secondary schools Environmental protection	36 to 82 hours

The media broadcast programs devoted to ecology and environmental protection. Increasing attention is being given to international cooperation in environmental affairs and to the roles of various organizations, especially NGOs. These broadcasts play a major part in raising public awareness of ecological culture.

To Light a Candle or to Curse the Dark?

If they are to shoulder their responsibilities, teachers must have a high level of professionalism, characterized by flexibility and innovation, in addition to pedagogical competence. This is part of the new ecological dimension of teacher training. However, during the difficult transition period, the effective application of the ecological approach in training will take time. The guidelines of CONFINTEA V should provide a basis for the development of higher education and adult education in Bulgaria.

According to the Hamburg Declaration, universal access to literacy and basic education can be achieved:

- by adjusting literacy and basic education to social, economic, and cultural development, and to the needs of learners; by integrating basic education into all development projects in health and the environment; and by helping organizations and social movements to implement education and sustainable development projects;[6]
- by raising the quality of literacy and basic education programs through the integration of traditional and minority knowledge and cultures;
- by enriching the educational environment.

It is necessary to work out a specific ecological approach for the educational environment, the implementation of which would bring about positive changes in:

- the content of programs;
- the organization of the education process, by emphasis on student participation, independent and collaborative work, and effective learning methods and techniques;
- school materials, so that these reflect the problems of the environment in everyday life;
- learners' commitment to the process of evaluating the results of educational activities, academic courses, training, etc.

Creating such an educational environment presupposes an additional appropriate training for those responsible for university teaching. According to the Hamburg Declaration, in-service training for teachers working with adults – and this includes university professors – should involve:

- improvement of basic training and a requirement to undergo continuing training;
- refinement and application of innovative methods;

- provision of information and documentation services that take cultural diversity into account.[7]

Changes are being made very gradually. Numerous questions and difficulties are still open and unresolved. Some of these are as follows:

- the lack of specialists in adult education. No institution is training adult educators;
- the absence of a strategic policy on adult education, and hence the lack of knowledge about the needs of adult learners. After a change at the Ministry of Education and Science, the team set up to prepare for reform in this field was dissolved;
- the lack of coordination between the universities and those working in this field;
- the absence of statistical data;
- the lack of information and of coordination between establishments providing education programs and training courses for adults;
- the lack of coordination with employers, who might be able to help in matching the training of adults to the requirements of the workplace and of employee training;
- the absence of research into the problems of different social groups and their needs in education, bearing in mind their cultural identity;
- the absence of a strategy for the development of ethnic minorities and for their integration into Bulgarian cultural life. For example, the Union of Gypsies would like to set up a cultural centre and to organize musical performances. However, nothing concrete has been done by the Movement for the Defence of Rights and Liberties, despite electoral promises.

All these difficulties give the impression that we are in the gloomiest possible impasse. The situation is disheartening rather than an encouragement to act. We are seeing a lack of interest in education among poor people, who are concerned above all with survival. We should remember Maslow's pyramid of human motivation, in which education and personal development come after the satisfaction of physical needs. At the same time, in this period of transition, the provision of educational services by the private sector has increased considerably, which confirms the opinion of Phil Race, that what distinguishes people from monkeys is their desire to learn, and the possibility of thinking about what they want to learn and, if they wish, of looking for new paths of development.[8]

'It is better to light a candle in the dark than to curse the darkness,' said the Indian Satish Kumar. Rather than depriving children of schooling because school transport has been abolished, parents have set up their own small school in Hartland, in the United Kingdom. In Bulgaria, we must seek to convince teachers and to touch their hearts, for in their hands is the future of the country – its children. People say: 'You have to sow before you can reap.' Teachers are the sowers of a new culture, the fruits of which will be the manifestations of human awareness.

Bulgarian education has strong traditions. Bulgarian teachers do seek out information for themselves, and are thoughtful and creative. Despite the difficulties, most do their work well and try to solve problems. They feel responsible for the future of the Bulgarian nation. They will, without a doubt, succeed in rising to the challenges of life. The application of the ecological approach and the awareness of the place and role of human beings in relation to the environment are also a challenge at the professional level. Despite the difficulties, I believe that teachers will enter upon the twenty-first century with creativity, humanism and optimism.

Notes

1 UNESCO, Fifth International Conference on Adult Education, Hamburg, 14–18 July 1997, *Hamburg Declaration: Agenda for the Future* (Paris: UNESCO; Hamburg: UNESCO Institute for Education, 1997), p. 5.
2 Jean-Paul Hautecoeur, ed., 'ALPHA 99 – Ecological Approaches to Basic Education' (1998), Report of the ALPHA 99 Seminar, Brno, September 1998, p. 4.
3 European Commission, *Formation des enseignants sans détachement du travail* (European Union and EFTA [EEA], EURYDICE, 1995), pp. 8–9.
4 International Commission on Education for the Twenty-First Century, *Learning: The Treasure Within* (Paris: UNESCO; London: HMSO Books, 1996), pp. 85–97.
5 *Dictionary of Our Time* (Bulgarian), vol. 1 (Hachette and Prosveta, 1997), p. 484.
6 UNESCO, Fifth International Conference on Adult Education, Hamburg, 14–18 July 1997, *Final Report* (Paris: UNESCO; Hamburg: UNESCO Institute for Education, 1997), p. 31.
7 Ibid., pp. 29–30.
8 P. Race, *Who Learns Wins: Positive Steps to the Enjoyment and Rediscovery of Learning* (Harmondsworth, UK: Penguin Books, 1955).

PART TWO

Stimulating Participation through Social Action ...

... in an ecological movement of regional revitalization
— *Jan Keller, Czech Republic*

... in the schools, and ultimately, on an environmentalist campus
— *Michal Bartos, Czech Republic*

... on a committee to save community gardens
— *David Barton, United Kingdom*

... combining environmental education with democratic practices
— *Adel Abu Zahra, Egypt*

... even civil disobedience in the face of the dangers of an international agreement
— *Brian Sarwer-Foner, Canada*

Education for Regional Sustainable Development

Jan Keller

The author calls for education that is more closely linked to regional life and better adapted to ecological needs than is the current school system. Ecological education presupposes ties with community life. He confronts the sociological theories of community with the practical problems that accompany attempts to revitalize community life in the Czech Republic. He examines the opportunities for creating stable, non-hierarchical networks that could facilitate contact among groups and individuals, and help them co-ordinate their efforts to renew community life.

The literacy rate in the Czech Republic is almost 100 per cent. Although the rate of higher education is lower than in the most developed countries, the general level of education is satisfactory. This education has naturally been forged by the needs of an industrialized society. It has aimed above all to prepare men and women to meet the requirements of the major industrial and bureaucratic organizations. In short, the population continues to be trained to fulfil the goals of mass production and consumption, within an orientation that shapes a particular mentality characterized by conformity and passivity.

Effective adaptation to a centralized regime suppresses sensitivity to local peculiarities and particularities. Accustomed to state authority, men and women relinquish responsibility towards their locality. At the same time, passive attitudes and abandoned responsibilities weaken, and even suppress, cooperation between individuals. Such developments necessarily lead to significant social and ecological damage. People lose the intimate relationship with their surroundings; they no longer know how to use local resources; they become increasingly dependent on forces that are further and further removed from their concerns. Their locality becomes a sort of temporary stopping place into which goods are imported and from which refuse is exported.[1]

At the same time, localities become temporary stopping places in the social sense. The number of community activities declines, the frequency of contact between people falls, and the whole of life withdraws into a private world. The consequences of this for the development of the civil society are disastrous. Without a strong and vital civil society, the process of democratization stops half-way.[2] This is one of the reasons why the process of democratization in this country has nearly ground to a halt, and why it has been limited to the games of the political parties, which are suspended in a wider civil void of stalled decision-making.[3]

The Need for New Forms of Education

As has been mentioned, the formal education system fulfils the needs of a centralized society, but it is far less useful from the perspective of the locality in which people live. The very form of this education system reinforces centralizing logic and at the same time restricts the opportunities to draw on the experiences of everyday life.

In order to correct this appreciable shortcoming, it is not enough to change the content of education. The overall effect of education is determined not only by its content, but also by the way in which it is delivered. The predominant form of education is also extremely centralized. The entire education system harks back to the eighteenth century, a time when the power of the modern state was systematically eliminating all the independent elements of community life. The chief task of a centralized system of schooling was to shape human experience in accordance with the political, economic, and cultural priorities of the state. The bureaucratized education system served the forces of centralization, forces that respected neither the particularity of the regions nor the singularity of individuals. Knowledge deriving directly from the regions and localities was marginalized.

If we wish to bring people's education closer to their needs, we need to transfer resources and decision-making from the capital to the regions and even the local communities. If education is to become ecological, it must above all regain its links with community life.

For education to interest people who are already educated (at least at the formal level), its programs must be well fitted to local circumstances. While people still remain in their localities, it is perfectly legitimate to suppose that this will stimulate a demand for 'localized knowledge.' The community level is, by its very nature, predestined to become a genuine school of regional literacy.

Education in and for a community presupposes that the basic model of pedagogical interaction will change profoundly. The classical model of education was limited to a one-sided relationship between 'schoolteacher and pupil.' This model expressed the inequality of power typical of the entire system. On the one side was omniscient authority, and on the other, the pliable material that was to be moulded to fit the criteria of tried and true methods.

Education at the community level does not set out to serve the image of an indivisible authority. The roles of teacher and student are not hierarchical. The teacher enriches his or her knowledge just as much as the student participating in the educational process. Education becomes a common ground that benefits two partners. Teacher and student both gain a deeper understanding of the local and historical context of all their knowledge. While television 'frees' us from every context by diminishing our capacity to distinguish what is important from what is banal, ecological education at the community level can give us back that capacity. It does so by improving our understanding of events that surpass life in local communities.

Efforts to Revive Communities

A great deal of sociological literature has examined the potential and limitations of community life.[4] Most authors agree on the fact that traditional communities are being successively destabilized by the processes of political centralization, industrialization, and urbanization. This dominant direction of the development process was described in the early 1960s by the American sociologist Maurice Stein.[5] Significant attempts have been made to cast community life in an idyllic light, which exaggerates the merits of spontaneous authority and non-formal relationships. These illusions of a return to a golden age of the community have been popularized particularly within the ecological movement. The dream of a return to community life is often a flight from unsatisfactory and threatening reality.

As a result, every effort to revive community life is called into question. The romantics fear that communities will be lost forever as a result of modernization. The partisans of modernity, on the other hand, fear that a community renaissance may lead to a return to pseudo-community forms of social organization.

Moreover, a return to 'blood and soil' was one of the slogans of the fascist movement. It is true that the community ideal can, under certain conditions, become a pretext for animosity towards anything 'from outside,' and even lead to the exclusion of those who are not part of the community of the elect.

Although these dangers exist, it has to be admitted that the community approach contains positive features. The local community can fulfil an important mediating role between the state and its citizens, who otherwise have few opportunities to influence decision-making in a centralized system. According to Alexis de Tocqueville, no democracy can survive for long in the absence of such institutions. Intermediary institutions foster the development of civil society.

Another argument in favour of a certain renaissance of community life has been put forward by the ecological movement. The supporters of the bio-regionalist movement stress the human need for attachment to an ancestral home as opposed to an abstract identification with international citizenship. They point to the need for a far more intimate and specific territory to which people can make a real commitment and see the results of their efforts. It is at the bio-regional level that social relationships are clearly and closely linked to the social and natural environment. This does not imply a return to the autarchy of the Middle Ages, but a far more efficient use of domestic and indigenous resources, and greater responsibility towards the natural and social environment in which we live.

The Particularities of the Czech Republic

Any initiative for sustainable development at the regional level in the Czech Republic must take into account a number of inadequacies in social life, but fortunately it can draw on a number of favourable circumstances.

The major obstacle is passivity among a large proportion of inhabitants, their unwillingness to take part in projects that demand some of their time and energy, which are in short supply. This passivity was confirmed in a research study on social actors and local politics (conducted in this country by the team of Alain Touraine in the early 1990s). Most people expect the politicians to take care of, and find solutions for, everything beyond the narrow confines of their families and home lives.

This mentality, which obstructs the development of local and regional activities, may be regarded as a hangover from authoritarian times, but such an explanation is too simplistic and inadequate. A similar mentality is surely also present in countries that were not affected by a communist regime. Such a mentality, determined by forms of production, decision-making, and consumption within the framework of organized modernity, is widespread in many societies today. Passivity is a major obstacle to the participation of the inhabitants in adult education projects. Nonetheless, a whole series of circumstances may be mentioned that may sustain such efforts. Paradoxically, most of these favourable circumstances were also to be found under the former regime:

1. The population is tied to a particular place (to a far greater extent than in the United States). The rate of geographical mobility is relatively low, people being accustomed to live for several generations in the same place. Regional loyalty is relatively widespread, although it is seldom based on a profound knowledge of the places to which people feel attached. There is thus considerable potential for adult education.
2. These historical regions are rich in cultural traditions and traditional values. In some cases (Slovacko, Valassko, etc.), these traditions are still alive, notably during festivals, and they keep their attraction for young people. Numerous non-formal associations pass on these traditions from one generation to another in the form of folklore. Under the former regime, folklore was one of the few fields in which it was possible to engage outside communist ideology. Currently, the same regional folklore is a cultural genre that is valued.
3. From the point of view of community animation, the specific form of urbanization is another advantage. Most towns in the Czech Republic are small, ranging from 10,000 to 20,000 inhabitants. There are no major cities outside the capital, Prague, which has a population of about one million inhabitants. The dense network of small towns and villages enables everyone to have close and easy contact with nature. Thanks to its modest dimensions, the social network is also relatively simple and clear, and community relations can, when needed, be established easily.

4. Among the other advantages is the high level of social homogeneity among the population. It has been pointed out that the former regime failed to achieve complete social equalization, but it is also true that social segregation did not develop to the same degree as in the rich countries. The different social and occupational classes still live in close proximity, and the social distance separating them is not so great. Current economic developments should not change this situation, at least in principle.
5. Finally, the last of the circumstances that favour the revitalization and reinforcement of community relations is a little absurd. It is well known that relationships of this kind become stronger in critical situations, when the problems of everyday life become more serious and the central institutions are incapable of helping to resolve them. We are now in such a situation. The system, which is still too heavily bureaucratized, is at a standstill, and the political and economic crisis is continuing to worsen. After their experiences of the former regime, it is unlikely that the majority of people will dream of a return to communism. But there is a third way: to overcome passivity and start using our own resources again. The central treasury is increasingly empty, and the crisis of the welfare state may accentuate the importance of community relations. Historically, the community is what is left for people who can no longer hope to receive help from outside.

The Process of Globalization and the Danger of Exclusion

What changes may be brought about in this situation by the process of globalization? This question remains wide open. Everyone can see that globalization is a necessary and irreversible process. Nonetheless, opinions differ widely as to the possible consequences of this worldwide process. According to the optimists, globalization will lead to a world in which the various cultures will draw closer together and nations will become richer. According to the pessimists, we must look forward to growing inequality and conflict among countries in terms of economic competition, politics, ideology, and culture.

At all events, the logic of current globalization is upsetting that of the welfare state. The increasing mobility of the major multinational companies contrasts with the immobility of countries and regions. Multinational companies are ever more adept at depleting countries and regions, and at imposing their demands and conditions on them, which include determining the price of labour and the extent of natural resource exploitation. At the same time, the multinationals attempt to set up shop wherever the tax regime is most beneficial to them. Governments are losing their traditional means of regulating the unemployment rate, and they lack adequate resources to stem the tide of under-employment or deal with its consequences.[6]

The new economic order is increasing the dangers of exclusion, not only for poorly adapted individuals, as in the past, but also for entire localities. It may trigger a revitalization of community relations in the regions at risk. In such a context, adult education may have an important role. Nevertheless, the problem of moving from the welfare state to active, entrepreneurial communities is, naturally enough, highly complex, and it cannot be hoped that education alone will be sufficient to the task.

In this critical situation, two possible strategies can be seen for helping the excluded. The first was widely practised under the welfare state. This consists in distributing social assistance directly to people who are in need. This form of aid has its weaknesses, which are well known. People become dependent on a constantly growing bureaucratic machine. They find it difficult to reconstruct a valid identity, and increasingly turn into a 'welfariat.' Worse, the very forms of employment that long allowed people to define a social identity have become rarer. It must not be forgotten that material security alone cannot guarantee that exclusion will be overcome since exclusion goes far beyond economic factors.

In short, the traditional policies of assistance and redistribution, which remain essential, will not allow the victims of exclusion to be helped to escape from their situation. These policies keep the excluded penned into their isolation and low self-esteem. Forms of state assistance further undermine the social bonds among people rather than restore them. The system of bureaucratized 'solidarity' itself requires people to relinquish all social links in order to benefit from social assistance.

From time to time, some thought is therefore given to an entirely different course: a renaissance of community life, a return to a world in which the role of the economy is less dominant than it is today. It is true that economic relations are only one aspect of exchanges between people. Undoubtedly it would be enriching to create new, wider, and more satisfying forms of solidarity.

Up until 1989, a system was established among us which, let us say, had certain community features. The market, which produces not only wealth and consumption but also unemployment and exclusion, did not exist. Society was relatively homogeneous, and economic marginalization was more or less absent thanks to the existence of various social networks of an informal nature, notably the family.

In an economy that produced only a minimum of social exclusion, there were nevertheless two other persistent sources of marginalization: the first derived from unequal access to power and political structures; the second from lack of access to the dealings of the informal economy.

The current situation in my country is unique because we are experiencing a transitional period, and, according to the greatest sceptics, we have succeeded in combining some of the faults of a market economy with the vices of the former system. Economic growth is practically nil, in contrast to growing social exclusion. The unemployment rate has reached almost 10 per cent and is continuing to rise; exclusion on the basis of ethnic origin is worsening dramatically (especially in the case of Gypsies); older people are in a difficult socio-economic situation; and the number of homeless people is constantly growing.

We have therefore to find some other combination that can bring together the advantages of the welfare state with a system that can better accommodate community relations. This path will lead us from the nation state towards localities, and from a purely economic approach to one that is more social and cultural. It will above all lead us from economic growth to growth in employment, which does not automatically derive from mere economic expansion, as can be seen today. We believe that no one in the community should be reduced to the status of a mere consumer or user of services, and that social ties that are not governed by state bureaucracy can protect people from exclusion.

Mala Sumava: A Failed Attempt at Reviving a Marginalized Region

Let us now try to document two attempts that set out to revive regional and community life through adult education. The first, called Mala Sumava, although unsuccessful, provided significant experience for its initiators.[7]

In the mid-1990s, the social and ecological movement DUHA (a member of the international organization Friends of the Earth) attempted to implement a project to revive community relations in a locality in southern Bohemia, which had barely been affected by industrial activities. The authors of the project assumed that changing the relationship between people and their natural environment would be impossible unless relationships among people were improved at the same time. The DUHA movement, in cooperation with the members of the local administration, was seeking an alternative development model for this marginalized region. Their project targeted a range of goals:

- help with the establishment of small primary schools;
- foster the return of educated people to agricultural areas and their integration into the cultural life of the region;
- prepare cultural activities (exhibitions, theatre, etc.) that might be embraced by local tradition;
- create cultural festivals in which local artists could come into contact with artists known throughout the country;
- establish a local newspaper;
- found a publishing house for books of local origin.

The DUHA movement found weak support for its activities from the local authority, and more active support from Zlata Koruna convent. Most of the inhabitants reacted to the project with some scepticism and with little real curiosity. Moreover, it was soon noticed that local interest groups were trying to win the newcomers over to their side in their incessant ideological disputes. These cliques did not take an interest in the aims of the project, but instead wondered how they could profit from it to the detriment of their local adversaries. Prominent figures in the region began jealously guarding their positions, which they believed to be threatened by the newcomers.

The project came to an end after three years. The chief cause was not lack of money or the inability to find the accommodation and premises needed for the cultural and educational activities. The initiators of the project failed to rally the various interest groups. The locals could see no reason to change their way of life. They did not feel that they needed to live differently.

The lesson of this failed project is both simple and complex. The major obstacles to implementing this project were indifference and even apathy on the part of local people. It should be remembered that people only become sensitive and open to education once they have attained a certain level of education. The problem that must be addressed is how to awaken awareness of and the desire for better education. The Mala Sumava project organizers did not succeed in discovering the dynamic that would have enabled them to pursue this purpose.

Libceves: The School for the Regeneration of the Countryside

This project is entirely different in terms of its goals and scope. It was initiated by the mayor of the little village of Libceves in western Bohemia. He wished to create a space in his village for regular meetings of active people, from a variety of occupations, to pursue a common aim – the revitalization and ecologization of the countryside. The school for the regeneration of the countryside set out to bring together specialists in different fields (energy conservation, low-cost construction of buildings, solutions to the problems of marginal groups, etc.). It thus aimed to create a forum for the exchange of information and ideas.

The main aim of the project is not to attempt to involve all local people in its activities, but rather to create a solid coordinating network to meet the needs of activists working to achieve similar goals throughout the country. The main advantage of this project is that it is addressed only to the people who already have at least some motivation for educational action.

The school is rooted in a network of free, non-hierarchical contacts which anyone can join voluntarily. The village of Libceves serves only as a natural rallying point from which impetus can be given to initiatives, and from which ecological action can be coordinated. The project's educational outlook draws on appealing psychological strategies such as role play.

The revitalization of the countryside does not mean a return to the past. The school intends to harness the Internet and all the useful technology of the late twentieth century. It also aims to bring the different generations together in its network. It will offer young ecologists the chance to discover alternative living in the countryside; afford experts the opportunity to apply their ideas directly in the field; and provide older people with the chance to settle in buildings without barriers. The school has merely begun its activities, and the future will show whether this approach is viable.

How to Advance Local Literacy

As mentioned in the introduction, it is at the community level that the literacy process may become appropriate from the ecological point of view, in comparison with the classic, centralized education system. It is at the local community level that the form can best serve the content. The key unifying concept is participation.

How can we move in this direction? It has to be said that local education has little chance of becoming a widely standardized, systematic activity. In any case, that would be contrary to its purpose.

In the Czech Republic, local education will likely benefit a small number of people for some time to come. Concern for the revitalization of poor and exhausted regions is not a widespread preoccupation in the present situation. Development occurs wherever resources are most abundant, often at the cost of causing very serious social and ecological damage.

If local literacy is not to be a purely marginal affair, rather extensive networks have to be created to put people of varying backgrounds, orientations, and potential in contact with each other. Fortunately such people are already keenly interested in their communities, and are easily contacted. For example, there is a group of people who have for a long time been fighting to save a hill in western Bohemia that is threatened with development. There are people in the north of the country who have refused to leave their homes under threat of expropriation. In the west of the country there is another group of young people who are protesting the building of a motorway in an area of historical and ecological importance. In the south of the country, another group has successfully prevented a Czech Disneyland from being built in their region.

All these people, young and old, from all social backgrounds, are not usually in touch with each other. Yet these people and groups often consult the same lawyers and seek help from the same experts. From time to time, they all sign the same letters addressed to politicians. It is not necessary that these people should work on the same projects. What is important is that they have the chance to contact each other whenever they need to do so.

One way of creating and maintaining relations between these groups is through our newspaper *The Seventh Generation*. This newspaper takes a great interest in local traditions, but it also addresses regions threatened by sudden socio-economic change in this 'greater society.' It does not resort, however, to nostalgic appeals in its efforts to raise readers' awareness of their roots.

Conclusion

The official education system continues to prepare students for life in a society that is highly centralized and hierarchical, and enclosed in the fixed framework of frontiers and national economies. The process of globalization is breaking down frontiers, and is creating new areas of uncertainty and new dangers. In this unprecedented situation, the strengthening of community relations linking people who are prepared to resolve common problems through cooperation may serve as an effective protection against these dangers and uncertainties. We cannot survive the flood of globalization by withdrawing into isolation. A wiser form of defence is to create flexible, non-hierarchical networks bringing together experts and all interested people and making it possible for them to work in a range of contexts. For these networks to be more than virtual, it is necessary to provide them with meeting places in a number of localities. New experiences might radiate out from these meeting places – experiences of the revitalization of social relationships and of the creation of a balance between human society and nature, a balance without which there can be no guaranteed sustainable development in the future.

Notes

1 From the ecological point of view, the transport associated with this way of living is becoming one of the most threatening activities in comparison with the activities of the other sectors of the economy.
2 The problems of 'half-way democracy' are well known even in developed countries, as Ulrich Beck has noted. See U. Beck, *Risikogesellschaft* (Frankfurt am Main: Suhrkamp, 1986) and *Politik in der Risikogesellschaft* (Frankfurt am Main: Suhrkamp, 1991).
3 According to sociological research, the number of citizens who are convinced that the present system does not differ essentially from the pre-1989 regime is still rising. Fifty per cent of citizens believe that conditions before 1989 were better for them than they are today. Indifference towards politics is growing appreciably; during the elections to the Senate, only 20 per cent of electors voted in the second round.
4 C. Bell and H. Newby, *Community Studies: An Introduction to the Study of the Local Community* (London: George Allen and Unwin, 1971); G. Crow and G. Allan, *Community Life: An Introduction to Local Social Relations* (London: Harvester Wheatsheaf, 1994); G.A. Hillery, *Communal Organisations: A Study of Local Societies* (Chicago: University of Chicago Press, 1968); D.E. Poplin, *Communities: A Survey of Theories and Methods of Research* (New York, 1972).
5 M.R. Stein, *The Eclipse of the Community: An Interpretation of American Studies* (New York: Harper and Row, 1964).

6 An exact analysis of the possible political consequences of globalization is sketched out by the Polish sociologist Zygmund Bauman in *Globalization* (London, 1968). On the social and economic consequences, see Richard Douthwaite, *The Growth Illusion: How Economic Growth Has Enriched the Few, Impoverished the Many and Endangered the Planet* (Dublin: Green Books, 1992). See also R. Douthwaite, *Short Circuit: Strengthening Local Economies for Security in an Unstable World* (Dublin: The Lilliput Press, 1996).
7 Sumava is the name of a mountain massif on the border between Bohemia and Bavaria. The Mala Sumava project was conducted in one locality, Vysebrodsko, situated in this region.

Environmental Adult Education in the Czech Republic

Michal Bartos

This article describes the current state of environmental education for adults in the Czech Republic within the context of the social changes brought about by the transition from totalitarianism to democracy. A newly open society has afforded the ecology movement a space for expression. Activists have begun – not without difficulty – to take their place and undertake awareness-raising and information activities for the adult population. The author provides an overview of initiatives in the ecological approach to adult education within networks, programs, governmental organizations, and NGOs. The focus is on the activities of the Slunakov Centre for Environmental Education in the district of Olomouc, where the activists, along with the municipal council, have developed a significant range of ecological activities targeting adults and school-aged children.

A Context of Difficult Transition to Democracy

The collapse of the totalitarian political system in former Czechoslovakia in 1989 brought with it the expectation that citizens would readily take an active personal role with regard to extensive ecological problems. Since that time, the former forcibly uniform ecological movement has become an extremely varied collection of ecological groups. Nevertheless, neither the creative dialogue nor the ideological clashes concerning serious social problems seem to have been appreciated by other sectors of the social life of the nation. In addition, minor ideological clashes arising within the ecological movement have threatened the hopes for any significant penetration of ecologically oriented thinking and behaviour into the everyday social lives of the nation's citizens.

Initially, significant improvements were made in many fields of environmental protection and its cultivation. Many desirable laws were enacted. However, an increasing number of problems resulting from the process of economic transformation, as well as legislative and social problems, contributed to a mounting disregard for ecological issues by state authorities. The hopes of individuals who were not concerned merely with future material abundance were the first to vanish in the post-1989 development. Political parties on every administrative level obstructed possibilities for achieving a reasonable consensus, an essential step in managing the period of social transition from a totalitarian system to a democracy. Those who dared express criticism were often accused of retreating into the past. When the people were finally given the opportunity to support the candidates of their choice, the gains of the democratic system seemed to amount to nothing more than the right to cast a vote on election day. Worst of all, when the election campaign was over, the only opportunity to meet the elected representatives was to look at the retouched portraits on billboards and read simplistic slogans such as 'It is normal not to steal.' Politicians, then, hidden inside the thick walls of their offices, do whatever they can to create heaven on earth, forgetting somehow the public, civic movements, the political opposition and the experts.

It is therefore no wonder that such exclusionist behaviour on the part of the administration, enclosed in its severely guarded chambers, results in mistrust and frequent accusations of corruption, which in reality are not always well founded. Public matters seem to be unclear, obscure, and dark. Citizens showing public concern find themselves in the familiar state of hopelessness, unable to improve things, knowing they have no opportunity to influence the final decision. People feel 'out of the game'; citizens are not partners with representatives, as they had been promised. Instead, they feel somewhat like serfs. Their interests and concerns turn into indifference. Such a state of things results in an open struggle between the citizens and their representatives, who are consequently distracted in their efforts on behalf of the public interest by people's incompetent and personally motivated claims. Politicians and officers working in such an unpleasant atmosphere do not always realize that it is their duty to take an active part in a dialogue with the public. Both local authorities and the state government should be obliged to risk bringing all their aims into the open. They should overcome reluctance and take the risk of open ideological discussion. Although the losses may be painful, the gains, in the case of success, are tremendously desirable. Every sign of increased public involvement should be the politician's most precious reward.

The enormous emphasis on economic policy has led to the neglect of the transformation of social mechanisms that is essential for the successful development of a future democratic society. Issues concerning protection of the natural environment have often been considered merely the icing on the cake. In other words, the environment is reduced to a problem that will not be addressed until all the real, objective, and urgent problems are solved – meaning, of course, after the successful accomplishment of economic transformation and the end of economic stagnation. This strategy could turn out to have dangerous long-term effects: the damage may be irreversible.

Unfortunately, at present, the activities of the ecological movement in our country are committed above all to the defence of certain basic principles: the right to be fully informed about environmental issues, the state strategy of the electricity industry, the defence of the validity of the concept of permanently sustainable development, etc. Consequently, time has run out for open dialogue with the general public outside of ecological circles. Despite all these difficulties, many ecological movements are engaged in developing large-scale cooperation and accomplishing the urgent task of connecting ecological thinking and its values with the concepts that apply to other areas of public life: social welfare, legislation, the economy. Unfortunately, the voices opposing the concept of permanently sustainable development keep employing a rather convenient tactic. They usually condemn the ideological background of the ecological movement and accuse those involved of attempting to retreat to the totalitarian era, claiming their activities threaten the democratic development of society. Even very moderate ecological groups have been put on a government-compiled list of extremist organizations. The idea of permanently sustainable development has often been rejected as a vague concept without intrinsic meaning, and has been long excluded from the terminology of the official program for environmental protection.

Ecological issues appear only as a peripheral topic in the media. More often than not, if they appear on Czech television at all, it is in the form of a news reports about cute animal offspring born in zoos! The media usually present the activities of the ecological movement in its most radical form (immediately apparent among social and anarchistic ecological groups), a radicalism which is simplified and interpreted as pure violence. Never does the media offer any clear explanation for dissatisfaction among youth. Globalization is readily discussed, but is seldom the subject of any serious or profound social analysis, even though it plays a substantial role in current changes to the world's social and economic order.

It should be said that many members of the ecological movement make fruitful dialogue difficult for both the public and the authorities by presenting their illuminating and absolute truths intractably and with overly confident resolution. One can guess at the reasons why the pre-Revolutionary movements have paid such great attention to environmental activities. The participants used to plant trees, worked at preserving endangered precious natural areas, organized preservation programs to protect rare species of plants and animals, and took part in excursions to the countryside. After 1989, many different ecological groups emerged, including Hnuti-Duha (the Rainbow Movement) and Deti Zeme (Children of the Earth). These groups call for a non-anthropocentric view of nature. The general public tends to ignore this kind of moral appeal, or worse, often reacts with hostility. Such reaction stems partly from the intransigent forms of revolt adopted by some of the 'greens.' It is also partly a relic of the country's history, marked by numerous proclaimed ideals that merely covered up a distorted and painful reality.

Despite all these difficulties, a number of noteworthy attempts have recently been undertaken to inform the public and encourage it to step up pressure on political representatives within the conditions of a pluralistic society. Ecological movements do their best to incorporate deep commitment and a sense of responsibility concerning environmental problems into every level of social life. They take great pains to develop a strategy for desirable social communication in order to secure decent and dignified living conditions for the present generation as well as for the generations to come. These efforts are extremely difficult to accomplish without positive public dialogue based on mutual trust amongst all participants. The participants in the dialogue should have access to full, objective information. Effective strategies have to be developed in order to make this flow of information reach as many citizens as possible. At present, attempts of this kind are isolated and locally limited. Nevertheless, it is possible to envisage the implementation of several regional and governmental projects aligning ecological and social aims with economic and technical needs in accordance with the principles of sustainable development. A network of this kind is being developed which, although fragile, could eventually establish a basis for future social changes and long-term strategies to improve quality of life in the regions.

A Network of Ecological Organizations

At present, no existing state institution for environmental adult education serves the complete adult population. Many people show no interest in this topic, and one can hardly imagine their reaction should they be presented with such a sweeping program. Despite this fact, many non-governmental activities attempt to awaken public interest by focusing on the environment where people live, work, and relax. There are, however, some governmental activities and programs that rely on the active participation of the public in the decision-making process in order to accomplish their goals. The promising programs that aim to increase public interest in the task of incorporating ecological activities into Czech social life are described below.

Non-Governmental Ecological Movements

The network of non-governmental ecological movements is almost overpopulated. Some movements present themselves by organizing various activities, demonstrations, happenings, and exhibitions, or by publishing books and journals, etc. These movements cooperate closely with similar institutions abroad (Hnuti Duha, Deti Zeme, Greenpeace). Such organizations currently play an important role in conveying information on environmental conditions to the public and putting pressure on governmental institutions to amend inadequate environmental protection legislation. Socially oriented ecological groups cooperate with other non-governmental movements involved in social welfare problems.

Alternative Subcultures and Communities

These consist of groups of mostly young people who are searching for an alternative lifestyle, independent of the conformist political and social standards of the majority society (counter-culture). There are many such groups, with diverse histories and sets of declared values and ideals (punk, anarchy, squatting), which place them in opposition to those of official culture. As early as 1990, a group of artists invaded an empty house in Prague and named the place the Golden Ship. They held meetings in a 'café' that was open to every visitor. There was an art gallery in the house. The community included families and children whose communal life was quite harmonious until the police cleared the building out. One of the most famous instances of squatting is Ladronka Autonomous Centre in Prague, established in an uninhabited, shabby building by a group of young anarchist-oriented autonomists. The group has been involved in many cultural activities (concerts, films, theatre, journals, vegetarian food, exhibitions, tea room, library, etc.). In addition to its cultural activities and its anti-racist orientation, the community pays particular attention to an ecological lifestyle.

Another subculture community has emerged in the village of Chvalec, focused on a traditional rural way of life. A similar project is about to be begun in Libceves. These communities offer released criminals and drug addicts a chance to return to everyday life. This effort, however, causes some difficulties as conflicts arise between the community and the neighbourhood. The groups are sometimes accused of supporting crime. Many people interpret the movement's critical approach as an attack on democratic principles in general, and, as a result, tend to reject these communities. There are definite signs of the existence of subculture ideals throughout the Czech Republic, even outside the walls of these communities. Unfortunately, the majority does not accept these ideals. Nevertheless, the energy and creativity of young people has the power to alter the most deeply rooted prejudices of the majority.

Ecological Consulting Offices

Ecological consulting offices emerged from non-governmental movements. They mediate among citizens, local representatives, specialists, government, and commercial representatives. They contribute to the everyday dialogue on environmental protection. Since 1995, the consulting offices have been working as a unified communication network. The offices differ, however, as to their specialization. They provide those interested with information services on ecological methods in agriculture, organizations committed to alternative electricity sources, natural landscape protection, ecologically sensitive tourism, household ecology, the most ecologically friendly types of washing powders, legislative aspects of nature protection, wastage, agriculture, ecological ways of building and living, etc. Unfortunately, because of inadequate funding, the consulting offices are not situated in town centres. This rules out systematic contact with the public through effective promotional activities. The successful consulting offices are: Veronica in Brno, Rosa in Ceske Budejovice, and VITA in Ostrava.

'Local Agenda 21'

This program is based upon several documents (Agenda 21) adopted at the UN Conference on Environment and Development, the Earth Summit, in 1992 in Rio de Janeiro. The conference followed up a report tabled with the UN in 1987 pointing out that human development so far had been unsustainable in terms of preserving the contemporary quality of human life for future generations.

The Local Agenda 21 program was designed to encourage local and regional authorities to adopt concrete strategies to increase public awareness of the need for permanently sustainable development to guarantee a healthy environment. Local Agenda 21 is supposed to become both a strategic and action plan for the development of municipalities, districts, and regions. This plan focuses on the revival of villages and the development of healthy towns and cities. It emphasizes tasks within municipalities and in the surrounding countryside, as well as regional ecological projects. Its goal is to interconnect and harmonize ecological, social, economical, and cultural activities by involving representatives of all groups in the local community (local authorities, citizens, businesses, industry, and private companies) in the economical and effective use of natural resources. In this way, the connection is made between local, individual responsibilities and the global goals of environmental protection.

Unfortunately, this program has encountered huge obstacles. Agenda 21 was evaluated by the UN General Assembly in 1997, and the findings were positive. In 1997, more than 2,000 municipalities in 64 countries were involved in the program. However, the declared successes mask many problems: the clash between the wealthy North and the poor South; an unwillingness to increase development aid; mere promises about slowing population growth, etc. With the passing years, one senses that many of these well-intentioned aims remain only as documents, for lack of willingness and courage to enforce them.

The situation in the Czech Republic is similar, or maybe even worse, as people do not believe in planning, an attitude perhaps based on their experience under the former totalitarian regime. The painful political situation in a number of municipal parliaments, combined with disputes among political parties, often make it impossible for authorities to reach any agreement on development, let alone arrive at an agreement on permanently sustainable development. Personal, local, and group claims often quash public interest, as does the indifference of formerly committed activists. The program is thus mainly advocated by a handful of non-governmental ecological movements. Highly cooperative regional projects are often realized in a tremendously difficult context, within a still stratified society that does not seem quite ready to accept them just yet.

Nevertheless, a whole range of Local Agenda 21 ideas has been implemented in the program of the Centre for Environmental Education in Slunakov. The city council's support, in the form of financial resources, enables the centre to raise public awareness of environmental values and to implement sustainable development principles. The centre is an important partner. It informs the public, raises awareness, and involves various communities in social events. It tries to develop cooperation among various municipal services, as well as between the city hall and various institutions, in addition to maintaining an active dialogue with citizens.

Unfortunately, the Czech Republic version of Local Agenda 21 still takes the form of clumsily written handbooks, which are often perceived as merely romantic fairy tales. Nevertheless, the program has been successfully developed in Brno (Veronica), and there are plans for a pilot project in the region of Novy Jicin. It is also being developed in Cesky Krumlov, where an attempt has been made to define permanently sustainable development indicators with the help of many organizations and varied scientific expertise.

Village Revival Program

The village revival program is a successful governmental program that was adopted in 1991 and endorsed by the Ministry of Local Development, the Ministry of Environmental Issues, and the Ministry of Agriculture. Every year Parliament distributes funds to projects of the local development program (over 100 million crowns). The purpose is to encourage the activities of those municipalities that have designed their own revival and development projects. Such projects are designed to preserve the traditional rural character of the country, as well as cultural and community activities throughout all forms of development.

They must respect the local historical background and traditional crafts while developing modern trade, business, agriculture, social welfare, and housing policy, etc. Achieving the goals depends on the active participation of local inhabitants.

The Country Revival Society informs the public of the lessons to be learned from successful projects and shares its know-how. The Society gave rise to the Country Revival School, at Libceves. Many village development projects were accomplished on the school grounds. The Society organizes the annual 'Village of the Year' competition on both a regional and a national level, which has a notably positive effect.

The Society is remarkably influential in the district of Olomouc. The Litovelske Pomoravi National Preserve Administration also belongs to this organization. It initiates annual meetings of the representatives of villages situated inside or nearby the preserved area. As a result of this exemplary cooperation, it is possible to harmonize the architectural design of villages with the surrounding natural environment as well as to create projects for environment quality improvement.

Given the problematic economic situation, most of the available funds have been spent on the reconstruction of long neglected rural infrastructures. As a result there is little left for other no less important tasks.

The development of ecologically sensitive tourism might meet with a positive response from the public. There are many immensely remarkable natural locations and historical monuments in the Czech Republic, all interconnected by a dense network of marked footpaths that converge in numerous villages. The network of footpaths was set up prior to 1989, when hiking was very popular, particularly among the young. Unfortunately, the opening of borders between countries resulted in a decline in the popularity of hiking at home. Nevertheless, activities which attract people to spend their free time in the countryside and introduce them to the natural surroundings remain an effective method of environmental education.

'Healthy Town' Project

This project is a worldwide movement associated with the WHO 'Health for Everyone' program. It basically aims to establish a balanced material and social environment that preserves healthy living conditions for citizens. It is endorsed by the Ministry of Health. In 1993 the Council of the National Network of Healthy Towns was established and is now a member of the worldwide Healthy Towns network – EURONET (1994).

Other attractive initiatives have emerged in Brno, Cesky Tesin, Boskovice, and Sternberk. However, like Local Agenda 21, such initiatives embrace existing projects, and their main purpose is one of coordination.

Strategies of Regional Development

The Strategies of Regional Development program was set up with a view to the entry of the Czech Republic into the European Union. The governmental program was carefully prepared before being implemented in 1998. It is endorsed by the Ministry of Local Development. In all the regions (their definite borders are now a subject of fierce debate), nine boards are responsible for various spheres of social life in compliance with the development project. Many local non-governmental organizations as well as commercial bodies are official partners, and their interests and opinions are incorporated in the final version of the adopted documents.

The project, however, has encountered a wide range of difficulties. Its ties to other current activities, such as Healthy Town, Village Revival, and Local Agenda 21, remain unclear. The ratified documents will become the basis for the distribution of state budget funds to infrastructures. It is still not clear, however, whether the project goals will be successfully accomplished in the present economic situation.

Association of Environmental Education Centres: Pavucina

Pavucina is a network of organizations specializing in environmental education. Representatives of all environmental education centres (EECs) held a meeting in Prague in 1995 to discuss the inadequate communication among the centres. The Association of EECs (Pavucina) was established as a result of long-term preparations in April 1996. It brings together organizations primarily focused on developing and implementing environmental programs for school children and young people. Today this association has ten regular and six associate members committed to close cooperation. They all meet strict entrance requirements. All participating centres must offer courses for school children of all grades. The courses are part of the regular teaching curriculum; they comprise 60 lessons per year with seminars and excursions for the teachers and at least 30 lessons per year for teacher-training students. The overall extent of educational activities at schools must encompass at least 250 lessons a year. There must be at least one full-time expert in ecological education available in each centre, and the EEC is supposed to own or rent at least one room. Many centres experience difficulty meeting these requirements.

Pavucina is striving, so far unsuccessfully, to ensure the operation of EECs from state funds. Nevertheless, it is an influential representative and defender of social benefits, supporting the mutual exchange of experience and solidarity. It guarantees service of superior quality and the credibility of its members. Newsletters and many additional materials that are delivered to all members are an important source of information. Pavucina presents the work of centres at various fairs and promotional events that target education institutions. Many members took an active part in the elaboration of concepts of environmental education, and in the development of an environmental state policy document. All through the year 1997, some members also participated in negotiations with members of parliament and senators to prepare the strategic materials for the Ecological Education Centres 2000. At present, many EECs are operating under the supervision of the Czech Nature Protection Association, an organization with a long history. In addition, there are also several independent centres in existence. These centres constitute a web that covers the entire Czech Republic.

In addition to children's education, the centres also organize seminars for teachers and the general public. One favoured method aims to influence the adult public by educating children. Hundreds of children's groups and school classes, as well as many families, take part in ecological projects (e.g., Globe, Ozone, Blue Heaven, Three Steps to Life, Where Europe Ends, Living Water, etc.), which develop a strong sense of solidarity and shared responsibility for the ecological situation. Children can sometimes communicate their experiences to participants from abroad. In the course of the program, children and their teachers have the opportunity to solve actual problems concerning their environment, their village, or town. Children learn to be sensitive to the natural environment and its protection. Their friends, well-known personalities, official representatives, the general public, and the media often get involved in these projects. In 1997, the ecological education centres that are members of the Pavucina association arranged one-day teaching programs for 46,346 children, long-term excursion programs for 1,938 children, educational courses for 6,802 teachers, out-of-school excursion programs for 4,899 children, and other projects for 21,500 school children.

The centres organize a wide range of activities for the adult public.

Earth Day and 'ecological' Christmas celebrations arranged by the EEC members are very popular in certain towns. In 1997, a wide array of events organized by the Pavucina association for the general public drew 60,829 people. One centre focuses primarily on the improvement of ecological education for the public in our region: the Slunakov Environmental Education Centre, Olomouc, operating under the supervision of the Olomouc City Council.

Slunakov Environmental Education Centre

In 1993, the Slunakov Environmental Education Centre (EEC) was established as a separate section of environmental education within the Department of Environment. It draws on the previous experience of non-governmental movements that have been in operation since 1989. Since 1994, the Slunakov EEC has initiated cooperation with public schools. These programs – operating at all levels of the educational system, from kindergartens to secondary schools – have become the basis for communicating its ideas to the public. The EEC also rented a kindergarten classroom in Horka nad Moravou, where the surroundings provide an ideal space for direct practical education in the countryside. The aim is to educate children through personal experience and direct contact with the natural environment, in order to enable them to understand its complicated structural relations, not merely through reason but with all their senses. This is accomplished through play, discussion, and dramatic performances in all forms of creative self-realization.

The Slunakov Environmental Education Centre strives for a continuous dialogue with the public through regular ecological evenings (since 1993, at least one evening per month) and the ecological days of Olomouc. In 1998, the eighth version of 'Ecological Days,' one of the largest festivals of its kind in the Czech Republic, featured many ecological awareness events spread over roughly fourteen days. These events attempt to promote a dialogue about the world and the environment in the form of a public meeting in a 'square,' or at a 'crossroads,' where people must stop and consider past and future directions. These public discussions are intended to be an evening university, providing citizens with abundant information. Covering a variety of social and cultural themes, the program stresses the relationship between global problems and human activities. Over the course of a few years, it has become an inseparable part of the cultural and social life of the city.

Various activities in progress have thus prepared the basis for well-balanced social development in the region that values the social benefits associated with environmental protection. Such a goal should be supported by the Olomouc Association of Non-Governmental Organizations (OANO). The EEC is a member of this association and substantially contributes to the promotion of the organization's social, health, ecological, sports, and humanitarian projects, as well as to the prevention of social problems such as drug addiction, crime, vandalism, racial intolerance, etc.

The dream of the Slunakov employees remains the hope of eventually building a fifteen-hectare site in the municipality of Horka nad Moravou to accommodate most of Slunakov's activities for children and adults. The site would be a beacon illuminating the activities of all NGOs in the region. It has been included in the area plans of the Horka municipality. The underlying vision will be incorporated in the Village Revival Program, as well as in other regional projects based on the principles of permanently sustainable development.

The Slunakov project, which aims to build a campus centre for environmental education and alternative research, transcends common educational practice, and is highly oriented towards the future. It deals with the human dimensions of development and will thereby contribute to a complex understanding of all aspects of public life in the region. The vision was given form in the Urban Area Project, designed by architect Tomas Lampar. It includes plans for an area campus linked to the Litovelske Pomoravi Nature Preserve (marshy woods, arboretum, orchard) and the construction of a tourist information centre with a restaurant, an alternative school, a farm, an electricity-saving house, and, last but not least, a new building for the Environmental Education Centre. The building will provide room for the implementation of ecological education, including capacity for long-term stays. The Olomouc City Council officially approved the project in February 1994.

The original version of the Urban Area Project of the Slunakov Centre had to be substantially revised after heavy floods in 1997 affected a part of the area zoned for the project. The revised version more specifically defines the steps of the implementation process, and should minimize expenses and facilitate fund-raising for the project. The new project will be carried out in cooperation with Dutch landscape gardeners, in accordance with an agreement between Olomouc and its partner city Veenendaal in the Netherlands.

The new project design has replaced the original 'agricultural' focus and now plans an alternative tourist centre providing visitors with information on the region's natural environment and recreation, while maintaining its basic mandate for children's environmental education. The fifteen-hectare site in the Horka municipality will be gradually cultivated as the EEC campus of environmental education. The project involves the construction of a new building for the Environmental Education Centre providing accommodation for children coming for long-term stays. The building will house an educational exhibition focused on the Litovelske Pomoravi Nature Preserve, a wetland of international significance. Another part of the building would accommodate visitors interested in ecological tourism. The outdoor classroom available for school programs is to be built near the main building.

The entire surrounding area is to be reshaped to highlight the region's various biotopes, especially the Litovelske Pomoravi Nature Preserve. An instructional pathway would lead through the whole area with a number of stopping stations, where visitors, including handicapped people, will have the opportunity to relax not far from Olomouc. The centre will also take advantage of the already existing and widely popular bicycle trails, conveniently connected to the international bicycle trail network (together with Poland, Austria, and Slovakia). It is hoped that the project will be put into operation with the help of certain institutions whose social programs concentrate on the reintegration of socially maladjusted people.

The Slunakov project is expected to be completed over the next fifteen years. The Olomouc City Council has recently launched the first phase, the redevelopment of a one-hectare pond. The City of Olomouc will receive financial assistance from the state revitalization program. The success of subsequent phases depends a great deal on the support of the public and local authorities, and on the long-term successful economic development of the country.

A Primary Idea

Every step, even the smallest one, that develops a commonly shared respect towards life, enables people to understand their dependence on the environmental condition. Are people able to transform their knowledge of the deepening global crisis into action that would develop mutual cooperation and communication, provide assistance to the most affected regions, and initiate social changes to improve life for the maximum number of people and sustain environmental quality?

The whole ALPHA project is very inspiring. It provides information on social conditions in specific areas of the world, and enables participants (and perhaps readers too) to understand local activities within a global context. It interconnects isolated activities and thereby breaks new ground for planning a sustainable future.

This contribution describes several practical examples of ecological activities in the broader social context of sustainable development in the Czech Republic. It has highlighted the very recent initiatives of the Slunakov EEC. Given the current difficult economic situation, it is not easy to push through the idea that environmental, cultural, and social issues must go hand in hand with the resolution of the economic crisis. Hence the importance of non-governmental movements in society.

I would like to express an idea that I believe is of primary importance. The concept of sustainable development aims to restore value to natural resources within a system of social indicators. The goal of this concept is not only to protect nature, it is also to protect the world. It is a praiseworthy and realistic mission, but it can lead to a common failing among rulers: arrogance or simply blind belief in human infallibility. Nature becomes an object of evaluation, measurement, trade-offs, improvement, and also manipulation. Can we avoid making nature a pawn in the big game of *how, when, and how much?* Although not quantifiable, the idea of 'sacred' nature must be an integral part of the concept of sustainable development. Failing this, we risk intensifying the environmental crisis. The state of the planet requires much more than merely 'correcting' people's attitudes; it requires a radical shift. Such is the goal of our work in environmental education.

References

Kosik, Karel. 1995. *Stoleti Markety Samsove.* 2nd ed. Prague: Cesky spisovatel, p. 208.

Ministerstvo Zp Cr a Cesky Ekologicky Ústav. 1998. *Práce s verejnosti a mistni agenda 21.* 1st ed. Prague, p. 88.

Literacy Practices in Local Activities: An Ecological Approach

David Barton

An ecological approach to literacy is one which examines the role of reading and writing in people's lives. This paper traces the development of the idea of ecology when applied to cultural phenomena such as language and literacy. It then takes the example of a local community organizing to resist land developers, documenting people's participation in this action, and examining the role of literacy in real activities. This example then forms the basis for a more general discussion of literacy as part of democratic participation and sustainable development.

In this paper I want to explain what I mean by an ecological approach to literacy, showing how concepts from ecology can enrich our understanding of literacy. The example of a local community activity serves as a case study to show what can be learned about the role of reading and writing in people's lives in one place in today's world. More generally it provides an example of vernacular activity, of literacy embedded in its ecological environment. This paper draws on my earlier work, particularly Barton 1994 and Barton and Hamilton 1998; it has also benefited from discussion with the authors of the other chapters in this book.

The Ecology of Literacy

Firstly, in this section I provide an overview of how the concept of ecology can be applied to literacy; this is a summary of a broader argument which can be found in Barton 1994, 29–32. In the natural world, ecology is the study of the interrelationship of organisms and their environments. When applied to cultural phenomena, it is the interrelationship of an area of human activity and its environment. An ecological approach is concerned with how the activity – literacy in this case – is part of the environment and at the same time influences and is influenced by the environment. It takes as its starting-point this interaction between individuals and their environments.

Shifting the notion of ecology from the natural world to the cultural world can be traced to the work of Gregory Bateson, who linked biological notions of ecology to anthropological and psychological concerns about the nature of human thought. He referred to his collected works as steps to an ecology of the mind (1972). Since then others have used the idea of ecology to situate psychological activity, placing it in a more complete social context and a dynamic social context where different aspects interact. An example of this development which provides an important parallel for those of us interested in reading and writing is Ulrich Neisser's work on the ecology of memory (1982). This showed the importance of studying how people use memory in natural contexts in their everyday lives. Neisser was highly critical of laboratory-based experimental studies of memory, and argued for a more ecologically based approach, that is a more naturalistic approach. His book begins with an article arguing point-by-point the importance of studying natural memory and criticizing the methods of experimental psychology. His argument about the importance of studying phenomena in their natural settings applies equally well to the study of reading, which needs to get beyond an over-reliance on purely psychological approaches.

Within linguistics there has been an important strand of work which uses the term 'ecology' and which is now becoming identified by some people as ecolinguistics. This started with Einar Haugen's work (1972) tracing the extent to which immigrants to the United States kept their own languages or changed to using the majority language, English. Another example is the work of Michael Clyne (1982) in Australia, who uses 'ecology' to mean a study of the environment that favours maintaining the community language. A more recent use has been that of Peter Mulhausler, who points out the need to focus on factors related to the ecology of a dominated language, rather than on the language itself, if one is interested in its preservation (1996). Marilyn Cooper has used the term 'the ecology of writing' in relation to literacy, attacking the limitations of process views of writing that ignore the social aspects of writing (1986). The phrase 'the ecology of literacy' has been used by Patricia Irvine and Nan Elsasser to demonstrate that literacy teaching designed in one society may not be appropriate in another (1988).

The framework of ecology is a valuable way of understanding the uses of literacy and the learning of literacy. One advantage is that it has been used in both psychological and social traditions. Ecology actually produces a whole set of terms that can provide a framework for discussions of literacy. Terms like 'ecological niches,' 'ecosystem,' 'ecological balance,' 'diversity,' and 'sustainability' can all be applied to the human activity of using reading and writing.

There are also several ways in which applying these concepts demonstrates that literacy is also an ecological issue in the current sense of being a political issue to do with the environment. Firstly, languages are vanishing at a remarkable rate: there are many languages that have a very small number of speakers and these are likely to disappear within a lifetime. Literacy may be aiding this, but it can also have a role in changing it. For ecological reasons there is a need to protect these languages and the cultures they often embody.

Secondly, dominating languages like English need to maintain their diversity and variety. There are English languages, not one English. The dangers of a push to a monocultural view of any language are great. The edges are its vitality, and variety ensures its future. There is much diversity in language: there are different genres of language, different languages, and different scripts. An ecological approach emphasizes diversity and sees it as a virtue: diversity is a source of strength, the roots of the possibilities of the future. Again literacy has a role in maintaining diversity; it can be seen as the main force of standardization of languages, or it can have an important role in maintaining the range of variation in language.

Thirdly, there are communication technologies that can change the balance of languages and cultures, often in ways that have not been thought out. In the natural world there is technology available that can destroy whole forests and transform the earth at remarkable rates, irrevocably and without thought of ecological effects. The same is true of language and literacy. Large-scale communication, such as satellite television, means that sudden and probably irreversible changes are taking place now in our generation. Technology beyond a human scale is speeding up ecological change.

Concentrating on reading and writing, ecology is a useful way of talking about literacy at the moment, and of bringing together its different strands. Using the term changes the whole endeavour of trying to understand the nature of reading and writing from a purely psychological phenomenon to one that is both social and psychological. Rather than isolating literacy activities from everything else in order to understand them, an ecological approach aims to understand how literacy is embedded in other human activity, its embeddedness in social life and in thought, and its position in history, in language, and in learning. An ecological approach to cultural phenomena such as literacy is one which examines the social and mental embeddedness of human activities in a way which allows change. Instead of studying the separate skills that underlie reading and writing, it involves a shift to studying literacy, a set of social practices associated with particular symbol systems and their related technologies. Inevitably an ecological approach starts out from people's lives, from what people actually do and from the sense and meaning people give to their activities. In this way, an ecological approach gets to concentrate on vernacular activities and vernacular values, often contrasting them with more dominant ones.

An Example of Literacy Practices in a Local Activity

With colleagues I have recently completed a detailed study of people's everyday reading and writing (Barton and Hamilton 1998). The study was carried out in Lancaster, a town in northwest England, over a period of several years. The study involved a wide range of research methods, the central form of data collection being a detailed study of life in one neighbourhood. This included repeated in-depth interviews with people in their own homes, some covering a period of more than a year. These interviews were complemented by observations of local activities. There was extensive photography of the visual literacy environment and the collection of documents such as letters, newspapers, leaflets, and notices. Most interviews were recorded and transcribed, and the study resulted in a large amount of data.

Reading and writing played an important role in people's everyday lives, within the home and throughout the community. There was also a great variety of different sorts of reading and writing, and many different ways in which people participated in literate activity. To summarize such diversity, we found it useful to identify particular everyday activities and to examine how people bring reading and writing into their lives. One such area is social participation.

We found that people participate in a wide range of social activities, and we were surprised at the large number of groups and clubs which exist in the town, and the fact that everyone in our study seemed to have connections to at least one such organization and several people had been officers of organizations. There are clubs and associations concerned with animals, nature, sports, religion, music, politics, care for the sick and elderly, and much more. These range from small short-lived campaigning groups to long-established local branches of national organizations. We estimate that there are well over a thousand such groups in this medium-sized town.

Participation in groups can involve literacy in many ways. People read and contribute to notices and newsletters, participate in meetings, raffles, and jumble sales, design posters. People write to local newspapers as members of associations and send in reports of activities and achievements. Records of memberships and finance are kept and there may be complex funding applications. There are different modes of participation; even when people are not actual members of associations, they may still go to meetings, and they may read about the activities of neighbours and friends in the local paper and display notices in their front windows.

One such group, which we studied in detail, was the local neighbourhood allotment association. Allotments are communal gardens. They are common in British towns and they are often provided by the local council. Everyone who has an allotment becomes a member of the association that collects the rents and liaises with the council. We observed the literacy associated with being a member of the allotment association in the neighbourhood we were studying. We did this partly because it might be thought that there is very little reading and writing associated with growing vegetables for one's family. We followed the regular repeated events of the allotment association, such as the meetings, and came across a broad web of literacy practices.

Here I want to give the example of an unexpected event that arose during the course of our study. The council tried to sell off some land to a developer for building houses. This included the land where the allotments were located, but it also included public open space used by the wider community. The event is only one example of the many social issues that arose during our study, and it is useful for examining the dynamics of locally organized activity and getting closer to the ecological basis of literate activity. Several other disputes were also about land, concerning issues of ownership, access, or use. Other broader issues included traffic problems, pollution, disputes about taxes, and schooling issues. The points which arise from this example are common to the processes involved in all these cases. We present this example as a case study offering a framework for analysing events in which a local community mobilizes and organizations are formed, and it provides a way of seeing how literacy is embedded in people's everyday activities. (See Barton and Hamilton 1998, ch. 12.)

Analysing the Problem

As a way of understanding this action as it developed, we interviewed a range of people who described this process from their differing perspectives. We tracked the set of events which followed the announcement of the council's intention to sell the land, in particular examining what role different literacies played in this process. The allotments were on land owned by the county council. The council was under pressure from the central government to sell any surplus land. They planned to sell this seven-acre site, used partly as public open space and partly as allotments, to a developer who would build houses on it. This meant that the gardeners would lose their plots and the locality would lose a significant area of open space – in a neighbourhood of densely packed housing. The problem was first recognized by the allotment holders who would lose their plots, but the potential loss of open space affected everyone in the local area.

In order to act on this issue, local people needed a range of information, which had to be assembled and then shared with interested people. They needed to know what had happened so far and who was affected by this issue, in this case, both allotment holders themselves and the other residents of the neighbourhood. They had to find out what the legal situation was, including the status of the land in question, who has the right to make and oppose decisions, what general rights residents and allotment holders have. They needed to understand what the possible solutions were, who makes decisions in the local and regional administration, and how these decisions are made. In this case, the situation was complicated by the duties and rights of the various administrative levels – both the city council and the county council were involved.

The Sequence of Events

Rumours about development began when some allotment holders noticed someone digging holes in the green area adjoining the allotment site. Then a representative of the county council visited the secretary of the allotment association to explain the plans; this was followed up by an official letter to the allotment association giving allotment holders formal notice to quit. The chair of the allotment association, although pessimistic himself about being able to influence the decision, showed the letter to an allotment holder who was also a student training to be a solicitor; she offered to write to the county council on behalf of allotment holders to express concern. The chairman also talked to a number of other interested people about the problem and a variety of individual initiatives resulted from this. Other people wrote letters and there was much informal talking and gathering of ideas. One allotment holder wrote to the local MP and sent round a petition to allotment holders on her own initiative.

Initially, people did not know how to react, and there were individual responses until a general meeting organized by the chair of the allotment association was held in the local church hall. At this meeting, plans for the proposed development were circulated and discussed, and an action committee was formed. The chair had lobbied some individuals beforehand to volunteer themselves for the committee. As well as some allotment holders, the committee included a resident who had been involved in a car-parking campaign previously and a man who offered to word-process and copy letters. He kept minutes of meetings, went to a legal-aid office in town, and organized other volunteers (for example, in the street distribution of the newsletter). At the meeting, people discussed possible strategies, such as petitioning, letter writing, persuasion of individuals, and organizing a press campaign.

The action committee held weekly meetings, sometimes at a local office, sometimes in people's houses. A collectively written newsletter was produced and distributed; this encouraged people to write to particular people, and it offered ideas on what to write. Meetings were held between the action committee and city and county councillors at which the compromise plan was put forward. This mobilization all happened in a short period of time, and within two months of the original letter to quit a compromise was offered by the council and put to the allotment association at a meeting. Half the land was to be sold for housing; the rest would be covenanted to the city for open space and the allotments would remain. No decision was taken immediately as there was some opposition to accepting the compromise. At a regular residents association meeting there was still some opposition to the compromise plan, but a short time later the compromise was accepted by the action committee and it formally notified the council.

Identifying the Strategies, Resources, and Texts

Our interest here is in the role of literacy in this community action. It can be analysed in terms of the strategies, resources, and texts used to solve the problem. There was a range of strategies used to solve the problem and people did a variety of things: they gathered and distributed information in the local community; they mobilized other local people; they organized a petition among allotment holders; they held general meetings to agree on what to do; they formed an action committee to act on behalf of the community; they held a letter-writing campaign directed at influential councillors; they carried out a press campaign in the local radio and newspapers; and they arranged meetings with local officials in order to try to influence them.

To do these things, people drew upon a range of resources. These included material objects, skills, knowledge, time and ideas, money, and meeting spaces. Examples include: the legal literacy knowledge of the trainee solicitor; the use of a word processor and a photocopier; the local library; accounting skills; fund-raising; local contacts in the council; dealing with the media; skills of persuasion and argumentation; other organizing skills, such as offering structure and being able to work with others; design skills, such as combining words and graphics on signs and posters.

These practices required the production of a variety of texts, including letters to newspapers, to councillors and to others, maps, historical records of the allotment association and more general histories of allotments, legal documents, newspaper articles, a petition, local newsletters, posters, and press releases.

Close observation of this sequence of events adds to our understanding of the dynamics of everyday literacy practices, and we see the strategies, the different sorts of resources, and the texts utilized as the basic elements of literacy practices. As we have seen, there was a wide range of ways in which reading and writing were brought into the activities. There are some similarities to more routine activities, for example, in the ways in which they draw upon both oral and written participation. Different configurations of practices were effective and appropriate for particular purposes, and in the meetings people discussed how to strike the right balance; for example, whether a petition was a useful strategy, or whether standardized or individualized letters should be sent to the council. Both individual and collaborative activities were involved. Because this was a new situation making unfamiliar demands on people, there was more discussion and negotiation of process and strategy than in more routine meetings and there was invention and creativity. People also had to search out and draw upon a range of different funds of community knowledge; for example: the history of the dispute and previous similar ones; legal rights and official structures; knowledge of local networks, including who has responsibility for making decisions, and who can influence outcomes; experience of other local campaigns and organizations, formal and informal.

Following the campaign through, it became clear that this was not a homogeneous community: conflicts and tensions rose to the surface. There were various interest groups involved – allotment holders, councillors, and other residents. Another source of tension was that both long-time residents and more recent in-comers were involved in meetings, with different ideas about how to solve the problem and what would count as a resolution. People with different personalities and resources contributed in different ways, some more visibly than others. Some people wanted to rely on more semi-official groups, such as the local residents association, while others wanted to organize separately from it. All this raises many issues about who gets to play the key roles in collective action, who gets the credit for doing so, and how this happens. The internal dynamics of the community are important.

Literacies in Local Action

From this example, we can see the vernacular response to dominant practices; we can see the ecological embeddedness, and how literacy fits in with people's lives and their everyday activities. Crucially, we can see how a global activity impinges on and is transformed by people's local organizing. Through this example, we can examine various questions, such as the work literacy does in groups and the connections between these forms of democratic participation and more formal bureaucratic structures.

We must reiterate that literacy fits in with other resources and practices available to groups. Any situation offers a choice about the ways in which oral and written practices may be used. Sometimes an oral invitation or face-to-face persuasion is appropriate. At other times, only a written communication has the right kind of authority to produce the response that is needed. Often, combining them proves more effective than either one alone. These choices have to be carefully weighed up, and, in the case of the allotments fight, where a new situation arose, people were uncertain about what to do, so that considerable time was spent in meetings discussing the value of different strategies. In routine contexts, such choices are less likely to be discussed since traditions have already been established.

We saw the ways in which people make use of discourses learned in other areas of their lives. For example, people draw upon knowledge they have acquired at work to carry out the roles of secretary and treasurer. A particularly useful aspect of employment-related knowledge is a trade union background with its close links to parliamentary democratic practice and traditions of training people in such skills as negotiation. Nevertheless, participation in many of these activities is not learned formally as part of the educational system. Rather, it is learned through the process of participation and is improvised as practical responses to new situations. In this way, it is part of the informal learning which is going on all the time.

In terms of participation, people differ widely in their formal and informal networks, in their knowledge of how to get access to official representatives, and in their confidence in literacy and in communication more generally. In part, this is to do with an individual's position in the community and the resources they control; for example, one person has a word processor, and other people are able to draw upon work resources. It should be pointed out that not all attempts to get things done in groups are successful. A local hairdresser successfully organized a march protesting local taxes, but she could not sustain the activity. She had strong informal networks, but very little experience of dealing with official agencies or formal organizations; she did not know what to do after her initial action. The local community did not have the resources to sustain the opposition to the tax, although the community of Lancaster, at large, networked with national organizations, did have such resources, and opposition to the tax continued in city-wide activities.

These examples illustrate that there is a diversity of ways in which people try to get things done in their locality and in which they make use of literacy in groups. Individuals contribute different parts of a collaborative effort. Some participate by simply being present at meetings, whilst others contribute through talk or actions. The level of participation is greater for those who take on official roles on committees. People do this according to their interests, confidence, resources, and expertise, as was the case with the allotment action committee. However, there are also issues about the existing power relationships and factors such as gender which may consistently marginalize some people.

The activities described are fundamental for understanding the nature of local democratic participation and the role of literacy in this. Many local organizations exist largely outside government influence and statutory control and are largely unsupported by the state. They draw on material resources available in the community. Where such resources are scarce, local organizations are vulnerable. Their activities are sometimes improvised, invented, or learned in the community, and then passed down through word of mouth and modelled traditions. This links in with the *bricolage* mentioned in other chapters of this book. There is little in formal education to prepare people for the roles they take on, for instance, or for working together in groups to solve disputes.

The relationship between literacy and local participation and democracy is more complicated than has been typically assumed (for example, in public discussions of literacy). Literacy has a role in democratic practice, yet literacy practices are not necessarily democratic in their own right. Neither can they, on their own, promote democracy. In terms of participation in formal political structures, people do not have to be literate to have an opinion, or to vote, or to take decisions, but the bureaucracy of the modern state assumes and requires literacy. Where people do not have the literacies society expects of them, this causes problems for both individuals and for the social institutions which require it.

The example given above demonstrates the validity of regarding literacy as a communal resource, rather than simply a set of skills located in individuals. The community had resources for resisting the land developers, in the form of time to research the issue, funds of knowledge, contacts in local government, physical resources such as computers and access to photocopiers, space for meetings, skills to produce posters and advertisements. However, no individual had all these resources, and it was in combination that they were effective. These local groups underpin political participation at the local level, and in addition to contributing to leisure and quality of life in a neighbourhood, the web of literacies in local organizations has much broader significance.

Finally, I have given just one example, and certainly parts of it are culturally specific, drawing on particular traditions of volunteerism and reciprocity in local relations and other aspects of life in a medium-sized British town at the end of the twentieth century. Nevertheless, there are broader lessons to be learned. These are local responses to global changes. The pressure on land leading to the council's original plan to get rid of the allotments is part of more global changes and governmental shifts to the private sector which are taking place in many countries. All over the world there are global changes which do not respect local identity and which are being resisted. It is by understanding everyday practices and everyday learning that we can support sustainable activities.

In summary, to provide some of the more general lessons of this specific case, we can see that much learning is in the routine, of observing, participating in, and reflecting upon everyday activities. Nevertheless, people also learn by participating in new practices and by engaging in activities such as negotiating and organizing. Vernacular responses to external dominant pressures involve inventiveness and creativity. Ideas such as *bricolage*, of making-do, of being resourceful, are a part of people's everyday experience. It is through *bricolage* that people invent local responses to global challenges. Local communities are complex and multi-faceted. People draw upon existing community resources, through networks in and beyond the community. Differences between people can be a strength; there are local experts and local funds of vernacular knowledge to be drawn upon. The challenge is to bring together local knowledge and global knowledge into new forms of knowledge and action.

References

Barton, D. 1994. *Literacy: An Introduction to the Ecology of Written Language.* Oxford: Blackwell.

Barton, D., and M. Hamilton. 1998. *Local Literacies: Reading and Writing in One Community.* London: Routledge.

Bateson, G. 1972. *Steps to an Ecology of Mind.* New York: Ballantine Books.

Clyne, M. 1982. *Multilingual Australia: Resources, Needs, Policies.* Melbourne: River Seine Publications.

Cooper, M.M. 1986. 'The Ecology of Writing.' *College English* 48: 364–75.

Haugen, E. 1972. *The Ecology of Language.* Stanford: Stanford University Press.
Irvine, P., and N. Elsasser. 1988. 'The Ecology of Literacy: Negotiating Writing Standards in a Caribbean Setting.' In *The Social Construction of Written Communication,* ed. B.A. Rafoth and D.L. Rubin. Norwood, NJ: Ablex.
Mulhausler, P. 1996. *Linguistic Ecology, Language Change and Linguistic Imperialism in the Pacific Region.* London: Routledge.
Neisser, U. 1982. *Memory Observed.* San Francisco: W.H. Freeman & Co.

Addressing Alexandria's Environmental Problems

Adel Abu Zahra

Alexandria was formerly a cosmopolitan city, a prosperous international cultural centre. The city has radically changed since the 1970s, when it faced mounting environmental problems and the deterioration of urban life. In 1990 the Friends of the Environment Association was founded. Its objectives are to protect, restore, and improve the environment of Alexandria. The Association uses a variety of methods in community education: dissemination of information, education for citizen-involvement, public demonstrations, and legal proceedings. It has been successful in informing a significant part of the population about their ecological and legal rights, as well as in protecting the architectural heritage of Alexandria and making substantial improvements in the urban environment.

Alexandria in the Past and Today

Alexandria was the economic, political, and cultural capital of Egypt from the time it was founded by Alexander the Great in 332 B.C.E. until the Arab Conquest in 642 C.E., that is, for 974 years.

When the Arabs decided to move the capital to Fostat – later known as Cairo – Alexandria started to wane in importance. In 1805, Mohamed Ali became 'Wali' (ruler) of Egypt. Four years after the French campaign, he found Alexandria to be a small village of merely six thousand inhabitants living in dire conditions in the midst of the ruins of the ancient city. Mohamed Ali recognized the importance of reviving Alexandria, and he focused a great deal of attention on restoring the city as part of his ambitious project to build a modern country. His efforts were pursued by the subsequent khedives, especially Khedive Ismail, who reigned from 1863 to 1879. Alexandria resumed its past eminence as one of the most important ports in the Mediterranean.

Alexandria ranks as the second most important Egyptian city, being the country's first seaport and summer resort, and its second industrial centre, accommodating about 36 per cent of Egyptian industry. The population, estimated at 4 million, is concentrated in the narrow coastal areas. Alexandria is bordered by the Mediterranean to the north, Lake Mariout to the south, Lake Edco and Abu Keer Bay to the east, and to the west, by the vast Western Desert. Because of its favourable geographical location, temperate climate, and historical sites and monuments that date back to the 4th century B.C.E., Alexandria has always been a major tourist destination. Until the late 1960s, it was a distinguished city, as reflected in its European architectural features. Indeed, it was – at the time – one of the cleanest and most beautiful cities of the world.

But in the mid-1970s, things changed. As a result of the great increase in population and the influx of people from other governorates, Alexandria began to suffer from pollution and urban degradation. Economic and social changes, concurrent with the weakening of administrative bodies and the spread of negligence and corruption, contributed to the degradation of the city's natural and urban environments.

The Friends of the Environment Association

To halt this deterioration, the Friends of the Environment Association was established in Alexandria in 1990. Its overall goal has been to protect, restore, and improve the natural and man-made environment in Alexandria Governorate. To attain this goal, the following strategies were adopted:

1. The founding of a broad public movement within Alexandria Governorate that supports environmental protection by providing accurate information regarding the environment, its components and resources, and the impact of human activities;
2. The establishment and operation of a pressure group to influence policy-makers and implementers, those who pollute the environment, and those who violate laws, as well as those whose responsibility it is to monitor law enforcement.

Participatory education and training have been one of the most important approaches adopted by the Association to achieve its aims. A key principle of its strategy throughout has been the preservation of ecosystems.

Education through Participation

From the outset, the Friends of the Environment Association recognized that is membership was limited in number and that it could not achieve its goals unless it was able to influence public opinion and generate support for FEA's goals among Alexandrians. To do so, the Association has used the following *methods*:

- awareness-raising
- education and training
- changing behaviour
- participation
- advocacy

And the following *means*:

- lectures
- seminars
- brochures and publications
- videos
- workshops and discussion sessions
- public hearings
- exhibits, festivals, and competitions
- press campaigns
- peaceful marches/demonstrations
- negotiation
- filing lawsuits

The Association's *targeted public:*

- school pupils and university students
- teachers
- police officers
- journalists
- radio and television employees
- workers
- housewives

- lawyers
- members of NGOs
- government employees
- industrialists

Through its varied activities, the association was able to form Friends of the Environment clubs, in schools and university colleges, in sports clubs, and within some NGOs in Alexandria. Nearly ten years after the founding of the Association, environmental issues have now captured the public's interest. Environmental problems have become some of the most commonly debated issues, whether in private or public gatherings. Examples include: sea and lake pollution, protection of biodiversity, global warming and ozone layer depletion, air pollution, sanitary drainage problems, industrial and agricultural drainage, solid wastes and the growing scarcity of certain animal species, and the importance of green areas.

I shall now describe some of the more significant activities which were undertaken in the field of environmental education through participation.

Public Hearings

These hearings were one of the most important means of raising awareness among citizens. Invited audiences comprised government officials, representatives of scientific research centres and faculties, ordinary citizens, illiterate fishermen, and representatives of NGOs and of industrial establishments. Dialogue among the various groups was animated and enriched by the presentation of all speakers' opinions and views, and all listened carefully to the different points of view.

One significant outcome of these hearings was the suspension of the governorate's plans to fill in and/or reclaim Lake Mariout, which lies within the boundaries of Alexandria Governorate. The discharge of sewage effluent into the Mediterranean Sea was also halted. Instead, the effluent will be redirected and discharged on desert land, to be reused for tree plantation.

Another outcome of such public-hearing sessions was to force one factory, which annually discharged about 12,000 kilograms of mercury into Mex Bay on Alexandria's Mediterranean coastline, polluting fish and negatively affecting the health of fish consumers, to change its production technology to a newer, mercury-free system. Another public-hearing session induced a cement factory located in a poor and densely populated district to use stack filters to prevent cement dust fallout. For years, the fallout had caused lung and various other chest ailments among local residents.

Peaceful Marches

The Association has regularly organized a peaceful march on June 5 of each year (International Environment Day) to raise citizens' awareness about environmental problems, existing legislation for environmental protection, and their rights to a clean and safe environment. The march is preceded by a musical band and four riders on horseback, followed by children wearing distinctive costumes, displaying self-designed slogans, and holding flowers. The children are followed by members of the board of directors of the Association together with consuls of foreign missions and local government officials. These, in turn, are followed in the procession by a large number of FEA members bearing placards depicting major environmental protection laws. Print, radio, and television journalists cover the yearly procession, and it ends at a specific location where all participants plant trees. This is followed by the opening of an exhibition of children's drawings about the environment.

Negotiations and Pressure

Through effective use of the media (newspapers, radio, and television) and mobilizing public opinion, the Association was able to persuade decision-makers in Alexandria Governorate to discuss certain major problems affecting the natural and man-made environments. One of the most successful achievements of the Association in this regard was the removal of private cabins along the seafront, which were owned by a limited number of people. The cabins blocked the general public's view of the sea and obstructed passage of the sea breeze to surrounding areas. The Association also succeeded, through pressure on decision-makers, in influencing the closure of twelve sewage outfalls along the seacoast, located at points near beaches used by people in summer. Through media campaigns, the Association was also able to prevent the planned demolition of various palaces and villas that have significant architectural and historical value.

Legal Action

FEA is the first NGO in Egypt to launch court action to stop decisions or actions harmful to the environment and, hence, to human health and safety.

The first case taken to court by the Association began in 1991 when the governor of Alexandria donated a street located in one of the most important squares in central Alexandria to the World Health Organization for the construction of an extension to its regional headquarters, a building which the WHO has rented for a nominal fee since 1949.

The Association decided that this action:

- constituted a serious legal violation;
- would deprive citizens of a street designated for pedestrians and vehicles;
- would deprive citizens of their basic right to adequate open space;
- would deprive citizens of a view of the sea and sky, and prevent the passage of air currents;
- would alter the characteristics of an historical city square;
- would deprive citizens of their precious architectural and locational memories.

The Association therefore negotiated with the governor to reconsider his decision, but he refused. The WHO regional director was also approached, but refused to decline the 'gift' in spite of the fact that the Association suggested seven different alternatives that could have met the WHO's need for a larger plot of land to expand its headquarters.

Throughout these negotiations, the Association clearly demonstrated its understanding of and support for the WHO's needs, and affirmed the important and vital role played by the WHO in Alexandria. When all attempts at negotiation failed, FEA felt it had no choice but to mount pressure through a media campaign and mobilization of public opinion, and, finally, through recourse to legal action. The Association dealt with this controversy in a carefully planned and distinctive manner. Members attended court sessions in large numbers wearing a clearly visible flower. This was quite new in court actions. Each week, members would place a wreath of flowers at the site of the excavated street. The issue of the Alexandrian street succeeded in arousing public interest, and became the subject of discussion in homes and coffee shops, and in clubs and workplaces across the country. Many lawyers volunteered their assistance to support the Association's case in court. And each and every national and opposition newspaper gave some coverage to the story during the course of the trial, whether through short news updates, commentary, or investigative articles.

After five long months, the court passed a breakthrough verdict annulling the governor's decree, ruling that it was illegal. The verdict stated that the use of public funds and property designated for public benefit cannot be set by an administrative decree. The court also stated that it is not only a right of citizens but also their duty to defend and safeguard public funds and property and all that is designated for public benefit.

The second court case concerned an area of public land in Smouha district which, according to the urban planning policy of Alexandria Governorate, had been designated for use as a public garden. However, the governor of Alexandria issued a decree to cancel this designation and turn this particular area into a car park terminal. Local residents sent numerous complaints to the governor, asking him to rescind this decree. They stressed the crucial importance of safeguarding this green area, and the fact that a public terminus serving hundreds of automobiles and buses would cause air and noise pollution in this residential area. But the governor refused, and residents approached FEA for help.

The Association then conducted a study of all the green areas available to Alexandrians. The study indicated that green space had decreased from one-third of a feddan per 1,000 persons in 1958 to one-fifth per 1,000 persons in 1994, and that the city is, in fact, in vital need of *more* green areas and leisure spaces. The Association sent the study to the governor and informed him that the officially ratified Alexandrian Urban Planning Policy placed such a plan on a par with the promulgation of a law, and that it was not within the power of the governor to cancel this land-use plan.

Such efforts at negotiation with the governor failed, and FEA therefore began a campaign in the newspapers and filed a lawsuit. After nine months of court proceedings, the court ruled to annul the governor's decree on the grounds that it was illegal. The court verdict also affirmed the right of citizens to green spaces and referred in its verdict to the findings of the study prepared by FEA.

The third case taken to court by FEA was in response to numerous complaints by Alexandrians affected by noise pollution caused by the city tramline. The tramline traverses residential areas in the city along its length of about 15 kilometres, starting from Ramheh Station and ending at Victoria Station. Noise levels reached 105 decibels, a level which affects the hearing of those residents living within the vicinity of the tramline, and causes tension, sleep deprivation, and lack of concentration. The vibrations caused by the tram also affect the stability of adjacent buildings.

The Association conducted a medical study and an engineering study. It was learned that the tram system was first established in 1862 and that it was initially horse-drawn. It later relied on steam-powered engines until the start of the twentieth century, when the system was converted to electricity. Maintenance for the tramline and its rails had been neglected for long periods, and the noise levels increased. The medical study revealed that those Alexandrians suffering most from hearing loss were residents living in zones adjacent to the tramline. That study also surveyed hearing deterioration in children.

Using the same approach as in previous situations, FEA wrote to the Public Transport Authority and the Governorate, requesting that they should undertake all necessary repairs of the tramlines to protect the health and safety of the public. But the Association received no response to its appeals. It therefore initiated a media campaign and contacted members of Parliament. When these actions failed to pressure the relevant authorities into taking appropriate action, the Association took the case to court.

During the court hearings and before a verdict was reached, the government approved the allocation of EGP 25 million for necessary repairs. Repair work on the tramlines took three years to complete, after which noise levels dropped from 105 to 55 decibels.

Lawsuits which FEA has filed on behalf of residents in certain poor districts exposed to pollution from nearby factories are still before the courts. The Association has also filed lawsuits against housing construction companies who have violated the Environment Law 4 of 1994 by not conducting the environment impact assessment study (prior to licensing and implementation) required for tourism or large housing projects.

Conclusion

Education is not achieved only through teaching reading and writing. Rather, it is effected through a variety of other means. Our Association has been able to use what is termed the ecological approach, utilizing non-traditional methods such as convening discussion sessions, symposiums, and public hearings; raising environmental awareness; training in communication; negotiation; mobilizing public opinion and action; organizing media campaigns, exhibitions, and public demonstrations; producing appropriate printed material; and filing court cases.

Such an approach has been successful in educating large numbers of people and eradicating their environmental and legal 'illiteracy,' increasing their self-confidence, and enabling them to be more positive regarding issues of environmental protection and improvement. People have come to realize that they are part of a wider and complex ecological system, and that they should live in harmony with it. Through the participatory approach, the Association has gained a large number of men and women, be they educated or without formal education, who are well informed and who support our cause with equal enthusiasm and commitment.

The Campaign against the MAI in Canada

Brian Sarwer-Foner

Non-governmental organizations (NGOs) have been increasingly recognized since the 1992 Rio Earth Summit as playing key roles in bringing about positive social change towards sustainable development. Amongst the varied functions they perform, NGOs are instrumental in educating the public, raising awareness, increasing the level of understanding and concern about environmental issues within society, and catalysing actions. Of all efforts to inform and educate the public in Canada, perhaps the most impressive of late has been the national campaign to raise awareness about globalization and the Multilateral Agreement on Investments (MAI) and the dangers they present to the economic, social, cultural, and environmental rights of citizens. The range of tactics used to link these issues and to disseminate information, from the Internet to civil disobedience, is highlighted.

The Information Age and the Global Environmental Crisis

As we sit in a new millennium, we are engrossed in what is being touted as the information age. Information is central to basic education; in fact, it is at the very heart of the matter.

Access to information is a key issue within basic education: people who have it can use it to support their goals and advance their causes; those who are uneducated or are left out of the loop of information access usually find themselves with limited options. Information is a form of power, but by no means is information the whole story.

The larger power in today's society, in fact the force which is the bottom line for motivating just about all aspects of human organization and that which dictates societal behaviour, is money. Human productivity is measured by monetary wealth, instead of by the health of people, the well-being of society, biodiversity, or the state of the environment, the true bottom lines upon which all human activity is inextricably dependent. The expression 'money makes the world go around' is in fact a fallacious anthropocentric notion that has run rampant as the dominant paradigm for humans this past century, and is ultimately going to undermine our own ability to survive on this planet.

As the Union of Concerned Scientists forewarn, in their 'World Scientists' Warning to Humanity' (1993), 'human beings and the natural world are on a collision course. Human activities inflict harsh and often irreversible damage on the environment and on critical resources. If not checked, many of our current practices put at serious risk the future that we wish for human society and the plant and animal kingdoms, and may so alter the living world that it will be made unable to sustain life in the manner that we know it. Fundamental changes are urgent if we are to avoid the collision our present course will bring about.'[1]

An ecological approach is needed in order to answer this challenge: both in terms of gaining a better understanding of the linkages between ecological processes, global patterns of human behaviour, and the myriad of environmental and sociological impacts that arise from the disequilibrium caused by this relationship; and in terms of educating people all over the world about the global environmental crisis and the changes needed in order to solve these problems, and helping them understand how they are implicated and what they can and must do to help start working towards positive social change and environmental improvements. This is no small task.

An ecological approach is holistic and encompasses diversity, rather than being disconnected and specialized. It is modelled on ecology, where the focus is not only on the sum of the parts, but on the linkages and interactions between them. An ecological approach to basic education involves relating the people concerned to the subject being covered, while exploring the linkages between the sub-issues and how their actions, or inaction, connect to the whole picture being studied. It is therefore fitting that an ecological approach be taken when studying and educating about the environment: the subject and method are both linkage-based.

Globalization

Globalization is one of the key processes that are shaping our world today. The ease of transportation, and the improvement and augmentation of communication technologies and systems, allow the movement of goods and people, and facilitate rapid communication, business transactions, political negotiations, and the distribution of information around the world. On the one hand, globalization can facilitate information flow, make the world seem like a smaller place, and bring unity to people; on the other hand, it is responsible for increased competition, downsizing of the labour force, governmental deregulation, and the homogenization of cultural differences and societal values.

Globalization has made it easier for corporations to do business, freeing up access to and the movement of currencies, resources, labour pools, markets, and production facilities. Corporations are given the freedom to acquire, locate, and move any of these components from country to country in order to maximize profit margins under such international agreements as the North American Free Trade Agreement (NAFTA), the General Agreement on Tariffs and Trade (GATT), and the failed Multilateral Agreement on Investments (MAI). The resulting impacts have been extreme for the natural environment and have caused a widening of the gap between the haves and have-nots – the rich and poor people of the world. As the neo-liberal agenda towards increased trade liberalization moves ahead, the restrictions on doing business decrease, facilitating activities that are environmentally deleterious and an ever-increasing widening of the gap.

This is a form of backward progress: increased trade liberalization, leading to increased governmental deregulation, increased environmental damage, increased sociological impacts, and increased levels of relative poverty. Somehow this process must be reversed. An ecological approach is called for; it must begin with basic education and public access to information.

A positive function of globalization is that it helps liberate the flow of information. With the advent of the Internet, information is no longer solely in the hands of the rich. Now people have a tool with which to fight back. The Internet is a powerful means for providing basic education and catalysing action. People can now take action and stand up for their rights on the basis of information made available via the Internet, and through the efforts of activist and public interest groups, and other types of non-governmental organizations (NGOs).

NGOs and the MAI

Since the 1992 Rio Earth Summit, NGOs have been increasingly recognized as playing key roles in bringing about positive social change towards sustainable development. Amongst the varied functions they perform, NGOs are instrumental in educating the public, raising awareness, increasing the level of understanding and concern about environmental issues within society, and in eliciting engaged responses from the public in addressing these issues through concrete actions. In Canada there are over 2,000 environmental NGOs (ENGOs), and together they perform a wide range of functions, represent a myriad of issues, and utilize a great diversity of tactics and strategies. Some have been more successful than others.

Of all efforts to inform and educate the public in Canada, perhaps the most impressive of late has been the campaign to raise awareness about the Multilateral Agreement on Investments (MAI) and the dangers it presents to the economic, social, cultural, and environmental rights of citizens. This campaign began in Canada in April 1997, spearheaded by the efforts of two individuals and their respective NGOs, and in the short time since has become a global phenomenon, with manifestations in many countries. Prior to this time the MAI was being negotiated behind closed doors, with the publics of all countries remaining ignorant of its existence and of the implications it poses to their democratic rights. Today, thanks to this campaign, the MAI and its ramifications are well known amongst both academic and activist communities, and concerned citizens around the world. People are taking a stand, speaking out and acting to ensure that the MAI does not become a reality. Their actions have already been unambiguously felt and have made a clearly observable difference.

NGO Strategies

In my thesis on the strategies of Canadian environmental non-governmental organizations (ENGOs) for protecting biodiversity, three questions were raised: Which strategies bring about success? Which barriers impede progress being made? Which actions can help to overcome the identified barriers?[2]

Although the study was focused on the biodiversity issue, the variety of life on Earth at all levels, and the threats that humans pose to its integrity, the findings of the study also apply to the environmental crisis in general. Throughout the participatory process, much of the discussion on strategies, barriers, and solutions was focused on issues related to basic education. From an NGO perspective, basic education about the environment involves making information available to the public, both in terms of general awareness-raising and in serving to motivate and facilitate public involvement with environmental struggles and protection initiatives. There is a clear link to communication in these endeavours at both the macro and micro levels.

There are very many different levels at which ENGOs can and do act, accompanied by a myriad of campaigns, projects, and programs. These follow the variety of environmental issues in both focus and scale, and include participating in international forums to represent the voice of the public and raise concerns; lobbying governments about policy development and new legislation; working at the grass-roots level and catalysing local community involvement; using many media to inform the public. All these means are used in struggles to stop specific environmentally degrading activities and/or to achieve protection in specific areas, as well as in efforts to stop macro-processes that are detrimental to environmental integrity.

No single NGO can effectively address all these issues and levels by itself: an ecological approach is needed. Taken together, ENGOs make up a sociological movement comprised of a diversity of groups, and this diversity of involvement spawns a diversity of tactics. Unfortunately there is not a sufficient number of NGOs to cover all the bases. Environmental problems are too numerous, human 'development' happens too rapidly, and the vested interests behind it wield much more power (i.e., money and resources, both physical and human) to sway and influence decision-makers and the public than do NGOs. Nonetheless, an oppositional force is needed, and people and groups do rise to this call. An ecological approach is taken by the movement as a whole to address all these concerns, although the movement is still not large enough to sufficiently change the tide.

NGO Strategies for Environmental Education

Some key barriers to the environmental cause faced by most NGOs involve inadequate environmental educational programs, accompanied by limited public perception, misconceptions, and ignorance. As well, there is the lack of engaged public involvement in environmental programs, accompanied by cynicism, denial, apathy, and a sense of powerlessness among people. Environmental issues tend to be marginalized by the media and by society at large, and this in large measure explains the degree of public ignorance about the details of environmental issues, and a tendency towards detachment from or even denial of ecological realities.

In addressing these enormous issues, NGOs need to strategically design their awareness-raising campaigns to present information in ways to reach as wide an audience as possible and to have the most significant effect. Raising the level of formal and non-formal environmental education, from kindergartens to universities, and from community centres to business boardrooms, requires an ecological approach and the involvement of many sectors.

In order for environmental communication to be effective, a balance must be struck between being sufficiently alarmist to raise public concern and elicit an engaged response; and not being perceived as preaching 'doom and gloom,' which tends to alienate the public and causes it to recoil. When raising concern about environmental issues, positive alternatives to the problems examined need to be highlighted in order to motivate action and engender hope.

Ultimately, a form of social marketing is required in order to analyse audiences and target messages appropriately, in accordance with the type of environmental issue, the level and scale at which it is operating, and the people and groups involved.

In Canada, a national communications strategy to promote sustainable development was developed between 1993 and 1995, the innovative 'SustainABILITY' program. It fulfilled the need for the development of proactive participatory programs that focus upon environmental education and communication in order to reach as wide a range of social players as possible.

The developers of SustainABILITY, in consultation with environmental experts across the country (many of them from NGOs), employed social marketing techniques to design the program. They had designed and appropriately targeted their messages to reach different sectors of the Canadian public to communicate environmental priorities in an uplifting manner. The program design used an ecological and multimedia approach for educating the public about linkages between economic, environmental, and social well-being and their need to be recognized in planning. It was also designed to help create a national movement towards a common environmental vision for the future, and to encourage greater public participation in existing programs.

In October 1995 the fully developed program was delivered to the government and ready to become operational, but, tragically, SustainABILITY was never instated because of a lack of financial backing. Sadly, only a handful of individuals ever heard of it. The Canadian public at large remains ignorant of it ever having existed.

A key strategy for basic education built into the SustainABILITY program, and a tool that has proved to be very successful when used in other settings, is the hosting of public-issue forums. These public meetings are an effective way of holding community consultations that foster two-way information flow, raise the level of environmental literacy, provide examples of successful environmental initiatives, and catalyse public participation in issues that are determined to be important.

At these forums, people are not pressured to join a group, or to commit to taking on responsibilities. They are only asked to attend a session so as to become informed and share their ideas. In this way, people become open to listening, learning, and participating, without feeling directly pushed to get further involved. The discussions need to be expertly facilitated, and truly participatory, involving a two-way flow of dialogue. The main aim of public-issue forums is to reach out to citizens so that they can gain information about the issues, express their opinions, hear those of others, and become engaged in discussions about options and involved in making decisions. Citizens usually leave such events being better educated, and feeling concerned, moved, and positively stimulated. When this happens, there is a good chance they will take the issues discussed to heart and naturally feel motivated to involve themselves in the actions suggested, and even do more, if they so choose.

Background on the MAI

The Multilateral Agreement on Investment (MAI) is an international treaty that was being developed by the Organization for Economic Cooperation and Development (OECD), which provided information and advice about economic policy for the world's richest twenty-nine countries. Until April 1997 this agreement, which had numerous implications for citizens around the world, was being negotiated behind closed doors, in complete secrecy from the publics of all countries.

It was at this time that information was leaked and the secrecy broke. A draft of the confidential agreement was smuggled, in March 1997, into the hands of two prominent Canadians who were tracking these issues. They analysed it, wrote a critique of it, and put the information on the Internet by early April 1997. The MAI was now no longer secret. People anywhere in the world (with access to computers) could consult the Web and begin to learn about the MAI and the dangers it poses to their individual and collective rights by reading the analysis, 'The Corporate Rule Treaty.'

As the principal author of this document, Tony Clarke, explains, 'the MAI is designed to establish a whole new set of global rules for investment that will grant transnational corporations the unrestricted "right" and "freedom" to buy, sell, and move their operations whenever and wherever they want around the world, unfettered by government intervention or regulation. In short, the MAI seeks to empower transnational corporations through a set of global investment rules designed to impose tight restrictions on what national governments can and cannot do in regulating their economies.'[3]

The implication of this is a fundamental transformation of the role of governments: from representing and protecting the rights of citizens, to securing and guaranteeing markets for investors, regardless of whatever social and environmental impacts arise from this augmented form of trade liberalization.

The MAI would have extended the free trade provisions of the General Agreement on Tariffs and Trade (GATT) and the North American Free Trade Agreement (NAFTA) by prohibiting signatory nations from impeding the free flow of money and production facilities from one country to another. The treaty, in effect, subordinates the right of elected governments to set national policy (economic, social, and environmental) in the best interests of their citizens to the right of transnational corporations and investors to conduct business, investing and divesting, however they see fit. The MAI is often refereed to as a 'Charter of Rights and Freedoms for Corporations.'

The MAI threatened the very nature of democracy, and bolstered the current global reality that power is money and that it is in the command of corporations and not in the control of people.

The Campaign to Educate the Public about the MAI

The campaign against the MAI was launched after the leaked draft broke the secrecy in April 1997. Central to this endeavour was the basic education of uninformed people about the existence of the agreement, the push to have it signed with no public debate (it was originally to be signed in May 1997), its implications, its impacts, and how it counters people's best interests. The campaign was spearheaded by a large Canadian NGO, a non-partisan citizens' interest group with the mission to provide a critical and progressive voice on key national issues: the Council of Canadians (COC). It began with a front-page story published 3 April 1997 in the *Globe and Mail,* Canada's daily newspaper, and the posting of information on the Internet warning people about the existence of the MAI and explaining its implications. This was followed by the publishing of a book.[4]

The principal implications that would arise from the MAI being instituted would have been enacted through governmental deregulation causing the following five types of negative impacts: economic, social, cultural, political, and environmental. The Council of Canadians produced fact sheets on these issues, and in the book by Clarke and Barlow, a chapter is devoted to each of these five areas.

A pamphlet produced by COC for the national campaign highlighted ten good reasons to oppose the MAI from a Canadian standpoint:

- The MAI would give corporations the right to sue our elected governments to protect their profits.
- The MAI would cripple our ability to create jobs through investment.
- The MAI would give new rights and powers to foreign investors and corporations.
- The MAI would open up our health care, education, and public services to transnational corporations.
- The MAI would give corporations more power to fight environmental regulations.
- The MAI would leave our culture at the mercy of U.S. entertainment mega-corporations.
- The MAI would threaten our ownership of fisheries, forests, energy, and other natural resources.
- All disputes would be settled in secret by trade experts with no public input.
- The MAI would impose tough, unfair rules on developing countries which are not even part of the negotiations.
- We would be locked into the MAI for at least twenty years![5]

One of the powerful things about the campaign against the MAI is that it linked the environmental and social justice movements, and connected them both to globalization and government decision-making, or the lack thereof. When people were educated about the MAI and concerned enough to take action, they found that they could link up with a great variety of interest groups and NGOs from any of the sociological movements (including trade unions, child care advocates, education and health-care organizations, professional associations, and women's, workers' rights, social equity, consumer, development, and environment groups), creating a powerful force of solidarity clearly aimed in opposition to the MAI.

In Canada this was manifested with the formation of the Canadian National Coalition (National Campaign) against the MAI, involving many thousands of individuals and over six hundred NGOs from a variety of sectors across the country (including all those mentioned above).

Environmental Impacts of the MAI

The environment is a subject that was basically not discussed in the MAI. Other than bracketed wording in the preamble of the agreement, and a reference in a limited exception to certain performance requirements, it was silent on environmental matters. The deregulation of international trade is essentially a set of rules that outline things that governments cannot do, instead of guidelines for what they should do.

The MAI had built into it no-distinction clauses, which did not allow preferential treatment of one company over another. These applied to governments favouring a company on the basis of whether it is national versus foreign, or on the basis of environmental standards. This means that under the MAI, governments could not be prejudiced against companies that have negative environmental practices: they must give them the same rights to conduct business as they do to companies whose practices are more environmentally benign.

Without a clearly stated broad exception or reservation, the investment obligations of the MAI would override environmental measures taken by governments. Under GATT, for example, to justify an environmental measure governments must prove the 'necessity' of a measure, and this is open to interpretation and can be argued against by a corporation with vested interests.

Not even international UN conventions and agreements can have an effect: trade agreements like the MAI supersede any environmental regulation. Recommendations made by UN environmental agreements are not enforceable regulations; they have no teeth. The UN Rio Declaration and Agenda 21, for example, are not legally binding. The MAI, by contrast, did have teeth – very sharp ones at that. If a company believes its business is negatively affected as a result of a government's policy, it can sue that government for loss of profit, even if it was an environmental policy.

The right, granted by the MAI, of corporations to sue governments is one that wielded enormous power. With this regulation held over the heads of governments, and thus people, corporations could block positive environmental initiatives, even before they are discussed in parliament, let alone disclosed to citizens or become subject to a public debate.

Such a case has already arisen under NAFTA. A large American company, Ethyl Corporation, launched a $350-million lawsuit against the Canadian government in April 1997 for banning a manganese-based fuel additive (MMT), a dangerous toxin linked to many respiratory problems. Ethyl was suing the Canadian government for loss of future profits. This set in motion a reversal of a tool for environmental protection. Instead of having a 'polluter-pays principle' executed, the exact opposite happened. The Ethyl case was an example of a 'pay-the-polluter' arrangement.

Rather than fighting the suit and risk losing, the Canadian government settled out of court in August 1998, withdrawing the ban, and issuing a written apology to the corporation and a payment of $19.3 million of taxpayers' money. MMT is banned in the United States, but when Canada tried to pass new legislation to better protect the health of its citizens, the Canadian ban on MMT was considered to be an illegitimate expropriation of Ethyl's assets, giving the right to Ethyl to sue to protect its market. Now Canada's shameful backing down and apology, including an admission that there is not clear evidence that MMT is in fact a health threat, sends an appalling message to the world ... two messages in fact. First, that MMT is not a health risk, and second, that a government policy is less powerful than a corporation's right to make profit. The Ethyl case arose from a clause in NAFTA, but in the MAI, protection against expropriation was a central pillar of the agreement. Under the MAI, it would be considered a form of expropriation if the federal government or a province moved to enact new laws to protect the environment, wilderness areas, endangered species, or natural resources.

Canadian environmental policy is rather limited and quite lacking in many areas to begin with, but whatever little is in place would be superseded by the MAI. As Barry Appleton summarizes, by being an active proponent of the MAI, 'Canada has chosen to voluntarily bind itself, its provinces and its municipalities to obligations which protect investments over the environment.'[6]

Opération SalAMI

In addition to the 'National Campaign against the MAI,' many offshoot actions occurred as well, organized by local groups. Perhaps the most impressive of these was 'Opération SalAMI,' a multi-faceted action which centred around a carefully planned civil disobedience intervention to block people from attending a major international economic meeting in May 1998, the 'Conférence de Montréal,' and in so doing protesting the MAI and performing the critical role of public education about the issue. In the French language, the MAI is l'AMI (Accord multilatéral sur l'investissement); 'ami' is the French word for friend, and 'sal' means dirty: hence, the double entendre of SalAMI, meaning 'dirty friend.'

A great deal of organization went into the operation, and a lot of people and groups were involved. These included Alternatives, a Montreal-based international development and social justice NGO, which provided office space and logistical support for the operation; and The People against the MAI (the Montreal chapter of the Council of Canadians), whose members produced and distributed information, and provided back-up support during the demonstration. At the centre of Opération SalAMI, however, were the organizers and the people who were willing to risk getting arrested.

They published and distributed a free information booklet on the MAI, globalization, and the backgrounds of the players involved in the upcoming Conférence de Montréal, and widely disseminated it one month before the operation. They also organized an alternative conference a few days before the blockade, a people's conference aimed at public education and empowerment. A critical part of the organization of the operation was special workshops on civil disobedience and peaceful-resistance training seminars in order to prepare individuals for what to expect, and ensure that they were ready to deal passively with any aggression or violence on the part of the police. Of course, they also took care of the many logistical details of planning and organizing the blockade itself, communicating with the media, and ensuring that everyone involved was sufficiently informed. A lot of activist experience was put into concrete action.

Taking all actions together, Opération SalAMI used an ecological approach to educating the public, not only about the issues, but on how to organize, stand up to oppose what is wrong, and be vocal so that people's collective voice is heard. It worked.

More than one hundred people succeeded in blockading the Conférence de Montréal with their bodies in an act of civil disobedience on the morning of 25 May 1998, and, indeed, as expected, most were arrested by the afternoon. But it went beyond that. Perhaps the most effective aspect of the operation was the effect that it had on public perception and the media, and on the publicization of the dangers of the MAI. Images of brutal arrests appeared on the front page of newspapers across the country the next day, with accompanying texts about the demonstration. It was the lead story on the national television news, and one station even provided some substantive coverage of problems associated with the MAI, which had not previously occurred.

Opération SalAMI pushed the issue of the MAI into the forefront of visibility within the media, whereas it had previously been an issue that the mainstream media had shied away from. The media had to explain to the public why these people were being arrested and, in so doing, give some coverage of people's concerns about the MAI. This was a great form of basic education for the public.

The MAI Inquiry

In September 1998 the national campaign against the MAI entered its most ambitious phase: 'The MAI Inquiry: A Citizens' Search for Alternatives.' This involved eight public-issue forums (public hearings), held in cities across Canada between 25 September and 27 November 1998. These events involved an evening session with a panel of 'national commissioners,' experts in a variety of fields, presenting their concerns to an audience, followed by a facilitated discussion. The next day a series of workshops were held in each city to allow for more input from participants. 'A Citizens' Handbook' was also produced, containing a great deal of information on the MAI, globalization, and their impacts, including a questionnaire and a section on recommendations for participants to fill out, and in this way it served as a community consultation process.

The inquiry was intended as an opportunity to raise the profile of the MAI and opposition to it; broaden interest and involvement in the campaign against the MAI and globalization; and to stimulate discussion and development of alternatives in various sectors and communities. As part of the inquiry, people were asked to think about what a citizens' MAI would look like and to present their ideas on alternatives to the process.

The inquiry was a grand success. All in all, more than ten thousand people participated by attending the evening forums and workshops the next day, and by filling out the 'Citizens' Handbook.' According to

Anna Dashtgard, one of the inquiry coordinators, 'the process gathered many sophisticated ideas on alternatives at the local, national and international levels, while deepening people's understanding of the impact of globalization on their lives.'[7]

The main themes emerging from the input of more than ten thousand people into the process were categorized by the Council of Canadians under the following four areas:

1. *Reclaim democracy:* Examine and reclaim existing democratic rights (civil, political, economic, social, human, and environmental).
2. *Control capital:* Monitor and limit increasing corporate control; push forward alternatives to investment liberalization at all levels.
3. *Civil society development:* Build an international citizens' movement and agenda which facilitates broad-based resistance.
4. *Nurture hope:* Develop a 'living' citizens' agenda with universal appeal that can be used as an educational and motivational tool.

Another sentiment felt at the MAI inquiry was that transformation occurs when enough people are struck by the same vision. As a result of the inquiry process, more than ten thousand Canadian citizens now share a common vision about their future and what must be done to protect it.

The End of the MAI?

On 14 October 1998, the same day as the Montreal session of the MAI inquiry, France withdrew from the MAI negotiations, officially renouncing it as not being in the best interests of their sovereign nation for many of the reasons discussed above. This occurred less than one week before talks about the MAI were to resume at the OECD and catalysed the OECD decision, on 19 October 1998, to shelve the MAI. The MAI was defeated.

But this does not mean that the MAI has gone away. The World Trade Organization (WTO) later put the issue of whether it should take up the call to develop an international trade investment deal on the agenda of its fall '99 meeting. This helped provide the motivation for environmental and social activists to band together and assemble in Seattle, in November 1999, for the now famous anti-WTO protest.

Whether trade investment deals continue to be negotiated within WTO or elsewhere, we can be sure that we need to remain vigilant about trade liberalization and globalization issues, because they affect all levels of society, the environment, and ultimately the very fabric of democracy and national sovereignty.

As Maude Barlow has explained, even though the MAI disappeared, the issues, motivations, and forces that created it have not. It is analogous to stepping on a bump in the rug – it may disappear from where it was, but it then resurfaces in another place, or in several other locations as a series of smaller bumps. Basic education will be necessary for keeping the public informed and wary.

Conclusion

Ecological approaches to basic education are crucial in helping ease and lessen the environmental crisis. The linkage between education and communication is a key one when considering basic education from an NGO perspective, especially within the area of public awareness-raising about environmental concerns.

The environmental movement functions at its best when an ecosystem approach is applied to organization. Following this model, each group and individual acts within a particular niche, strategically performing their roles in a coordinated fashion within a collaborative action plan. Public education and communication plans also function best when an ecological approach is applied, providing multifaceted avenues through which they can be expressed.

The success of the campaign against the MAI was that it brought people together from a broad range of backgrounds and sectors of society, from students, to mothers, to retired elders, each with their own concerns. It united the different social and environmental movements and got them working in a coalition to raise awareness of the threats posed by the MAI. This was a crucial factor allowing for the mobilization in Seattle in 1999. Information was disseminated to members of the public and served as a critical form of basic education about issues they were previously unexposed to.

The campaign was a manifestation of the liberalization of information and the need for its freedom of flow, while at the same time, it actively opposed to the notion of liberalization of trade and freedom of capital flow.

The use of the Internet was critical in this endeavour by making information that was previously classified and secret, freely available to citizens around the world. It was around this liberalization of information that the movement galvanized.

Once concern was raised and the basic information was beginning to be spread via a multifaceted ecological approach – through the Internet, a book on the subject, the alternative press, and word of mouth – public meetings were organized to further educate those who were concerned and to reach new people who wanted to become better informed and educated about the MAI.

These public forums, held across the country, really worked and gave the people attending – a colourful mix of all ages and sectors – a positive boost. Many formed their own local groups that continued to meet and plan their own actions.

Opération SalAMI shook the establishment through the education and mobilization of people. Protesters stood united against what they knew to be wrong. By putting their bodies on the line and getting arrested on 25 May 1998, they became the biggest news item across Canada that day, causing all news media to run stories on the MAI, thereby sending a strong message and serving an invaluable public education function.

The MAI inquiry served to further educate, inform, enlighten, and empower people to get involved with the cause – to take back democratic rights (both social and environmental) and not let the powers of corporations continue to increase at the expense of human liberties and our best interests for the future. Citizens have not stood down; all walks of life mobilized because of dislike for what the MAI represented. This was positive and helped build an international citizens' movement.

People power is the only hope for the future. Change will only happen when we stand united, take ownership of processes, and demand what is right for what we need now, for future generations, and for the environment. Basic education has been, is currently, and will remain forever a critical factor in the catalysis and fostering of this process. It is most effectively achieved when an ecological approach is used, multifaceted, interlinked, and diverse in terms of both content and execution.

Notes

1 Union of Concerned Scientists, 'World Scientists' Warning to Humanity' (1993). This document was signed by over 1,670 scientists from 71 countries, including 104 Nobel laureates – the majority of living recipients of the prize in the sciences.

2 Brian Sarwer-Foner, 'Strategies of Canadian Environmental Non-Governmental Organisations for Protecting Biodiversity: A Participatory Action Research Study' (Master of Science thesis, McGill University, Montreal, 1998); supervised by Dr Stuart B. Hill. Those interested in a summary of the results (the key strategies, barriers, and ways to overcome them) may contact the author, or can download a research report from the Internet: http://iisd1.iisd.ca/rio+5/canadian/finalreport.rtf.
3 Tony Clarke, *MAI-DAY! The Corporate Rule Treaty* (Ottawa: Canadian Centre for Policy Alternatives, 1997).
4 Tony Clarke and Maude Barlow, *MAI: The Multilateral Agreement on Investment and the Threat to Canadian Sovereignty* (Toronto: Stoddart, 1997). Although this book focuses on a Canadian perspective, as does the Council of Canadians (COC) and hence much of the campaign against the MAI, the issues raised and impacts covered largely apply to any country and the concerns of people throughout the world.
5 Council of Canadians, *Ten Good Reasons to Oppose the MAI* (pamphlet for the campaign against the MAI, 1998).
6 Barry Appleton, 'The Environment and the MAI: A Presentation to the House of Commons Sub-Committee on International Trade, Trade Disputes and Investment' (Council of Canadians web-site, 1998).
7 Anna Dashtgard, 'The MAI Inquiry: A Citizen's Search for Alternatives' (unpublished tour and campaign notes, 1998).

References

Canadian Perspective [quarterly magazine of the Council of Canadians], Ottawa, Spring, Summer, and Autumn 1998.
Clarke, Tony. 1998. 'Towards a Citizens' MAI: An Alternative Approach to Developing a Global Investment Treaty Based on Citizens' Rights and Democratic Control.' Ottawa, Polaris Institute.
Council of Canadians. Fact Sheets.
– Web-site: www.canadians.org
Dashtgard, Anna. 1999. Personal communication.
Lalumière, Catherine, Jean-Pierre Landau, and Emmanuel Glimet. 1998. 'Report on the Multilateral Agreement on Investment (MAI).' Paris, Ministry of the Economy, Finance, and Industry. 1998. Available on the Ministry's Internet site at: www.finances.gouv.fr/pole_ecofin/international/ami0998/ami0998.htm
National Campaign against the MAI. 1998. *A Citizens' Handbook on the MAI.*

Prepared for The MAI Inquiry: A Citizens' Search for Alternatives. Ottawa: Council of Canadians.

Opération SalAMI. 1998. 'Opération SalAMI.' Information bulletin. Montréal: Opération SalAMI and *Alternatives*.

Pippard, Leone. 1995. 'Background Situation Research and Analysis for: SustainABILITY' – a National Communications Program in Support of Sustainable Development.' Toronto, ParticipACTION.

Sarwer-Foner, Brian. 1993. 'Rio Revisited: Exploring The '92 Global Forum.' *The Explorers Journal* 71(1): 40–3.

PART THREE

For Sustainable Endogenous Development ...

... based on what people are and can do differently
— *Anthony Flaccavento, United States*

... that draws on the creative energy of communities
— *Salah Arafa, Egypt*

... in which cultural heritage guides economic initiatives
— *Valeria Nagy Czanka and Ildiko Mihaly, Hungary*

... through the combined efforts of a professional association and indigenous knowledge
— *Ismail Daiq and Shawkat Sarsour, Palestinian Territories*

Sustainable Development Literacy in Central Appalachia

Anthony Flaccavento

Communities in the Central Appalachian region of the United States continue to struggle with high levels of unemployment and poverty, a dependence on external capital for jobs, and severe pressures on the natural resource base. In this context, Appalachian Sustainable Development is working to build a more locally rooted, ecologically sustainable economy, focusing on agriculture, forestry, and wood products. Drawing upon this experience, this article explores the opportunities and obstacles encountered in the process of building a more sustainable economy. Specific attention is given to the process of educating people through experience: farmers, loggers, entrepreneurs, as well as consumers and professionals in these fields. This 'habitual learning' process is seen as central to creating not only new values, but the new behaviours and relationships needed for sustainability.*

> *There is a myth that the purpose of education is to give students the means for upward mobility and success. The plain fact is that the planet does not need more successful people. But it does desperately need more peacemakers, healers, restorers, storytellers and lovers of every kind. It needs people who will live well in their places. It needs people of moral courage willing to join the fight to make the world habitable and humane. These qualities have little to do with success as our culture defines it.*
>
> David Orr

On 1 November 1996, the day-shift crew arrived at the Louisiana Pacific Waferboard factory in Dungannon, Virginia. Greeted by a small group of security guards and a management representative, they were told to go home, that the plant was closed. Permanently. No notice had been given. Ten years after opening its doors in this richly forested Scott County community, the plant precipitously laid off nearly one hundred workers. The profits from this plant, it was said, were not sufficient, even though it had been earning profits.

The Appalachian regions of Tennessee and Virginia are not in crisis. The situation would better be described as one of long-term economic stagnation and marginalization, steady, usually subtle ecological deterioration, and inexorable cultural decline. In the snapshot of the present, it is a region striving mightily to come astride the rush of global, post-industrial capitalism. In the longitudinal view of the past two hundred years, it is a frustrating story of cultural and economic subordination, of individuals and communities gradually relinquishing the skills, knowledge, and bonds that made this part of the world different from countless others. It is a 'place' becoming a 'region,' a community – flawed but distinct – degenerating into an ever more eager body of consumers. As such, Central Appalachia is a success story in the global economy, a people once 'left behind,' now rapidly integrating into the worldwide web of consumption.

But there is another Appalachian tale unfolding, one that will perhaps be instructive for rural communities throughout the United States and much of the world. It is the evolving story of community-based initiatives to regenerate the Central Appalachian economy and culture *from within*. This story includes:

- fledgling organic farmers' cooperatives, learning and sharing sustainable agriculture skills, while developing marketing partnerships with families, restaurants, and grocery stores;
- grass-roots community planning processes which are bringing relatively broad cross-sections of people together to imagine and work towards a better, more self-reliant future;
- value-adding initiatives utilizing solar wood-drying kilns, commercial 'kitchen incubators,' and joint marketing efforts to help increase local revenues while improving environmental conservation practices;
- hands-on, farm- and field-based educational efforts designed to improve agricultural and forestry practices *and* to broaden the understanding of those involved in agriculture education and training, forestry management, economic development, and vocational education.

Appalachian Sustainable Development, a key player in this process, is focusing its efforts on a ten-county area of southwestern Virginia and northeast Tennessee. This part of Appalachia has sustained high jobless and poverty rates, even as the economy of most of the United States has boomed. Unemployment rates are two to five times higher than U.S. rates, approaching 20 per cent in some counties. Underemployment – people working fewer hours than they would choose or at jobs with wages and responsibilities far below their capabilities – is quite common. These low-wage, usually benefitless jobs used to be the domain of young people, providing basic job experience. Now it is an increasingly common form of employment for laid-off, semi-skilled workers or homemakers entering the workforce out of necessity. This underemployment contributes to poverty rates exceeding 30 per cent in some counties.

The Central Appalachian economic pillars of coal mining and tobacco agriculture are in decline. Although the region's rates of coal extraction remain at historic highs, employment has dropped steadily and dramatically: jobs in Virginia's coal mining industry fell by more than 50 per cent between 1986 and 1996. While tobacco remains a relatively profitable crop, the margin for tobacco farmers is shrinking, with net profitability declining by nearly one-third since the early 1980s. This has led to increased consolidation and mechanization in tobacco, with fewer farmers growing on a larger scale.

With nearly 60 per cent of the region's land mass in forests, the timber industry is expanding rapidly, creating some new jobs and spawning opportunistic logging firms. Because some of these loggers lack adequate training and experience, and because much of the harvested wood is destined for chip mills and other lower-value manufacturing, pressure on the forest resource base is increasing dramatically. Whether on farms, in the forest, or in factories, Appalachian communities increasingly face 'jobs or the environment' trade-offs, a conundrum from which there often seems little escape.

Appalachian Sustainable Development (ASD) is a non-profit organization working in partnership with community-based organizations, entrepreneurs, and public sector agencies to overcome this jobs versus environment trade-off through education and community development. The author of this article is the director of ASD. Utilizing the experience of ASD and its public and private partners, this essay will examine educational issues relevant to fostering sustainable community development. In this context, informal dissemination of experience and knowledge is considered of equal importance to more formalized educational activities.

This article begins with the assertion *that most adult learning and value formation occurs within the context of our everyday experience and the institutions that shape and delimit those experiences.* That is to say, we act primarily out of *habit*, for it is nearly impossible to ponder each of the hundreds of daily decisions we must make, particularly in fast-paced, high-stress 'modern' societies. These habits become our teachers, forming our consciousness of the world. They predispose us to see, hear, and consider some things, while devaluing or ignoring others. This is especially true in individualistic societies like the United States, where opportunities for challenging these behaviours and the beliefs that propel them are constrained by an obsessive protectiveness of personal space and personalized ethics.

This assertion of the profound importance of 'habitual learning' will be explored in the first section of this article. It begs further, more rigorous examination, which the author would welcome. If it is valid, then strategies for improving education – of young people as well as adults – must go far beyond the classroom and into the lives, the culture, the commerce, and the institutions of daily life, what David Korten calls the 'social economy' (Korten 1994).

In the second section, a set of *sustainability working principles* developed from experience in Central Appalachia will be posited. The final section will consider emerging alternative models, particularly the effort to *create an infrastructure for sustainability*. The social and market relationships unfolding in this effort will be examined, with particular attention to alternative adult education strategies. Sustainable development literacy as it is, or is not, expressed in the educational, social, and market infrastructures of our region will be evaluated.

Everyday Living, Everyday Learning

> *It isn't enough just to advertise on television ... You've got to reach kids throughout their day – in schools, as they're shopping at the malls ... or at the movies. You've got to become part of the fabric of their lives.*
>
> Senior Vice President, Grey Advertising

A young boy played on the fringes of the woods surrounding his large suburban Kentucky home, while his mother spoke with a visitor in the doorway of the house. At some point, he approached his mother, arm outstretched to reveal a handful of wild strawberries. He started to put one in his mouth, but his mother slapped the berries away.

'Why did you do that?' queried the visitor. 'Wild berries are safe.' The boy's mother retorted: 'Are you kidding? I would never let him eat anything that *just grew.*'

Our values and our world-view are shaped by many factors: our parents, schools, church, the media, our occupational peers, and more. Of fundamental importance in our childhood, these influences continue to affect us into adulthood, directly and through our children, permeating 'the fabric of our lives,' as advertising executives know all too well.

One of the most subtle but critical factors in shaping our consciousness, and our relation to the world, is our eating habits. In agrarian, subsistence-oriented cultures, what is eaten is directly related to the local ecosystem and to the skills and occupations of the members of the community. Most of what is eaten is clearly connected to what is found or cultivated, and the rituals of both raising and eating food are central to the 'collective memory.' Under such circumstances, an intimate understanding of local soils and habitats, and other environmental knowledge, is indispensable, a central component of basic adult education.

The British development expert Robert Chambers writes of an encounter between Western soil scientists sent to a region in southern Africa, and the farmers they were sent to help. After some time spent mapping and sampling soils, the agronomists developed a soil classification scheme that included sixteen types. After the experts' work had been completed, the local farmers shared their own classification scheme, which included nearly *two hundred* different soil types! This finely tuned understanding came out of need, and a long and intimate relationship between those people and their land (Chambers 1983).

Along with other sustenance skills – building homes, securing heat and energy, rearing children – the raising, preparation, and eating of food shapes the celebrations and stories of the community. This can be seen even in modernizing rural cultures such as Central Appalachian communities, where the cooking of sorghum molasses, or the preparation of apple butter remain big attractions in community gatherings and festivals.

In most modern communities of the West, food continues to play a central role in the rituals of family and community life. There is a profound difference, however, vis-à-vis subsistence cultures, or even most urban communities of previous generations: the *consumption* of food now occurs virtually without reference to its production. The constraints of seasons, rainfall, soil type, and topography are virtually eliminated, along with distinctive local varieties and palates. So too is the need for food preservation skills, once so central to maintaining a healthy – and interesting – diet in the non-growing season.

Nowhere is this divorce between the production and consumption of food more pronounced than in the modern supermarket. The produce section of a typical U.S. supermarket stocks from sixty to one hundred different types of fresh fruits and vegetables – in the heart of winter! Concern for taste and quality, not to mention the health of soils or farmers, has largely given way to an overriding emphasis on uniformity, convenience, and availability. One example suffices: An Appalachian organic farmer presented boxes of fresh, beautiful peppers to the senior produce buyer of a regional grocery store chain. The buyer pulled a box of peppers from the shelf, stating that they'd been grown in Holland, in hydroponic greenhouses. These peppers were considerably smaller than the local ones, nearly a week old upon receipt, and amazingly uniform. 'Look at these!' the buyer proudly exclaimed as he picked one up. 'They look like they came out of a mould!' The local peppers – larger, fresher, and of comparable price – were refused.

With fewer than 3 per cent of U.S. citizens now involved in farming, their primary experience of food is grocery stores and, increasingly, restaurants. The industrial-style uniformity and season-defying availability of the modern supermarket are extended further by the fast food complex. In the United States, over half the population lives within a three-minute drive of a McDonalds, enabling Americans to buy over 700,000 hamburgers every hour (Rifkin 1992, 1). Over the past fifty years, the percentage of food dollars spent *away* from home has nearly doubled, approaching half of all U.S. household food expenditures (Rifkin 1992, 2). Even with this dramatic growth in restaurant and fast food consumption, U.S. citizens continue to pay proportionately less than any other people for food, roughly 10 per cent of total income.

These experiences transform our relationship to food, to farms, and to the agricultural ecosystem. The lesson is clear: food is cheap, plentiful, and easily produced. The 25 billion tons of topsoil annually lost to erosion worldwide, or the estimated 60 per cent of global rangeland damaged by overgrazing since the Second World War, are not just hidden by this ubiquitous cornucopia. They are virtually unfathomable to the average 'consumer.'

The lessons of the global economy go beyond our understanding of food and agriculture, permeating nearly every dimension of our lives. With forty-eight of the hundred largest economies of the world now *corporations* rather than nations, the ideology of convenience and the desirability of huge 'economies of scale' have achieved near global acceptance, at least among political and economic elites. Even our language for 'size' has been swayed: The U.S. Small Business Administration's definition of a 'small' business can now include companies with as many as 1,500 employees and as much as $5 million in annual sales (Small Is Beautiful, Big Is Subsidized, *The Ecologist* 1998).

Our language defines and reflects our understanding of the world, our relationship to it, and our sense of opportunities and obligations. These habits of eating, shopping, travelling, and consuming teach us constantly, at times insidiously. They instruct us, as an advertisement for Gimbels Department Store once stated, that 'economic salvation, both national and personal, has nothing to do with pinching pennies. Economic salvation depends upon consumption. If you want to have more cake tomorrow, you have to eat more cake today. The more you consume, the more you'll have, quicker' ('Small Is Beautiful, Big Is Subsidized,' *The Ecologist* 1998, 2).

This message of consumption has transformed once frugal, substantially self-reliant communities such as those of the Appalachian United States and many 'developing nations.' Disguised under the banner of solidarity (IBM's 'Solutions for a Small Planet' advertisements), couched in supranational efficiency ('Archers Daniel Midland: Supermarket to the World'), the global consumer culture is becoming so pervasive, so *necessary*, that we can barely imagine an alternative, let alone build it with our minds and bodies. It is precisely that remnant of imagination, those rebellious minds and bodies to which we now turn our attention.

Working Principles of Sustainability

David Orr, quoted at the outset of this article, states that 'success' as defined in Western, consumptive societies is overwhelming the biosphere. David Korten argues that sustainability will only be possible with healthy, resourceful households and vibrant local communities and institutions, what he refers to as 'sustainable livelihoods' (Korten 1994). Yet many people see no other option than the consumptive vision of success, and few basic educational programs prepare them for a meaningful alternative. This next section outlines five 'working principles' of sustainable development, perhaps providing a foundation for an alternative vision of success, both in education and community development.

*

> *I spent the summer travelling.*
> *I got halfway across my backyard.*
>
> Louis Agassiz

Principle 1: *Sustainable development is first and foremost locally rooted.*

It 'fits' within the ecosystem of a particular watershed or bio-region, and it builds upon the opportunities and challenges embedded in the region's human community. This does not imply parochialism or a clinging to the past, as some would characterize it. Rather, it means that economic and technological choices are made locally, in consideration of ecological limits and the more basic needs of people.

This is no easy task, especially within a broader culture so enamoured with mobility, globalization, and change. But it is essential if our development is to be both sensible and innovative. As the theologian Dallas Willard has said, 'the first act of love is always the giving of attention.' And it is only in this *attention to the particular* that we can begin to understand complex biological relationships or see unique cultural strengths.

*

> *Before any course of action, we should first ask:*
> *What is already here?*
> *What does nature allow us to do here?*
> *What does nature help us to do here?*
>
> Wendell Berry

Principle 2: *Sustainable development takes place within the context of both the local ecosystem and the larger biosphere. It is guided – and limited – by three essential ecosystem facts: diversity, community, and regeneration.*

Ecosystems vary dramatically in their natural levels of biological *diversity*. In all but the coldest extremes, however, ecosystems evolve towards a level of increasing species differentiation. This diversity provides the foundation for ecological resilience, adaptability, even productivity

(*Nature*, February 1996, as quoted in the *New York Times*, 5 March 1996). Broad diversity creates numerous symbiotic opportunities, such as rhizobial bacteria colonizing legume roots, facilitating nitrogen fixation. It also limits disease or pest epidemics, and increases the total amount of solar energy (productivity) which can be harnessed.

The human community and economy derive comparable benefits from diversity, to the extent that we do not shrink from it. A wider range of human cultures and traditions broadens our potential for insight and creativity; economic diversification makes communities less vulnerable to plant closings, 'downsizings,' and technology-driven changes in demand for particular products (e.g., the relatively rapid shift from glass to plastic bottles, which has dramatically reduced the number of jobs in glass manufacturing).

This species diversity is interconnected through an extraordinarily complex web of relationships, including biological, climatic, and physical elements. If this *community of relationship*, the second ecosystem fact, is not understood, the consequences will eventually be felt downwind or downstream. The eutrophication, or over-enrichment, of streams from agricultural run-off not only chokes out fish, but will gradually change the very composition of species in a particular waterway.

In economic terms, these communities of interrelationships create both opportunities and challenges. Some firms, such as Full Cycle Woodworks in Rogersville, Tennessee, are undertaking *full cost accounting* in an effort to minimize side effects and 'externalities,' instead integrating *all* the impacts of an enterprise into its bottom line. This has led Full Cycle to develop high value products from wood scraps and so-called low-value tree species.

The third ecological reality is regeneration: In the natural world, everything takes place within cycles of decay, death, and rebirth. Simply put, in nature there is no trash, for everything – and all of us – eventually yields to decomposition, the source of fertility and new life.

Gigantic hog and cattle feed lots create millions of tons of manure. To minimize water pollution, these enormous firms are required to implement 'manure management systems,' including expensive lagoons and monitoring systems. Meanwhile, neighbouring corn farmers, operating on a large, highly specialized scale, watch their soil steadily decline, in large part from a lack of organic matter. Thus the manure, a renewable and inexpensive source of fertility and organic matter, becomes a waste and a cost for one farm, while another buys increasing amounts of petroleum-based fertilizers to compensate for declining soil health. According to a Worldwatch Institute study, this system generates about 35 lbs of eroded topsoil for every one pound of steak produced (Isaac Walton League).

Holly Creek Farm in Greene County, Tennessee, exemplifies an alternative approach based upon integration with the community and the ecosystem. This small farm includes two acres of commercial organic vegetable production, most of which is sold to forty to fifty neighbouring households through an arrangement known as community supported agriculture. Additional markets for farmer Cathy Guthrie's produce include local restaurants and the farmers' market. Chickens, which provide eggs to the households, are integrated into the crop rotation plan of the farm; their manure adds nutrients and organic matter to the soil, rather than becoming a source of water pollution. No off-farm chemical inputs are used.

*

Any physical subsystem of a finite and non-growing earth must itself also eventually become non-growing.

John Cobb and Herman Daly

American culture was founded on a pioneering spirit. The increasingly pervasive 'global culture' rests in large part on a similar notion of no limits, no constraints. In this context, serious conservation is difficult, and radical reductions in consumption, primarily in the Western world, are urgently needed. In ecological terms, excessive consumption depletes our sources and overloads our sinks, compromising the cycles of regeneration discussed earlier.

Principle 3: *Another means to better fit our human subsystems within the finite biosphere is by maximizing the value added to resources within or close to the place where they're found.*

An oak log brings 60 cents per board foot; when sawn into a board it brings U.S. $1.00; kiln dried it is worth about U.S. $3.00 if directly sold to a neighbour building book shelves. This fivefold increase in value, in addition to generating more revenue within the local community, creates opportunities for more and higher skilled jobs, reduces energy used in transportation, builds relationships between 'producers' and 'consumers,' and increases the likelihood that the resource – trees, soil, fisheries – will be managed for the long term (since it is more economically valuable).

*

Principle 4: *The fourth element of sustainability which we have discerned is that of empowerment: building skills, creating assets, and opening the doors (or creating new ones!) to decision-making power within and beyond the local community.*

Often these different components of empowerment have been fragmented, with community organizers and political scientists focused on power relationships, while development professionals addressed skill building almost exclusively. In our experience, the two are closely linked if not inseparable. In the community of Pennington Gap, in Virginia's poorest county, a grass-roots visioning process spawned the creation of a farmers' market and a community services directory. Facilitated by ASD partner, the Coalition for Jobs and the Environment, the process brought elected officials and agency staff together with grass-roots folks, some of whom had never before participated in community decision-making.

The combination of a more broadly empowered citizenry and a value-adding infrastructure together provide the foundation for a more regionally self-reliant economy and community. Regional self-reliance does not imply complete self-sufficiency or isolationism. It *does* mean a healthy degree of regional independence based upon innovative, diverse enterprises, skilled and creative households, and a fundamental integration with the ecosystem.

*

A passerby: 'That horse logging does a good job alright, but it's slow. At the rate you're going, you'll be here forever.'
The horse logger: 'Yeah. I know.'

Principle 5: *The final and most obvious principle of sustainable development is simply that it lasts. Indefinitely.*

This goal is not disputed; the question is only how to get there. This next section will discuss the strategy being used by Appalachian Sustainable Development based upon the principles outlined above.

Building an Infrastructure for Sustainability

> *The economy is vitally dependent on meaninglessness. The whole commercial community is geared up to exploit and play to meaninglessness. When you feel bad, you go out for a nice lunch or buy yourself something nice.*
>
> Dr Thomas Naylor, Duke University

Nearly two centuries ago, economist David Ricardo forwarded the theory of 'comparative advantage,' describing an international system of exchange in which each nation specialized in the production of a limited number of goods, which for various reasons, it could produce relatively more efficiently than other nations. All of these efficiently produced goods, according to the theory, would then be 'freely traded' among nations, spurring a global proliferation of goods, rising export income, and steadily expanding consumer choices.

The idea of comparative advantage has proven to be more than just theory. It has been the centrepiece of economic development strategy for the World Bank, the International Monetary Fund, and every other major Western development institution in the twentieth century. It also describes the relationship between Central Appalachia and the urban-industrial centres of our nation since railroads first 'opened' mountain communities a century ago.

For Central Appalachian communities, and much of the so-called developing world, the problem with comparative advantage lies in its assumptions. These can be stated as follows:

- An ever expanding array of consumer choices is necessarily good.
- The best means to achieve that expansion is through specialization and the substitution of capital for labour.
- Local, regional, even national self-reliance is at best impractical, at worst anti-progressive.
- A free-market, consumer-driven economy is the best means to allocate resources, including decisions about what to produce and how to produce it.
- The economic playing field is a level one.

Comparative advantage as an economic development strategy has been ruinous to Central Appalachia, indeed to the culture and economy of countless local communities around the globe. Its major success, the global proliferation of cheap food, fibre, and stuff, has only marginally benefited the poor, and has degraded the ecosystem in an almost unfathomable number of ways.

In the communities of southwest Virginia and northeast Tennessee, this approach has led to an extractive, low-value economy and a high level of dependence upon external capital, markets, and experts. The infrastructure for such an economy began with the railroads, necessary to ship large amounts of coal and timber, and continues today with the almost religious belief in roads and industrial shell buildings (large metal buildings constructed to lure industries to a community). Beyond this important physical infrastructure lie equally critical systems of education – worker training and preparation supported by state and federal programs – and institutional marketing, largely taking the form of extensive and expensive industrial recruitment programs.

What is being produced in these shell buildings usually has little if any relationship to community needs or priorities, and only occasionally takes account of the bio-region's attributes and constraints. This estrangement of community and ecosystem from economic strategy is sometimes perpetuated by key institutions. In 1996 an 'economic development expert' from the Tennessee Valley Authority dismissed the role of agriculture in building a stronger economy, in spite of several thousand tobacco, beef, and dairy farms, an increasing number of commercial fruit and vegetable operations, and a terrain well suited to small livestock production. This is another instance in which the prevailing development paradigm, as Thomas Pruiksma has said, 'conceives of the majority of the world's people in terms of *what they are not*' (Pruiksma 1998, 344).

A sustainable development strategy begins with what people *are*, where they have come from – their culture, heritage, skills, and knowledge – and the attributes and constraints of the bio-region. Wendell Berry's questions, *What is already here? What does nature allow us, help us to do here?* provide the starting point.

As our efforts have unfolded, we have realized the need to go beyond creation of a variety of environmentally friendly businesses, or providing general education on 'sustainability.' Instead, our strategy is now predicated on *building an infrastructure for sustainability* based on the working principles described in the previous section. This infrastructure has five main elements:

1. *A diversified base of ecologically sustainable local businesses*, ranging from farmers, loggers, and wood manufacturers, to environmental service providers, energy and waste reduction firms, and more. In a more sustainable community, a high proportion of these businesses would be providing goods and services that help meet essential needs, rather than 'gearing up to exploit and play to meaninglessness.'
2. *Ongoing education and training for sustainable entrepreneurs which spawns innovation, resourcefulness, and adequate profitability*. This educational process uses peer training – 'farmer to farmer' workshops, for instance – while also bringing university and technical expertise to the farm, forest, and firm. Several ASD partners, including Jubilee Project, Rural Resources, and Lonesome Pine Office on Youth focus particular attention on high school students and young adults in an effort to reverse the out-migration of youth.
3. *Asset building and access to capital for low- and moderate-income entrepreneurs through micro-enterprise, revolving 'green business' loan funds, and cost-sharing opportunities for conservation and innovation.* Business Start, one of ASD's partners, has made nearly one hundred microloans in the past four years, while the Nature Conservancy is offering support to environmentally sound small businesses. The Lonesome Pine Office on Youth and the Coalfield Regional Tourism Authority are working to capitalize an ecotourism fund, providing training, loans, and equipment to beginning entrepreneurs. ASD's sustainable agriculture program includes nearly a dozen pilot farms, where cost-sharing has facilitated the adoption of sustainable practices and systems.
4. *Value-adding facilities to increase jobs and revenues retained in local communities, and to reduce extraction pressure on soils, fields, and forests.* These facilities now include a small solar wood-drying kiln, which processes sustainably harvested logs into dried lumber, and a recently opened commercial kitchen incubator developed by Jubilee Project in Tennessee's poorest county. Development of additional incubators and commercial food-processing facilities is planned, and a much larger solar and wood-waste dry kiln became operational in April 2001. Without adequate dry kilns, high-value logs are shipped out of the region as raw material, increasing waste and energy use, and, ironically, leaving hundreds of local crafters and wood manufacturers to purchase imported lumber for their

products. So-called 'kitchen incubators' provide facilities in which small-scale entrepreneurs can develop, test, and market high-value food and agricultural products, from sauces and preserves to soaps and vinegars.
5. *Regionalized marketing systems, including producer-consumer networks that build public commitment to sustainable entrepreneurs, and increase the viability of these businesses.* These marketing systems are usually cooperative in nature, enabling small-scale farmers or other producers to 'pool' their product, increasing its marketability. A regional growers co-op provides one example: Nearly two dozen producers from five different counties have built a network that now sells organic produce and other farm products to restaurants, health food stores, and, more recently, grocery stores. The farmers realize 75 per cent of the retail value of their product compared to the 20 to 25 per cent which U.S. farmers on average secure. In-store educational materials, including profiles of participating farmers, help build public understanding and customer loyalty.

This infrastructure for sustainability is based, fundamentally, upon the three ecological principles of diversity, community, and regeneration. While all three principles might be widely embraced rhetorically, in practice they present a radical challenge to the dominant development paradigm, for it is based upon specialization, the estrangement of producers from consumers, the mobility of capital and people, and the convenience of cheap, ubiquitous, disposable products.

A Strategy for Sustainable Development Literacy

Developing an effective adult basic education strategy begins with a recognition of prevailing norms and beliefs, among educators and development professionals as well as average citizens. To ascertain some of these beliefs, a community sustainable development literacy survey was conducted during the winter of 1998 and 1999. Given limited resources and time, two sample populations were chosen: public schoolteachers (primary and secondary) from four different schools, and a random sampling of 150 people, taken from both rural counties and a small (45,000 population) urban centre. The results of this survey are summarized in the accompanying box.

In addition to this survey, Appalachian Sustainable Development staff and partners have been gathering information about people's

SUSTAINABILITY SURVEY

In the winter of 1998–9 surveys were mailed to two groups: a random sampling of 150 households in the region; and to teachers at four different public schools in the area. The questionnaire attempted to determine respondents' understanding of economics, ecology, and community and sustainable development. A total of 30 individuals from the general public and 16 teachers responded.

While it is clear that this survey pool was not sufficiently large to draw broad conclusions, some interesting attitudes and definitions consistently emerged:

* Three-quarters of those surveyed defined *economics* entirely or primarily in terms of finance, investment, growth, and jobs, with no mention of a local or household economy, of natural resources, or natural capital.
* Thirty per cent included some element of sustainability (conservation, equity, self-reliance, future generations) in their conception of *economic health*.
* Forty per cent had heard of *sustainable development* (general population – 38%, teachers – 44%), but only 13 per cent displayed a moderate to strong understanding (were able to name two or more elements of sustainability).
* Just over half included some mention of 'place' in their description of *community*, with a nearly equal number (46%) naming helpfulness or neighbourliness; only 4 per cent mentioned heritage, history, or culture.
* Regarding *free trade*, teachers were far more likely to view it as primarily good: 50 per cent of teachers compared to only 14 per cent of the general public; *technological change*, similarly, was generally positive for 44 per cent of teachers compared to 19 per cent of the public.
* Teachers views of the *role of education and literacy* reflected a strong belief in the efficacy of local efforts, as well as in personal growth and development; two to three times over broader social, cultural, or political goals.

> * Conversely, in terms of their *food buying habits*, 3.5 times as many teachers named personal considerations (appearance, price) over environmental or equity considerations; a similar trend was followed in priorities governing the purchase or construction of a house – 3 times as many naming 'comfort' and 'location' as chose energy or environmental considerations; for choice of automobile, it was a fivefold difference.

beliefs, priorities, and behaviours. Much of this is anecdotal, all of it growing out of our efforts to promote sustainability. From this ongoing and practical 'research,' a number of obstacles have been identified which must be dealt with in order to expand and strengthen the sustainability infrastructure discussed earlier. These obstacles include:

1. *A strong and extremely widely held faith in the global economy as a means for both greater personal satisfaction and increased job creation.* This belief is particularly strong among elected officials, educators, and development professionals. One example: Recent test results from public schools in our region revealed particularly low scores in history and math, falling far short of so-called standards of learning in those subjects. When asked, a senior official from the state's Department of Education reiterated the importance of standards 'to help prepare students to be competitive in the global economy.' No mention was made of students being better prepared to address local needs, to better understand other cultures, or to become more intelligent citizens.

   In discussions with educators and community development leaders from Central Europe and Arab nations, it is clear that this faith in the global economy is *not* widespread in their communities, except among elites. In fact, the disenfranchisement from the global – and even national – economy experienced by most poor and working-class people may, ironically, be advantageous: the work of Laila Kamel with garbage workers in Cairo's poorest communities demonstrates extraordinary creativity, resource conservation, and community empowerment, all of which are central elements of sustainability.

Our own experience is similar: locally derived, resource-conserving solutions to problems often present themselves in the poorest communities or among 'less educated' people. An example: two local farmers described how they achieved outstanding insect pest control using guinea hens, a chicken-like fowl that patrols vegetable crops every morning, cleaning them of beetles, bugs, and larvae. This simple, renewable, on-farm solution not only avoids hazardous chemicals but reduces the need even for purchased *organic* controls.

2. *The profound and pervasive estrangement of most modern people from the source of their sustenance, including the people who raise or harvest it.* As Wendell Berry has said:

> The name of our present society's connection to the earth is 'bad work' – work that is only generally and crudely defined, that enacts a dependence that is ill understood, that enacts no affection and gives no honor. Every one of us is to some extent guilty of this bad work ... All of us are responsible for bad work, not so much because we do it ourselves (though we all do it) as because we have it done for us by other people.
>
> Living as we now do in almost complete dependence on a global economy, we are put inevitably into a position of ignorance and irresponsibility. No one can know the whole globe. We can connect ourselves to the globe as a whole only by means of a global economy that, without knowing the earth, plunders it for us.

3. *Following from this estrangement comes the frequently articulated idea that average people cannot afford to support organic farmers, sustainable loggers, and other socially responsible entrepreneurs.* This notion was recently articulated by several individuals who were part of a group of ministers and seminarians visiting the Appalachian region. The same sentiment is expressed when the subject of tennis shoes and child labour is raised or when 'buy local' campaigns are confronted with Wal-Mart superstores.

But this price sensitivity may be changing. A second, much larger survey recently commissioned by ASD focused on food-buying habits and preferences in our region. Encouragingly, of more than 1,200 (randomly contacted) respondents, 79 per cent expressed a preference for organic or sustainably raised foods, and almost 90 per cent preferred *local,* organic foods. Of this number, almost half stated that they would be willing to pay significantly more for such products.

4. *The implicit belief among many indigenous Appalachian people that non-academic knowledge is inferior, that local, homegrown solutions to problems are not adequate.* This manifests itself in a number of ways, most commonly as reliance upon professionals and experts, not to supplement local knowledge, but to supplant it.

    Alternatively, hands-on, peer-based networks of working people can effectively teach and support sustainability innovations. In rural Russell County, Virginia, a dozen traditional farmers met to plan for the opening of a new local market. One of the farmers in the group, who also ran the local farm supply store, described a biological soil treatment which significantly improved soil tilth and workability, especially on worn-out land. 'Exactly how does that stuff work, Buddy?' asked one of the farmers. 'See,' Buddy replied, 'you all buy chemical fertilizers from me and they increase your crop yields. But they kill the life in your soil. They kill your soil. Now you're coming back to me to buy this other product to put the life back in your soil.' Some of those farmers are now pursuing sustainable agriculture practices.

5. *The economic and infrastructural biases that favour growth, mobility, and external capital over locally based, modestly scaled development.* Two decades after U.S. secretary of agriculture Earl Butz told farmers to 'get big or get out,' these biases continue. Virginia Department of Transportation statistics show that the Commonwealth spends nearly *fifteen times* as much on road construction and maintenance as it does on all forms of mass transit, bike paths, and other energy-conserving transportation systems. Convenient, ever-expanding roads, of course, encourage more and more driving, with all its consequent ecological costs. More insidiously, it erodes local production and local commerce by making imported goods cheaper and virtually ubiquitous.

    Additionally, the very same outside companies which are recruited to replace the vanishing local economy receive myriad incentives to leave one community and set up shop in another. Local businesses rarely find comparable support because, they are told, they simply aren't big enough to merit substantial tax breaks or other subsidies.

    Recognizing these obstacles, ASD and its partners are working to create educational opportunities based upon the *practice* of more sustainable living, at home, in the community, and in the workplace.

The *practice* of sustainability neither precedes nor follows an intellectual choice to change one's values or lifestyle. At least not for most of us. Instead it appears that there is a constant interplay between intellect and experience, between the formation of values and priorities, and life in the real world. The habitual learning that each of us experiences day in and day out accumulates, strongly shaping not only our values but our *sense of possibilities*. The latter is perhaps the most important factor of all. Many so-called modern people experience cognitive dissonance: they 'believe' in one thing but do another, and they know it. Many people, for instance, express a preference for organic food but are unwilling to pay more. Social activists will boycott grapes because their production is poisoning farm workers, but few seek out local farmers who might be interested in alternative practices.

Why is this? From our experience, we believe it is primarily a limit of imagination, a limited sense of possibilities. Sustainable development and sustainability education are to a large degree based upon the sense of possibilities, specifically the possibility of alternative ways of living, working, and relating. This sense of possibility must be based first and foremost in experience, or it will quickly degenerate into wishful thinking and naivety. Sharing in the *experience* of a diversified organic farm, or the *experience* of a low-impact horse-logging operation, or the *experience* of a table made from scrap wood and low-value lumber species all engender a sense of possibility. The most critical role of educators and non-profit community development organizations may well be in helping to cultivate this renewed imagination based upon creative experiences and meaningful relationships with one another and the world around us.

References

Berry, Wendell. 1992. 'Conservation Is Good Work. In *Sex, Economy, Freedom and Community.* New York and San Francisco: Pantheon Books.

Chambers, Robert. 1983. *Rural Development: Putting the Last First.* London and New York: Longman.

Cobb, John, and Herman Daly. 1989. *For the Common Good: Redirecting the Economy Toward Community, the Environment and a Sustainable Future.* Boston: Beacon Press.

Korten, David. 1994. 'Sustainable Livelihoods: Redefining the Global Social Crisis.' *Earth Ethics* (Fall).

Orr, David. 1998. 'Technological Fundamentalism.' *The Ecologist* 28:6 (Nov./

Dec.). (Ecosystems, Ltd, Cissbury House, Forze View, Slinfold, W. Sussex, RH13 7RH, U.K.)

Pruiksma, Thomas. 1998. 'Stranger at Home.' *The Ecologist* 28:6 (Nov./Dec.). (Ecosystems, Ltd, Cissbury House, Furze View, Slinfold, W. Sussex, RH13 7RH, U.K.)

Rifkin, Jeremy. 1992. *Beyond Beef: The Rise and Fall of the Cattle Culture*. New York: Penguin Books.

'Small Is Beautiful, Big Is Subsidized.' 1998. Special supplement to *The Ecologist*.

Sustainable Community Development with Human Dimensions: The Basaisa Experience

Salah Arafa

This paper discusses the concepts and practices used in the Basaisa village project and the New Basaisa community project. The aim of the Basaisa village integrated field project (started in 1974) was to develop innovative educational and training practices appropriate for sustainable development, in the village and its surrounding rural communities in the Nile Delta. The success of the projects implemented in Basaisa are based on open dialogue, interactive learning, access to information, the community's active participation, and its commitment to assuming social responsibility. Education and training programs reflect the interests and the concerns of the villagers, and are based on the development of human resources – present and future – and their environment. The NGO initiatives in Basaisa will serve as examples for human development, the implementation of renewable energy resource techniques, income-generating projects, and education and training activities for communities affected by unemployment, poverty, and illiteracy.

> Knowledge is power.
> Half the knowledge is to know where to find it.

An Ecological Approach to Lifelong Learning

A common misconception often equates learning or education with schooling. It is true that some important learning does take place in schools and that schools can promote some types of learning better than any other institution. It is not true, however, that all learning takes place in schools and that no important learning takes place outside of schools. Indeed, for most people, some of the most important learning and the largest part of their education take place outside of classrooms and schools.

Learning takes place in three channels: incidental, non-formal, and formal. *Incidental education* is what occurs automatically through the process of living, resulting from what individuals absorb from the environment in which they live or grow up. It is both universal and lifelong. It also enables an individual to acquire all that education is expected to provide: (1) information, knowledge, and wisdom; (2) skills; and (3) values.

Various forms of *non-formal education* were deliberately organized by society and functioned in their own right, supplementing incidental education. Oral literature, including proverbs, tales, and songs, has also played a role, and it has conveyed all three educational objectives in tangible forms.

Formal education became necessary when knowledge or skills developed to such an extent that their preservation, promotion, and diffusion could not be managed through incidental or non-formal channels. It became necessary to create a new social player – the teacher – and a new institution to perform these functions – the formal school.

All three channels have coexisted in many countries and regions for centuries. Non-formal education cannot be developed in isolation: it has to be an integral part of a major education and social reform movement. A supreme effort must be made to create an egalitarian society which assures a decent standard of living for all, and where the evils of poverty, unemployment, illiteracy, ignorance, and ill health have disappeared. This requires a coordinated effort to improve and integrate all three channels of education. This can be achieved through the creation of a learning society with a comprehensive educational system that integrates the three channels and provides facilities for lifelong learning and adequate opportunities for all individuals to learn throughout their lives what they want to learn at their own preferred pace, from whomsoever they choose, and to teach what they know to those who desire to learn it from them.

Jacques Delors, as chair of the International Commission on Education for the Twenty-First Century, reported that 'bringing out the talents and aptitudes latent in everyone fulfills the fundamentally humanist mission of education, the requirement of equity that should inform all educational policy and the genuine need for an endogenous development that shows regard for the human and natural environment and the diversity of traditions and cultures.'[1]

Adult education programs have often ignored the ecological vision. An ecological approach to basic education implies critical attitudes towards the current practices of education and training, as well as the investigation of creative local actions as alternatives to global markets. This was the main objective behind a unique integrated project known as 'Basaisa Village Project' in the Nile Delta of Egypt.

Adult Education for Sustainable Community Development

As grass-roots groups in developing countries accelerate efforts to introduce new and appropriate technologies to their communities in order to increase the productivity of land and labour and improve the quality of life of the masses, effective education and training programs and new communication technologies are playing an increasingly important role. The question that has occupied my thinking since 1973 concerns the role educated intellectuals could play to actively participate in sustainable community development. The question was: Can we so-called intellectuals, technical experts, thinkers, etc., be involved in and play an active role in the process of sustainable community development. If yes, then how? It was clear that this could only be achieved with clear goals, effective plans, and commitment to the implementation of this process.

Other questions came to mind, as well. Is it enough to teach people to read and write? Is it enough to provide them with information on how to protect the environment or increase productivity? Are people in the Egyptian countryside willing to learn? Do they know what they need from adult education? Do they possess an ability to read and write? What can motivate them? Are there new factors, new techniques?

In mid-1974, I decided to set myself the challenge of seeking answers to these complex questions. From intensive readings of the published surveys in the university library at that time, it was clear to me that what were labelled as 'satellite villages' represented the lowest socio-economic group of the population within the pyramidal socio-economic structure of Egypt.

Since all my childhood and part of my youth were spent in the town of Zagazig, capital of the Al-Sharkiya region, I started my research efforts by selecting a satellite village in the vicinity of my hometown. After a week of consideration and some days of field search, I chose

Basaisa, a small satellite village at the centre of a number of small villages with a total population of about 25,000 inhabitants. Basaisa, like nearly 30,000 other satellite villages in Egypt, is a small rural community. Basaisa village itself has a population of 320 persons grouped in 45 households, forming 62 families. Life in the village is dependent upon and organized around the cycle of agriculture. All men, women, and children play a vital role in the production and processing of crops and residues that provide their livelihood. The village lies in the heart of the Nile Delta, 100 kilometres northeast of Cairo and 15 kilometres northwest of Zagazig. Basaisa land holdings consist of about 80 feddans (one feddan = 1.038 acres), all of which are cultivated by the village inhabitants.

Basaisa was selected as the nucleus for most activities on the assumption that successful actions at the Basaisa site could be easily diffused to other communities in the Basaisa village region and elsewhere. The main objective behind my intervention in Basaisa was to educate and train the local inhabitants to become well aware of their environment and their own potential, and to foster and support cooperative and active participation, in a free democratic manner, in a sustainable community development process. I always believed that a prerequisite for sustainable community development is having well-educated, well-informed, and technically skilled citizens living in a healthy and democratic environment. This was and continues to be the main goal of my teaching and my leadership within the university, among NGOs, and within society.

The milestone achievement of the Basaisa experiment has been open dialogue, in which voices are heard and opinions freely expressed, or searched for, and in which new ideas are introduced, or evolve, and old technologies and indigenous ideas revisited and re-examined. The dialogue has not, in most cases, ended with a decision: it continued informally, for a long period of time, before concrete action crystallized.

Weekly visits by the project team helped the continuation of the process and all contributions were considered. From the first moment I entered the village, the following three rules and approaches were strictly followed:

- Our role as outsiders to the community was to teach, train, direct, sponsor, and support grass-roots initiatives, but not to do anything without the active participation of community members.
- Our on-site activities were to elaborate plans concerning what the

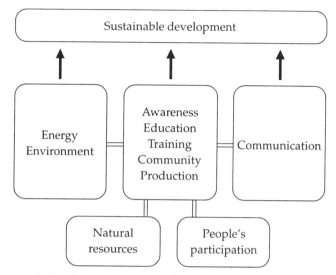

Figure 1. Model for Adult Education and Participation in Sustainable Community Development

villagers decided and expressed as needs, and to do it in a scientific way based on self-help.
- Our main objective was to identify, train, and support local educated leaders from the community itself.

The model we were working with and were committed to is illustrated in figure 1. We chose Fridays for holding public meetings and group activities, after prayer time: we found this to be the best time, as most villagers of all age groups and every socio-economic status were present on site.

No pressure was placed on the villagers to accept any new idea or specific action. The group discussion process provided the time necessary for new ideas and technologies to emerge, be understood, and implemented to meet expressed needs. When planning a teaching class or a training workshop, the essential step was asking the primary beneficiaries, and those who expressed the need, about the most appropriate time for the proposed activity. Such consultation was key to the success of on-site activities.

No promises were made. We could not offer money or privileges, but we could offer ideas and vision which could be translated into plans and actions whenever accepted by the majority of community members. Because we only acted with the villagers' active participation (through their input, money, and work), they intervened by and for themselves, which made them ultimately responsible for all successes and any failures.

Any community has among its inhabitants men, women, boys, girls, youth, students, workers, the landless, private workers, parents, graduates, the unemployed, religious conservatives, leaders, trustworthy persons, endogenous authorities, the elderly, the disabled, etc. Each of these groups has different needs, ambitions, inspirations, and capabilities. Different activities designed to respond to these different needs must be integrated into a comprehensive program for sustainable community development. Sustainable community development has to be in the mind of each individual and be part of his or her thinking, thus directing daily behaviour. Continuous education and training is a prerequisite for such a process.

The Basaisa Village Project

The project was concerned with exploring the possibilities and relevance of utilizing natural and renewable energy sources in appropriate ways to meet the needs of rural villages in a process of sustainable community development. It was designed as an integrated action research field study. The Basaisa project is unique in that it is the first integrated field study that explored how scientific developments and knowledge can be meaningfully linked to the concerns of community development in the rural sector.

The main aim of the project was to develop educational and training practices in the village and other neighbouring rural communities in the region and link them to broader actions of human, endogenous, and sustainable development. The project illustrates that genuine development can be better achieved through cooperative knowledge of the physical and social sciences when it is rooted in the basic concern of understanding how this knowledge can serve and benefit human settlements. In spite of the fact that the project activities were concentrated in the small village of Basaisa, awareness of solar energy utilization and the integrated approach to adult education and training for sustainable community development have spread throughout the Basaisa region, and the nation, as well as internationally.

In the Basaisa region, we were faced with a high rate of illiteracy and a low level of awareness among the different age groups of the population. There was also a low level of cash income, well below the poverty line, and a need to improve living conditions for most of the inhabitants. Each gender and age group had its own unique needs, interests, and aspirations. The need for alternative and innovative approaches for public education was crystal clear.

Main Principles and Approaches

Since its inception, the project has been based on certain fundamental principles:

- The proper development of any community starts with the social awareness of its problems and the full utilization of all the available natural and human resources.
- The definition of the urgent needs for any community must come from within the community itself, and not from people living outside it.
- Any technical innovation must be seen within the context of economic, social, and cultural factors, and therefore by its very nature demands basic social anthropological study. This includes continuous field observations.
- The actual participation of well-informed people in any community project provides a stronger basis for its acceptance and continuity than plans that are imposed from outside.
- The field workers participating with the village inhabitants in an integrated field project have the greatest responsibility for the success or failure of the project. Hence, they should be well chosen and well trained before the start of the project, as well as during its implementation.
- The active participation of the villagers themselves in discussing the basic outline, objectives, and goals of the project, and in making decisions at every stage of its practical execution is absolutely essential.

The main approaches used in the Basaisa project were as follows:

- Provide something that the target group wants and has internally expressed as needs, through which one can also provide for externally identified needs. Examples: football tournaments between teams from different villages among the young and educated;

games and competitions among children; skills for income-generating activities among girls and women; religion lessons among the elderly, in the village mosques; solar-powered television for all.
- Introduce environmental issues and awareness into the curriculum of training and adult education. Examples: renewable energies and environment protection in English teaching; literacy in knitting and sewing training; a library for the village and especially books on do-it-yourself and technical skills; good books for the educated to read and record on tapes for the illiterate groups; bio-gas technology promotion; solar-powered television and video training systems.
- Support and encourage the educated groups to participate in the awareness, education, and training of other groups in the community. Examples: bicycles on credit system for schoolchildren and workers to reduce commuting time, and the use of part of the time saved for adult education/training programs; on-site soft loans for professional development training to train others.

Practices and Programs

The Basaisa model has seven elements: awareness; education and training; participation; appropriate technologies; integration; sustainability; diffusion and networking. The model is described in more detail elsewhere (Arafa, 1996).

The Basaisa village project created a program division devoted to awareness, information, and public education and training. This program was founded on the concepts of cooperation, participation, networking, and maintaining in-house capacity to improve access to development information and the human resources to effectively use it. To be functional, appropriate, and cost-effective, every program, or development project, had to draw on the productive and creative energy of the community. The local knowledge had to be researched and encouraged so as to create a bridge to modern knowledge and to enhance respect for people who are the repositories of traditional lore.

A technical centre for training and production was created in Basaisa village as a grass-roots initiative in 1984. In 1985 the African Development Foundation (ADF) provided a grant to construct a central building for the centre. The idea for creating a technical centre started with faculty and student volunteers from the American University in Cairo (AUC). Later their efforts were amplified through the assistance of volunteers from the Basaisa community itself. Everyone focused his/her efforts on educational and training programs in areas where the village inhabitants had expressed interest and concern. It was our belief that sustainable community development should be centred on human resources, present and future generations, and their environment.

Long before the centre was built, the villagers gave it a name: the Integrated Rural Technology Centre for Training and Production (IRTECTAP). It was one of the earlier field projects that had extensive evaluations by the participants. With the available resources at the time (1984), the centre was expected to contribute to the development of the whole Basaisa region by providing:

- a continuous flow of information and upgrading of skills;
- a locale for awareness, education, training, and consultation;
- village-based expertise for upgrading production;
- a locale for research, studies, and the dissemination of knowledge related to appropriate technologies for rural development in the region.

Building a centre in the village was a village community dream. Everyone remembers the long hours spent in the village talking about the idea, and planning the structure and the functions of each square metre of the centre. The building was to house many of the scattered education and training activities already taking place in the village and to facilitate better management. Initially, however, there were many obstacles to be overcome. The first problem was the access to land, the second was the cost of construction, and the third was the needed equipment. The fourth was the operating costs, the fifth was the management of the centre, and the sixth was financing the sustainability of the project.

Before the development of the centre, the villagers had little opportunity to participate in the process of development – locally, regionally, or nationally. In the past, their social and economic conditions had allowed them little status, information, or power. Their economic assets were too small to make them credit-worthy by conventional standards, to permit them to take risks with new technologies, or to market their meagre surpluses at reasonable prices.

Through the activities of the centre, with an emphasis on action research and open democratic dialogue and participation in planning, decision-making, and evaluation of activities, Basaisa IRTECTAP has put the present and the future in the hands of the people. Today the centre's activities revolve around awareness, training and education, services, research and field studies, and production. The achievements of the centre are much more than had been previously expected.

Realization of the Dream

By the end of 1987 the cement structure of the whole building had been completed, only two years from the start. It has two floors, in addition to the ground floor that houses workshops in carpentry, machine repairs, metalwork, and woodwork. The first floor is devoted to training and production in knitting, embroidery, sewing, dress-making, carpets, and handicrafts. The second floor houses the village library, lecture hall, educational facilities, and the centre's administrative office. The open roof of the building is devoted to experiments, field-tests, and demonstrations of renewable energy technologies.

The enthusiasm of the villagers was demonstrated by the number of people who attended training courses, even during the construction of the centre. Between the period of 18 March and 16 April 1988, seventy-two people completed their training in different fields, thirty-two of them from the neighbouring communities. This is a concrete demonstration that depending upon the local people to maintain the continuity of IRTECTAP's activities is a more viable and appropriate strategy for community self-reliance than is possible through the sporadic visits of experts, or training in faraway towns.

On 26 March 1988, Dr Mahmoud Sherif, former governor of Al-Sharkiya, visited Basaisa with over five hundred representatives from different community development associations in the governorate. Everyone was very impressed with Basaisa IRTECTAP and its activities, and the governor urged all other associations to follow the Basaisa methodology and benefit from its experiences.

The Impact

The centre and its field projects have been an open-air classroom for students, professors, and researchers from many disciplines. It has served also as a working model for similar rural areas in Egypt and elsewhere. Members from more than forty-five communities outside Basaisa, with an uncommonly large number of women, have shares in the Basaisa cooperative and make use of the IRTECTAP's training courses and other services.

Three innovative programs (grass-roots initiatives) are worth mentioning here. The first is a program for women's education. This program has four main components: income-generating activities; home improvements; health; and environmental literacy. The second program is a training/education program for young graduates. This program has six main components: driving training for vehicles and tractors; income-generating activities; renewable energies and the environment; needs assessment and feasibility studies; computer literacy; communication, information, and creative thinking. The third is a program for technical training of adults for forming local cadres for dissemination and installation of renewable energy technologies, especially in new small desert communities. This program is an intensive one which lasts for ten days in a new desert community. All these programs are modified and repeated, some once every two years, and others as often as every month.

Because of the heavy expenses and economies of scale involved in providing technical training, and technical and managerial assistance, to the village, and to the many scattered and isolated rural communities worldwide, the video training system can boost the education and the technology transfer process. Nationally and internationally, Basaisa has gained wide recognition for pioneering the use of video as a tool for training on local development, activism, and adult education and for transfer of knowledge and appropriate technologies. It was used in the early 1980s at Basaisa village to educate the inhabitants, to stimulate people's thinking, and to encourage and motivate them to take action.

At that time, since the village area was not connected to the national electricity grid, the video system was powered by solar energy (Arafa and Zwibel 1987). A listening and viewing club was initiated in the Basaisa community. This system has proven effective in organizing, training, and raising awareness, as well as in advocacy, at the village community level. The instant playback characteristic of video is one of its most empowering qualities. The system was found useful for other organizations working in the fields of awareness, education, and training related to environmental and developmental issues.

In February 1995, a company was initiated and registered by a number of young graduates, after they finished their training with the IRTECTAP program for training youth for employment. The company name is Al-Sharkiya Youth Company for Environment and Solar Energy Services

Ltd. (SHAYESCO). It has the capital of 60,000 Egyptian pounds and thirteen shareholders. The company aims to protect the environment and provide a range of services that promote and support the use of renewable energies in Egypt, in the context of sustainable development. Today, the company offers a wide range of services to its customers and offers many products for different applications of new and renewable energy technologies. It has trained many other young graduates in its five divisions: water technologies; bio-gas; solar heaters; solar electricity; and awareness, training, and marketing. Each of these activities has different actors with different backgrounds and qualifications.

After a great effort devoted to people's education and awareness, and after achieving an admirable level of literacy among the communities in the area, we were still faced with the problem of unemployment among the university graduates. Opportunities for jobs at the village level are very limited, especially for university graduates, and their ability to compete for jobs in the open market was lacking. The members of Basaisa NGOs came up with a unique initiative: a cooperative project to move a group of young graduates out of the village area into the desert. The main objective was to build a new eco-community in the desert based on cooperative farming and the use of renewable energy. It was called 'New Basaisa.'

The New Basaisa Community Project

There is an acute population distribution problem facing Egypt today, and for future generations. According to most conservative estimates, population in Egypt is expected to increase, over the coming twenty years, by around 20 million people, despite sustainable family planning efforts to achieve gradual reduction of population growth rate. This increase will bring Egypt's population to more than 80 million in 2017. As this occurs, plans will be required to distribute the population throughout the country, and consequently out of the Nile Delta and the Nile Valley towards the desert. Also, about half the present Egyptian population is less than twenty years of age. This large group represents the future of Egypt, and it should be the focus of major development investments. Social institutions, cultural, educational, and scientific organizations, and religious and political institutions should coordinate activities to provide an integrated development program tailored to meet the needs of Egyptian youth.

Through analysis of the demographic information on population distribution, it is possible to divide the country into three categories:

- heavily populated urban areas with population density = 3,200–1,200 persons/km^2;
- areas of intermediate density: medium-sized cities and small towns with 22 persons/km^2;
- low density zones with population density below one person/km^2.

Currently, there is a three-pronged effort to solve the demographic problem:

- to reduce the natural population growth rate, especially in large cities, through efficient family planning programs;
- to strengthen socio-economic development in rural areas to stem the flow of internal migration to large cities;
- to establish new desert settlements and satellite cities to absorb the growing population.

Egypt is losing valuable agricultural land to the expansion of housing, and thus it is necessary to get people to settle on non-agricultural land. The twenty new cities constructed to date in Egypt have a problem of a low rate of absorption (only 7% of the target rate). What are the constraints? And what are the solutions to the problems in new settlements? What is the role of NGOs?

In 1991, Basaisa-IRTECTAP responded to the problem of population redistribution and unemployed university and high-school graduates, by initiating a program to train youth for employment. During one of the community open discussions, a group of three or four young graduates indicated an interest in moving out of their crowded villages and seemingly hopeless working situation, to migrate to a desert area of Egypt to work together and form a small community based on cultivation. Their main question was: would the Society (Basaisa-CDA) be willing to support such a project and secure a collective loan for their start-up? The idea was extremely interesting and was appealing to many. The next meeting of the Basaisa-CDA board had the issue on its agenda. The board approved the principle of supporting this initiative and the idea of a New Basaisa community was born. The Basaisa-IRTECTAP was asked to design an integrated training program for desert development.

The overall aims of the training program reflect the following considerations:

- to provide an adequate level of awareness, education, and training in technologically and economically viable development strategies for desert communities, with special reference to renewable energies and irrigation techniques, as well as to habitats and environmental protection technologies;
- to provide this education and training through acknowledged experts, recognized field practitioners, and NGO leaders;
- to structure the program in modules, so that participants would first be given basic knowledge and information on the different fields of interest to desert community development in module A. In module B participants would be exposed to a specific technology for further in-depth treatment. Module C is more technical and oriented to practical hands-on workshops to train local cadres who are interested in using their knowledge and training for paid work within the region of their communities. Also, an integrated program (modules A+B+C) was structured for intensive training courses.

The above aims have been translated into specific learning and vocational objectives:

- understanding the limitations, efficiency, costs, environmental impact, and conversion technology of non-renewable energy sources;
- assessment of the needs in desert communities in terms of cultivation, energy, environment, and sustainable development;
- basic knowledge of solar, wind, and biomass/waste source power;
- in-depth knowledge of at least one of the above renewables and at least one of the appropriate technologies proposed;
- experimental skills in instrumentation, data collection, and data processing, and operation and maintenance of at least one of the proposed (and available) technologies;
- practical involvement through a field project;
- collection and comparison of data in order to make appropriate choices;
- integrating the various subjects within a framework related to the main question of energy, environment, and community development.

Emphasis was placed on enhancing knowledge and awareness among the trainees about the relationships among population, energy, environment, and sustainable community development. The video training system was also used within the training program (Arafa and Zwible 1985), showing other field experiments and experiences, as well as technical presentations that were difficult to perform adequately during the allocated time.

Basaisa-CDA has played a successful role in providing the training for the local cadres, and Basaisa co-op provided an appropriate credit system for the construction of bio-gas plants as well as other renewable energy systems, including solar water heaters and photovoltaic power systems. Also, in Sinai, the Kenouz Sinai Association provided education and training for the public, and the agriculture co-operative of the new land provided appropriate technologies with a credit component.

Guidelines

From our experience, a few basic concepts need to be highlighted so that others can take them as guidelines for successful projects with good results:

- To get people from the community actively participating in the development process, the responsible people or project team should show the people an element of volunteerism and a commitment to help solve a problem facing them or their community.
- To read and write letters, words, and short sentences is a means of communication. But awareness and access to information are necessary for acquiring knowledge and are as important as formal education and training.
- Environment is concerned with all the resources around us, and also the resources within people. All awareness, education, and training programs should be concerned with how to protect these resources and make the most intelligent and effective use of them for present and future generations.
- Open dialogues, interactive learning, access to information, and active participation of people are key components of any successful adult education program.
- Chain actions (teaching a small group, so that each one of them can teach another group) are a way of getting everyone involved and of transmitting the sense of social responsibility that will empower a community to tackle its problems of illiteracy, population growth, and environmental pollution.

We are proud to report that most of the above mentioned programs and practices have been successful and have led to an exceptional increase in literacy and to improvements in the living conditions of the inhabitants of not only the Basaisa village in Al-Sharkiya or the New Basaisa community in Sinai, but also of their neighbouring communities. Many examples of human development can be cited. The Basaisa NGOs are now among the leading Egyptian NGOs in the field of environment, promoting and developing renewable energy technologies, small income generating projects, credit schemes, and public education/training activities.

Note
1 Jacques Delors, *Learning: The Treasure Within: Report to UNESCO of the International Commission on Education for the Twenty-First Century* (Paris: UNESCO Publishing, 1996), p. 87.

References
Abdel Aal, Hassan. 1994. 'The Activities of Rural Women in Farming and in the House and the Need for Information, Skills and Appropriate Technology.' In *The Circumstances and Legal Problems for Rural and Urban Women: Workshop at Menya (Atsa)*, June 1994, pp. 142–56.
Abu Bakr, Hassan. 1994. 'Women and Environmental Issues and Human Rights.' In *The Circumstances and Legal Problems for Rural and Urban Women: Workshop at Menya (Atsa)*, June 1994, pp. 165–86.
Alaa El-Din, M.N., et al. 1984. *Rural Energy in Egypt: A Survey of Resources and Domestic Needs. The International Conference on State of the Art in Biogas Technology Transfer and Diffusion.* Cairo, 17–24 November 1984.
Aly, Sayed, and Safaa Gamal Eld Deen. 1997. 'Egypt by Numbers!' *Al-Ahram.* 3 June: p. 13.
Amartya, Sen. 1995. 'Poverty and Participation in Civil Society.' UNESCO, World Summit for Social Development. Copenhagen, 7 March 1995.
Arafa, S. 'Basaisa Village Integrated Field Project.' 1985. In *Butterworth Integrated Rural Energy Planning*, ed. Y. El-Mahgary and A.K. Biswas, pp. 131–54.
– 1988–9. 'The Basaisa Project.' *Advance* 2:21–39.
– 1990. 'Basaisa-IRTECTAP Project: Final Report.' African Development Foundation, Washington, D.C.
– 1996. 'Sustainable Community Development: The Basaisa Model.' In *Proceedings of the 3rd AUC Research Conference.*
Arafa, S., and S. El-Shimi. 1995. 'Biogas Technology for Egypt's Rural Areas.'

In *Proceedings of the Conference on Settling Technology for Industrial and Social Development*. Alexandria, 24–6 Jan. 1995.

Arafa, S., S. El-Shimi, and A. Morcos. 1997. 'Development of Rural Technology.' Project Report. Egyptian Academy for Scientific Research.

Arafa, S., A. Ibrahim, S. Fadel, and W. Elnashaar. 1995. 'A New Solar Community at Ras Sudr; Sinai, Egypt: New Basaisa.' In *Proceedings of the ISES Congress*. Harare, Zimbabwe, 1995.

Arafa, S., C. Nelson, and E. Lumsdaine. 1978. 'Utilization of Solar Energy and the Development of an Egyptian Village: An Intergrated Field Project.' (Project proposal approved and supported by the U.S. National Science Foundation, Grant No. 78–01127, and sponsored by the American University in Cairo, June 1978).

Arafa, S., and N. Zeitun. 1997. 'Poverty and Natural Resources: Lessons Learned from Basaisa Experiment.' In *Proceedings of the National Symposium on Poverty and Environmental Deterioration in Rural Egypt*. Minia, 20–22 Oct. 1997.

Arafa, S., and H. Zwibel. 1987. 'Solar-Powered Video System for Village Training and Production.' ISES Congress, Hamburg 1987.

Aylwln, P. 1995. 'Poverty: Reduction through Participation.' UNESCO World Summit for Social Development. Copenhagen, 7 March 1995.

Carr, R.K. 1992. 'Technology Transfer Processes.' *Journal of Technology Transfer* (Spring-Summer).

El-Katsha, Samiha, et al. 1989. *Women, Water and Sanitation: Household Water Use in Two Egyptian Villages*. Cairo Papers in Social Science, vol. 12, Monograph 2, Social Research Centre, American University of Cairo. Cairo: American University Press.

El-Shennawy, Laila Hummad. 1995. *A Study of Environmental Behavior of Rural Women in Some Egyptian Villages*. Research Bulletin, no. 1, Scientific Society of Agricultural Extension.

Mink, Stephen. 1994. 'Poverty and the Environment.' In *Making Development Sustainable: From Concepts to Action*, ed. Michael Cemea et al., pp. 4–5. Washington: World Bank.

Schultz, P. 1974. *Communications and Social Change: Videotape Recording As a Tool for Development*. Rome: FOA.

Schumacher, E.F. 1984. *Small Is Beautiful: Economics As if People Mattered*. New York: Harper and Row.

Serag-Eldin, Ismail, and Andrew Steer. 1994. 'Making Development Sustainable: From Concepts to Action.' In *Making Development Sustainable: From Concepts to Action*, ed. Michael Cemea et al., p. 22. Washington: World Bank.

Revitalizing a Depopulating Region in Hungary

Valeria Nagy Czanka and Ildiko Mihaly

The citizens of a small area in southwestern Hungary which was slowly going to ruin have mobilized to save it. In order to arrest depopulation, they set out to develop a modern infrastructure of roads, and then they improved inhabitants' living conditions. The organizations taking part in the recovery program have paid particular attention to reviving traditions and events commemorating the history of the region. In order to keep, or bring back, the region's inhabitants, it has been necessary to create a new economic environment that will fulfil the local population's need for jobs and favourable working conditions. It has also been necessary to create new training opportunities locally in order to support sustainable development.

The Area and Its History

The region of Zselic is one of the areas of greatest natural beauty in Hungary. It is situated in the south of the country, not far from the capital of the District of Somogy, Kaposvar. Despite the beauty and diversity of the countryside, dotted with woods and small lakes, life is not easy for the villagers living in small valley settlements that are relatively isolated from each other. Traditionally, the population has led a simple existence, living from what it could find in the forest, from collecting mushrooms and medicinal plants, and stock-rearing. No major industrial activity has been developed in fifty years, and the labour force has not been able to find work except in the agricultural co-operatives and state farms, or in the enterprises and public services in

Kaposvar. Young people have therefore chosen to try their luck elsewhere, in larger towns, and as a consequence, village populations have aged and the region has gradually begun to suffer from an inevitable depopulation. The constant financial difficulties facing the local authorities have only aggravated living conditions, which were already suffering, and the authorities have started to have problems satisfying the basic social, cultural, and educational needs of the people who have remained. In other regions of Hungary, this phenomenon has been felt in the same way and has led to urban migration. In some villages in the region of Zselic, the boarded-up windows of abandoned houses today provide evidence of the same state of depopulation.

In the face of this steady erosion, a number of committed citizens of Zselic decided to confront the situation, which they still regarded as reversible. They proposed to alleviate the isolation of the villages by building initially on the attractiveness of the natural environment. Ten years ago, they set up an organization called the Banya Panorama Association, which has since become the driving force behind development in the region. This non-governmental organization is the leading light in a movement aiming to restore the environment and to exploit the advantages of the countryside, and, by doing so, to create the conditions necessary to guarantee inhabitants a suitable quality of life while safeguarding the traditions and culture of the region.

The Creators of the Program

From the outset, the creators of the program invited public personalities to associate themselves with it and to help in getting it off the ground, which has had the effect of persuading the local population to join in. The contribution of well-known intellectuals, scientists, university professors, parliamentarians, artists and sportsmen and -women has indeed given credence to the program. The president of the Association is still Mr Andras Hargitay, one of the most popular sportsmen in Hungary and the winner of several Olympic medals. In recognition of their contribution, and as a way of reviving the traditions of the past, an order of chivalry has been established. The Order of Zselic, the enthronement ceremony of which is based on ancient rites, offers membership to all those who have worked or are still working for the region.

With the support of energetic, responsible experts, the Association has succeeded in overcoming local chauvinism in favour of a regional vision, the long-term goal of which is to safeguard the values of the environmental inheritance and local customs, to develop them in order to improve local people's living conditions and conditions of employment, and to encourage people to feel that they belong to the locality.

The Program

In order to achieve this goal, the Association has worked out a program that will run until 2010 and comprises specific objectives for each of three proposed stages. The first stage, which was completed in 1996, set out to establish the basic infrastructure required for an ecological way of life, and to attract to the area the intellectual capital essential to carrying out the program. In the second stage, the aim was to create the largest possible number of jobs locally, and in the third stage, which will last until the first decade of the new millennium, the intention is to evaluate the results, to consolidate them, and to prepare the ground for new initiatives. Those managing the program have recently even outlined their tasks for the following period, up until the year 2020.

In the first stage, priority was given to building roadways (not only for vehicular traffic but also a network of cycle tracks), to restoring the former post road, and to adding a motocross track. The building of roadways made it possible to link the small localities in the region to each other and to the district capital. Major work to improve facilities for community services was carried out in this first stage. Inhabited areas and new housing developments were also provided with drinking water, electricity, sewage systems, and telephone networks. Those managing the program clearly understood that it was impossible to attract new inhabitants or tourists without offering them essential comforts and, above all, that the local population should no longer be deprived of services. Moreover, without the many permanent residents who were still living in the twenty-three communes in the area, the program would undoubtedly fail.

In order to make the area yet more attractive for visitors, a lake has been dug for fishing and water sports, and a golf course has been laid out. There is horse riding and archery, a 'new' sport that is very much in vogue despite its ancient origins. A leisure centre called the New Way of Living Centre has also been built: it provides accommodation, meeting rooms, and facilities for training courses. The houses being built in the new developments are the starting point for the creation of a network of 'village inns.' It should be mentioned that regulations have been laid down governing all new building: for example, only natural building materials may be used. This decision has been generally welcomed, and in 1997 it won for the area the prestigious Pro Regio Prize. There is no need to emphasize the job opportunities provided by such a project since they are all too obvious.

Safeguarding the Heritage

Those managing the program have attached great importance to safeguarding the cultural inheritance: the castle, which is classed as a historic monument, the hunting lodges, and the village museum have been restored and handed over to promoters for the development of the luxury tourism that is taking off. In order to strengthen regional provision for tourists, thought has also been given to the widespread passion for health centres. The growing of medicinal plants using biological methods will enable non-interventionist medicine to be practised, and a centre specializing in herbal therapy to be established.

The group charged with implementing the program believes that cultural traditions are an integral part of the infrastructure of development. A number of historical remains have been rediscovered by the historians attached to the project and turned to good account: for example, a park laid out with ancient lime trees by one of the most illustrious kings of Hungary. The Zselic Development Association is reviving the memory of the king in order to make economic capital out of it: it is marketing the local honey under the name 'King Mathias's Honey.' Many imaginative initiatives of this sort have been started.

The Preservation of Traditions

As part of the Zselic Historic Games, an event that takes place every year, there is always an activity in costume, a sort of historical walk over 14 kilometres, which allows schoolchildren and their parents to rediscover the past. The craft workers in the region benefit from these cultural activities since the organizers order historical objects, tools, and instruments from them. Furthermore, the theme camps organized in the summer go even further in keeping traditions alive: well-known craftspeople come and teach local girls and women the arts of twisting and weaving as well as the making of traditional ceramics and earthenware, not only to satisfy family needs but also for sale to tourists. During this event, traditional Zselic dishes are prepared and eaten by participants, in the same spirit of preserving traditions and spreading them as widely as possible.

A project called the Valley of History 2000 encourages the running of such programs about traditions and customs. As part of this project, local people come together once a month to discuss their ideas and make proposals. Another measure designed to make inhabitants aware of preserving their inheritance consists of selecting the most beautiful and best-maintained houses and publicizing their locations. Signs are set up in the communes directing visitors to these model houses.

The Creation of a New Economic Environment

A reassessment of the region's economic potential was essential if the developments launched were to be profitable. For example, potatoes have traditionally been grown in the area, but the conditions are more suited to the growing of strawberries, raspberries, and cucumbers. Given that there is no regional industrial infrastructure, products have to be transported after picking. Similar constraints apply as much to medicinal plants and chestnuts, and to meat, deer skins, and otter skins.

One economic project is to set up a plant in the near future to process timber so that the inhabitants can transform the raw material into finished products, which have a far higher return. Those managing the program also propose to change the agricultural profile of the region. Climatic conditions and soil in Zselic would suit the growing of tobacco, and it appears that the growing of elders, a medicinal plant that is in heavy demand, would be of benefit to the region. The exploitation of local peat is also among the intended short-term changes.

Labour Force Training: A New Requirement

In order to bring about sustainable development, it was absolutely necessary to set up a food-processing industry in the region. The training needs of the labour force were then quickly felt, which has encouraged the creation of better-structured training enterprises. Adults are trained in short courses in the techniques of picking, drying, sorting, and processing medicinal plants. Training is also given in the marketing of chestnuts, venison, and timber. There are also plans to train the labour force in the marketing of fish (there are natural and artificial ponds in the region, and new facilities will be opened) and animal skins.

Experience shows that it is above all small enterprises that have created the largest numbers of jobs, particularly in tourism and crafts.

As there was no expertise of this nature in Hungary, it proved indispensable to acquire technical and organizational skills. The short courses therefore provide an excellent opportunity to teach a basic knowledge of commerce, law, and finance. An initial training program lasting 160 hours, made up of short courses and organized on demand for local inhabitants, came to a successful conclusion last year.

The greatest success of this program is in fact the rapid use made of the knowledge acquired, through the almost immediate entry of all the participants into the labour market as employees or entrepreneurs.

Prospects

It is clear that far more complex skills in coordination will be required to meet the challenges after the year 2000. The people concerned are fully aware that only projects which are rigorously prepared and run by very effective local training establishments will enable them to meet the various organizations' need for specialist workers, whether business consultants or experts in tourism or environmental protection. And since regional development is closely linked to tourism, it will be necessary at the same time to create the necessary conditions for the learning of foreign languages, at least at a basic level. Plans have already been drawn up for language-teaching projects outside the school system; all that remains is to implement them on a permanent basis.

In the Arts and Crafts Centre, which has been built to revive traditional crafts, funding for the learning of folk trades has been obtained through a call for contributions. Every year, ten young people are thereby enabled to receive a student grant, which encourages them to pursue their careers locally, the priority being to attract skilled resource persons who might choose to set themselves up in the region.

Funding

We have described the most positive outcomes of the development of the region and have outlined the measures to be taken in future programs, but we have not addressed the issue of funding these investments, which are sometimes very costly, and the details of financial support for the projects. The whole program is part of a civil initiative managed by the Banya Panorama Association; at the same time, it is intended to serve as a catalyst for the creation of new associations. The actual projects come into being thanks to the members, who are the only management resources, helped by experts who take part on a voluntary basis. In the final analysis, even the drafting of the program can be seen as a significant 'financial contribution'! The support and ideas which the organizers of the program have received through their participation in international meetings, such as the study visits to Sweden and Ireland funded by the PHARE program, and the inputs from foreign guests at conferences held in the region also amount to a considerable 'capital' of experience.

It is thanks to their own enthusiasm and hard work that those managing the program have found the financial resources to run it. Since the local authorities do not generally have funds available (local budgets and taxes hardly cover the costs of maintaining infrastructures), the program managers have had to start their activities with funding obtained through grants. Cooperation between the associations and the local authorities has made it possible to have access to funds allocated to regional development and has opened the doors to various aid programs for community organizations. Every positive result has raised the hopes of those who are committed and has helped to persuade those who have been sceptical because of the difficulties.

The Development of Human Resources

The results in terms of the number of jobs created locally have been more than encouraging. Help with job creation has come from successful bids for funding, which shows that regional and national authorities value these initiatives, which are something of a rarity in current practice. The Public Works Program, for instance, has not only provided jobs for 190 unemployed persons, but has also demonstrated its effectiveness in the positive impact on the environment, in the cleaning and enhancement of the twenty-three villages in the region.

The Association was also successful in its bid for funds to the Ministry of Foreign Affairs for a program to raise Hungarian public awareness of integration into the European Union. Its proposal, as part of this program, was to create a European Information Office and to start a tradition of 'Zselic European Days.' In addition to the significant support given to setting up an experimental training program to promote regional development, there will be effective participation in transnational programs, which will open up a European perspective for the community. The Office that is set up under this program will be linked to the computerized Information Centre of the District Authority. The projects that are specific to the region, which have been worked out in detail up until the year 2000, will also serve to provide users with information on the strategic advantages of the integration process, and will give them an introduction to how to submit documentation in competitions launched by the European Union.

The program adopted under this scheme embraces a wide range of proposed topics and methods. The aim of all the conferences, competitions, working groups, exhibitions, and cultural events will be the same: consciously to shape the minds of the participants, both secondary-school children and adults, so that they combine the image they have of their future with a European perspective.

Advantages and Disadvantages

During the initial assessment, those managing the program have looked particularly at the positive effects of the program. It would nonetheless have been very wrong not to have informed citizens of the disadvantages that they might expect.

As for the advantages, the most obvious is that every inhabitant and visitor to the region can immediately see the beneficial effects of the program on the environment. The complete respect for ecology shown in carrying out the work, the protection of the natural environment, and the observance of building regulations have all worked to preserve the local cultural inheritance, to make the villages more attractive and more harmonious, and to reduce pollution, which is currently causing increasing problems. Alongside the investments in infrastructures, the dredging of the river bed has benefited the whole community by creating a more even flow of water.

The positive economic effects are visible above all in the creation of places of work, the employment of local labour, and the rise in income for businesses and individuals, and hence in higher revenue from taxation. In consequence, the modernization of the economic structure (the unprecedented upsurge in the tertiary sector through tourism) and the growth in the demand for some goods and services, are also among the most valuable effects. Other sectors also profit from the situation since all this activity is pushing development and stimulating the overall economy of the region.

These projects also have social and cultural effects, which will become more noticeable in the future. In the light of the rise in the employment rate among the labour force, the social mobility of the inhabitants is increasing, and a significant change is being felt in the model of the family, given women's access to the labour market. The increase in 'free time' and the diversification of leisure activities indicate that the local population, like the tourists, are enjoying a higher quality of life. The strengthening of socio-cultural integration could also be mentioned as a consequence of greater collective solidarity. The opening up to the culture of other nations, and the favourable welcome given to them, derive from the efforts made to promote an attitude of respect for the local cultural inheritance. It may be assumed that the political awareness of the citizens of the region will be strengthened by the implementation of the European integration programs; people's sense of responsibility towards themselves, the community, and the region will grow, laying the groundwork for the further development of democracy.

It is likely, however, that the development of tourism will be thought to have some negative effects. It might be supposed, for instance, that large amounts of household waste will be created by the influx of tourists. It may also be supposed that the new popularity of the region will attract investments that may lead to environmental damage. Strong economic performance will inevitably lead to a rise in consumer prices because of the increase in tourism. Other harmful effects can be anticipated: the concentration of cultivable land on single crops, the seasonal nature of employment for the local labour force, the growth in criminality caused by the circulation of too much money, and prostitution. Should such repercussions occur, they will likely be viewed as a threat to the social fabric and the natural environment, and they may mar the program's success. They must be taken into account at the outset of the program, and mechanisms must be put in place to avoid them as far as possible. New tasks will therefore fall to the civil population and the local authorities since the favourable economic climate will certainly give rise to further projects.

References

Balipap, Ferenc, Dezso Kovacs, and Endre Markolt. 1996. 'A Community Development Foundation in Jaszsentlaszlo.' In *ALPHA 96 – Basic Education and Work*, ed. J.-P. Hatuecoeur, pp. 215–25. Hamburg: UNESCO Institute for Education; Toronto: Culture Concepts.

Bocs, Attila. 1996. 'A Higher Education Project for the Gypsy Community in Aranyosapati.' In *ALPHA 96 – Basic Education and Work*, ed. J.-P.

Hautecoeur, pp. 145–60. Hamburg: UNESCO Institute for Education; Toronto: Culture Concepts.

Hautecoeur, J.-P., ed. 1997. *ALPHA 97 – Basic Education and Institutional Environments*. Hamburg: UNESCO Institute for Education; Toronto: Culture Concepts.

Touraine, Alain. 1997. *Pourrons-nous vivre ensemble? Egaux ou différents?* Paris: Editions Fayard.

UNESCO. 1997. *Fifth International Conference on Adult Education, Hamburg, July 14–18, 1997*. Final Report. Paris: UNESCO; Hamburg: UNESCO Institute for Education.

Agricultural Development and the Preservation of Indigenous Knowledge

Ismail Daiq and Shawkat Sarsour

The Palestinian Agricultural Relief Committees (PARC) began in 1983 by providing services to Palestinian farmers on a voluntary basis. The organization wanted to maintain the identity of Palestinian society, especially after many farmers had become labourers in Israeli settlements. This was a negative turn for the way of life in the villages, making them into consumers instead of producers. The committees began by providing aid to needy farmers and have reached the point of establishing partnerships in development with the farmers, as a basic component in defining and approving their needs, and also with friendly funding organizations. Now PARC can help make more efficient, cost-effective, and sustainable the role of the local farmer organizations in providing services for themselves. The most important providers of extension services are the farmers themselves, through their daily lives. The role of governmental and non-governmental organizations remains secondary compared to farmer-to-farmer extension.

The Palestinian Agricultural Relief Committees (PARC) were established in 1983 in Jericho, Palestine, the fruit of the efforts of a group of volunteer agronomists. Volunteers began to provide free agricultural extension services to the farmers of the region because of the lack of governmental services provided by the Israeli civil administration at the time. That administration did not concern itself with developing the Palestinian agricultural sector. When the Palestinian Authority took over the agricultural sector in 1995, it found the staff of the civil administration unchanged since 1974.

PARC's services expanded in the late 1990s, and it institutionalized its management of projects and developmental programs. PARC has four main types of programs, for the service of farmers: crop extension, livestock services, women's programs, and environmental programs. Its activities and projects have helped develop the abilities and experience of the rural population from a social, economic, and environmental point of view.

The Palestinian Agricultural Relief Committees employ a staff of nearly 110 for the core program, and approximately 80 more people are employed for projects. The whole staff is focused on extending services to Palestinian farmers, both men and women, throughout the West Bank and Gaza Strip. The average age of PARC employees is thirty-three. Forty per cent are women. Most hold higher university degrees in various agricultural sciences, in social sciences, or in development and management. Most are from villages. In order to maintain and expand their understanding of development issues, all staff members annually take specialized and general courses given by internal trainers and, occasionally, by specialized trainers from both local and international universities and training centres.

One of PARC's strongest features is its decentralized administrative system. Projects are managed by eight regional branches. Field workers implement an annual work plan prepared through workshops attended by farmers, PARC's staff farmers, and representatives of other organizations. PARC aims to achieve integrated and sustainable agriculture by putting emphasis on the development of human resources, and by reinforcing transparency and participatory approaches.

The work reinforces local governmental and non-governmental institutions and associations in Palestinian villages, and contributes to building the capacity of farmer leaders and cadres, both men and women, who can assist PARC in the fulfilment of its goals and objectives. First and foremost is increasing farmers' social, productive, and environmental capabilities, and activating the utilization of local resources.

PARC publishes an annual report describing the most important achievements of the past year, as well as future plans proposed by representatives of all sectors of society and of organizations, including international organizations, especially development and funding partners. PARC receives various forms of support from non-governmental organizations and other partner organizations that believe in the need for solidarity and cooperation for the benefit of mankind.

Since its establishment, PARC has played an active role in various sectors throughout the shifting political and economic circumstances that the Palestinians have experienced over the years. Following are some of those achievements over the past fifteen years:

1. Support for farmers in reclaiming their lands, building agricultural roads, cultivating trees, and organizing demonstration activities. PARC realizes how important it is to reclaim unused land in order to prevent Israelis from confiscating it. More than 55 per cent of the area of the West Bank and Gaza Strip was confiscated for the establishment of settlements and military bases.
2. Raising farmers' awareness in technical issues related to plant and animal production. More than 65 per cent of the Palestinians live in rural areas and consequently depend directly or indirectly for their livelihoods on agriculture.
3. Encouraging and promoting women farmer leaders, who have initiated and inaugurated thirty women's clubs in a number of villages. PARC would like these clubs to advance and reinforce women leaders' abilities and potentials. In the beginning, traditional local leaderships expressed great opposition to the establishment of these clubs, but currently the situation is evolving rapidly towards unanimous approval and acceptance of them.
4. Promotion of the abilities of Palestinian agronomists in the realms pertaining to needs assessment, communication, extension, planning, and farm work.
5. Providing Palestinian institutions with agronomists trained in scientific methods through the newly launched Agronomists Training Program.
6. Participation in the infrastructure of agricultural training by publishing agricultural books, leaflets, and educational video films.

The Palestinian Farmer

History has had a great impact on the formation of human societies and the life of their members. This is especially true in the case of the Palestinians, given the strategic location of their territory. Many historic conflicts have been inflicted upon the Palestinians, such as that between the civilizations of the Tigris and Euphrates and of Egypt, or the Persian-Greek conflict, which persisted up to the Roman regime. Other significant events were the British Mandate and the Arab-Israeli conflict, which resulted from the establishment of the State of Israel in Palestine.

The impact of the Ottoman regime remains evident in the life of the farmers and Palestinian people. The continuing prevalence of chaotic land registration is the result of the Ottoman policy of imposing taxes on agricultural land, which pushed farmers to refrain from cultivating their lands and to transfer the property of land to heads of clans and tribes who were supposedly representatives of the Ottoman governor of the region. In addition to this, farmers' children were deprived of educational opportunities, which remained exclusively accessible to the children of the rich class and the pro-Ottoman men. At that time, education was connected to jobs offered by the Ottomans.

At the beginning of this century, Jewish immigration to Palestine started from such European countries as Russia and Spain. The Jewish Socialist Youths established cooperative colonies (Kibbutzim and Moshavim), which encouraged immigration to Palestine, especially during the British Mandate. Jewish immigration coincided with internal immigration from rural areas, to cities, and from highlands to coastal areas as people sought work in the aftermath of the decline of the role of agriculture and the intensive attention paid to the development of cities and the coastal area. Until Al-Nakbah (the Catastrophe of 1948), 80 per cent of the Palestinian people led a rural life, depending greatly on agriculture as their means of income. Although the policies of the British Mandate aimed at developing Palestinian agriculture for export purposes, this was not obviously reflected in agricultural development because of the expansion of the Jewish settlements' control of the arable land. This period ended in the occupation of most of the agricultural lands in Palestine in 1948 and the emigration of tens of thousands of families from rural and urban areas to the West Bank and Gaza Strip and neighbouring countries.

Agriculture is a key part of Palestinian life, playing an important role in the political, economic, and social life of all Palestinians, regardless of gender. The economic importance of agriculture is evident from the percentage it comprises of the gross domestic product and the fact that it has created job opportunities for more than one hundred thousand rural families. Its cultural value cannot be measured in economic terms alone because the Palestinian farmer continues to connect his honour to the land. Politically, farmers protect huge amounts of land from confiscation by the Israelis by reclaiming and cultivating it. They continue to cultivate the land and plant it with different kinds of vegetables because this food will be the only resort when crises occur. We should not forget the great cultural inheritance handed down in the form of farmers' folk songs. Also, women participate in various stages of the farming process because women's work in the fields is considered socially legitimate.

Indigenous Knowledge of Palestinian Farmers

In many countries, indigenous knowledge and know-how is still a major influence in rural people's lives, and the agricultural sector in particular. The know-how varies from one country to another according to the degree of agricultural development and the use of modern agricultural methods.

In Palestine agricultural experience and know-how has evolved, and has been developed and transferred from one generation to another, with the aim of improving the produce quantitatively and qualitatively. The following factors have shaped Palestinian agriculture:

- Palestinian farmers have always been considered among the most experienced and accomplished. Throughout history, they have made optimal use of the fertile coast by cultivating legumes, grain, and fruit trees. They also cultivated the highlands with olives and different fruits. These farmers were directly dependent on agriculture.
- This situation lasted until the late 1940s, when the first Nakbah and Israeli occupation of the Palestinian territories – especially of fertile land – occurred. Then, most of the Palestinian farmers became refugees living in camps. They lost their main source of living as well as the farmland required for resuming agricultural work and rural life. Consequently, they could not transfer their accumulated experience and know-how to their children. Most of these farmers became labourers outside the agricultural sector. Others emigrated outside the country after they had obtained a good education and worked in Gulf States as teachers, physicians, and engineers.
- A small number of Palestinian farmers resumed agricultural work on what was left of Palestine (West Bank and Gaza Strip). They transferred their experience to the highlands, and this had a direct impact on the development of agriculture in Palestine throughout the past fifty years.
- When the West Bank was integrated with Jordan, it produced 80 per cent of the agricultural produce of both banks of the Jordan River, although the West Bank merely makes up 15 per cent of the total

area of the two banks. It comprises 6,000 square kilometres, whereas Jordan comprises 90,000 square kilometres.
- Following the Israeli occupation of the rest of Palestine in 1967, the Israelis followed the policy of land and water resource confiscation and the transformation of Palestinian farmers into labourers in Israeli factories and workshops. This resulted in increasing the number of settlements, the refusal of youth to work in agriculture, which became exclusively the occupation of the elderly, and the abandonment of thousands of hectares. Thus, for the second time during this century, the process of integrating indigenous knowledge and inherited traditional experience was interrupted and discontinued.

PARC's most important activities in the field of indigenous know-how aim:

- to improve local seeds and species used by Palestinian farmers through the natural selection process;
- to organize mutual extension visits among farmers who have less experience and farmers with more experience; Furthermore, farmers accompany extension workers on their extension visits.
- to support rain-fed crops, especially those that use sustainable traditional methods. At the outset of development, PARC helped to expand this practice with respect to irrigated crops, which do not exceed 5 per cent of the total farmed land;
- encourage and support farmers who use organic fertilizers and alternatives to chemicals, whether biological or mechanical.

Preserving Indigenous Know-How

The idea of researching indigenous know-how emerged as part of PARC's programs that aim to develop sustainable Palestinian agriculture. The experiences of PARC's extension workers indicated that there are a number of agricultural processes performed by farmers that have a positive outcome, whether in terms of pest management, issues related to soil and water, or ploughing and storage of agricultural produce. Therefore PARC, in cooperation with the German University Hohenheim, started a study encompassing all inherited agricultural methods in five Palestinian villages. The research aimed at documenting these methods and utilizing them in agricultural extension, as well as developing them through field and practical experience.

Agricultural Development and Preservation of Indigenous Knowledge 233

The research is executed through individual and collective interviews of farmers, both men and women, young and old, in their own workplaces by means of different techniques, such as participatory rapid appraisal. Five villages were selected according to specific criteria that offer demographic and geographic diversity. We can summarize the most significant preliminary results as follows:

- There is considerable weakness in the assimilation and integration of indigenous knowledge from one generation to another. During the meeting of the research team with the farmers, a conflict in solving the technical problems faced by farmers was obvious among the different age groups. The young farmers tend to move towards modern technology in solving their agricultural problems, and the elderly farmers depend more on their own and their grandfathers' experience in solving these problems. For example, the young farmers use tractors in ploughing the land, and elderly farmers use animals and traditional tools.
- Generally speaking, youths do not have a great attachment to agricultural work. They evaluate the land in terms of its economic feasibility, while the elderly farmers are connected to it through their souls, socially and culturally, without any regard to economic feasibility. This was reflected in the young farmers' disapproval, for economic reasons, of cultivating olive trees, while the elderly farmers, despite their difficult economic situation, persist in looking after and developing the cultivated trees.
- Farmers' loss of their lands in 1948 and 1967, and its disastrous consequences – the emigration of farmers to other neighbouring countries to live in refugee camps – greatly inhibited the development and application of inherited agricultural knowledge.

Most inherited knowledge exists in highlands or rain-fed areas, especially those lands where technology has not been introduced. Irrigated crops in Palestine are connected to Israeli agricultural production, which depends mainly on irrigation. By contrast, the farmers depending on rain-fed agriculture are still using traditional cultivation methods.

Agricultural technology has influenced traditional knowledge in irrigated farmed lands, which comprise 5 per cent of the farmed lands in Palestine. This is reflected in the widespread use of chemicals and agricultural machines, with great dependence on exporting the produce instead of marketing it in the local markets.

Developing traditional knowledge through applied practice may help in transferring it to coming generations in a way that fits them. A good example of these practices is the ploughing of mountainous lands depending on rain more than twelve times, with different depths, especially for vegetable crops. Traditional knowledge in Palestine, especially in rain-fed crops, will beget practices that fit with environment and fulfil the principle of sustained land utilization. This is evident and manifested in farmers' practices pertaining to pest management and maintenance of soil and water.

Principal Working Strategies

It is necessary to understand the roles of different actors and stakeholders in the development process before conducting any studies or putting forward any plans in this field. A good example of this is reflected in Ein Sinia village in the Ramallah district. The farmers in this village depend mainly on agricultural production. A team of three consultants – one of whom is an agronomist – visited one farmer and started discussing his agricultural, social, and economic situation. They concluded that the farmers in this village are facing one major problem, and it is the excess use of pesticides for fighting the white fly. The only way to overcome it is by the use of gauze, which is not available in the local markets.

The same team later visited agricultural shops in the city of Ramallah, and it was concluded that the factory that works on production of gauze is not regularly producing this material, despite farmers' need. The team decided to visit the factory and from their discussion with the owner concluded that shops are not placing regular requests for this material. The taxes on the threads for production of gauze are high, making gauze expensive. Since this thread is considered a textile instead of an agricultural product, it is highly taxed. To be able to solve this technical problem, we have to depend mainly on the Palestinian Ministry of Agriculture. The same team then visited the general director of extension at the ministry, who expressed his deep concern about this issue. He expressed the ministry's interest in making gauze available to farmers, but said he could do nothing to alleviate the high taxes, which are the responsibility of the Ministry of Finance. This incident reveals the complex web of different stakeholders enmeshed in an apparently simple matter that affected only one farmer. What about an issue that affects an entire community or society?

We conclude that behind any deed or action is an actor affected by other actors. Accordingly, we stress the importance of having a comprehensive view of all actors and integrated issues in achieving any necessary rural development.

PARC used the following main intervention mechanisms:

1. Improving the Abilities and Capabilities of Rural Women

This intervention is directed at the role of rural women in the social, educational, production, and environmental sectors. It aims to lay the groundwork for increasing their input to all facets of life.

Women conduct about 65 per cent of the agricultural work in Palestine. They also carry out the maternal tasks of the family, which in the rural areas consists of more than nine people (the average Palestinian family has seven members). But Palestinian women still face huge obstacles created by centuries-old traditions and customs. They have a high illiteracy rate, few chances to obtain secondary or college education, and are subject to early marriage (in many cases at the age of fifteen years) and polygamy. So PARC focuses on providing awareness programs for women in more than eighty Palestinian villages through a network of groups of thirty women each.

A program of lectures, workshops, films, and mutual visits among women are conducted on the basis of a prior needs assessments. Women's social activity and production are promoted and advanced through the empowerment and reinforcement of local women's associations. This gives women a greater opportunity to participate actively and effectively in both household life and the life of the village. PARC has found that many of the awareness-raising programs have met with greater success and support among women than among men.

2. Training

The expansion of capabilities is a basic part of the success of rural development programs. Thus the rehabilitation of farmers in the areas of social, economic, cultural, and political life is the foundation for the various development projects.

But the strategies of institutions working in raising the capabilities of farmers in various areas should focus on their participation, while taking into consideration their conditions, their abilities, and their future outlook. Most important is the simplification of methods and an emphasis on collective work. So PARC has prepared a rural-training building program for this purpose, and it is expected that by the end of next year two others will be completed, to be used to train farmers of both gender, along with newly graduated agronomists and rural development workers. PARC concentrates on practical training through applied demonstrations, and the creation of new methods of training that fit different age categories.

3. Raising Environmental Awareness

The provision of infrastructure services such as water, electricity, garbage collection, health clinics, and maternal centres is weak in Palestine, especially in the rural areas. Bad habits concerning the use of natural resources and energy resources have taken hold. There are health and pollution problems. There is also the problem of waste being dumped by Israeli settlements and industrial zones onto Palestinian arable land, with the consequent destruction of soil and trees.

PARC focuses on teaching rural families to establish water treatment stations. These are inexpensive systems that work at the household level. Treated water is used in agriculture, and PARC focuses on different programs dealing with the digging of water-collection wells and water conservation.

4. Encouraging Ecological Agricultural Production Systems

Most arable land in the mountainous areas depends on rain-fed agriculture, and this has forced Palestinian farmers over the years to adapt their working methods to their environment. But the application of technology in many of the surrounding countries, like Israel, has led to widespread irrigated farming. This, in turn, has encouraged many Palestinian farmers to change their old farming ways and to take on modern methods that might damage the soil and quality of produce, and threaten the longevity of the farmland. It has also caused farmers to lose their indigenous expertise.

PARC is currently focusing on developing a Palestinian agriculture that depends on sustainable systems by using organic agriculture and integrated pest management through the training of farmers and the use of practical demonstrations. Organic farms have been set up in the rural areas and are used in training, experimentation, and the transfer of knowledge.

5. Developing Animal Production

The Bedouins of Palestine, whether in the south or in the various desert areas, depend totally on the products of animal resources. PARC provides veterinary services and training programs in a PARC farm that was established for this purpose. PARC has made it its priority to develop suitable extension and training programs that closely address the reality and needs of farmers and rural women.

6. Building Institutions and Relations with the People

In implementing its work, PARC cooperates with village institutions and farmer organizations, who best know their own needs. This method also makes implementation less expensive because of the direct participation of the farmers, who are trained to manage their programs and projects in a sustainable manner. PARC has a department devoted to strengthening village institutions according to principles of transparency, democracy, and volunteerism.

These developmental projects are conducted in cooperation with the Palestinian Ministry of Agriculture along with non-governmental organizations. The ministry and other governmental agencies see a need to reinforce the work of NGOs through cooperation and consultation. The Ministry of Agriculture has established an office to manage relations with NGOs and a coordinating committee that holds regular meetings to exchange information and coordinate plans and programs.

Agricultural Extension Methods in PARC

Agricultural extension in Palestine is one of the desired and basic tools of adult education because farming is tied to all aspects of rural life: economy, politics, and social affairs. Revitalizing the role of agricultural counselling in the education process for farmers of both genders is a pressing need.

PARC began its extension program on a voluntary basis in 1983, through conducting regular visits to the fields of small groups of farmers in the Jordan Valley. As PARC grew in human and financial resources and in developmental concepts and methodologies, its extension methods expanded over the past ten years. The training and rehabilitation of extension workers in agricultural extension concepts – by focusing on the social and environmental dimensions, planning ahead, and having the farmers participate in establishing their needs – are essential elements in achieving the goals of the agricultural extension program. This program focuses on providing a good life for farmers by helping them match solutions to the problems and issues they face.

The most important agricultural extension methods used in PARC are the following:

1. Field Visits

These aim to develop social relations with farmers and a familiarity with their daily problems, in order to work with them in solving those problems. They are also used to organize and plan for future extension agendas. The visits are costly, and no more than seven farmers can be visited daily. Sometimes visits are not welcomed by the farmers, especially during the seasons when they must be busiest.

2. Lectures and Workshops

Usually farmers – especially the older ones – like to attend lectures and workshops, where they listen for a short while, but also like to talk a lot, especially when the extension topic concerns something in their own experience. The skill of the agricultural extension worker in facilitating the discussion and listening to the experiences of farmers is useful in fostering the exchange of expertise among farmers. The discussion of relevant, timely topics is the key to getting farmers to attend these workshops and lectures. To be effective, workshops and lectures must be aligned with the farming seasons.

3. Publications

PARC annually publishes a number of agricultural publications to reinforce and strengthen other extension methods. Simple posters, stickers, flyers, and booklets carrying extension ideas are published to initiate awareness programs, and other materials are brought in later.

4. Demonstrations

These are carried out in two ways. The agricultural extension worker invites five to seven farmers to the fields and, in cooperation with the farmers, conducts a farming practice that the farmers have never seen before. Then he asks them to repeat what he just did in front of him. The other method is to make use of a model farm with a farmer, and to ask other farmers to watch.

5. Mutual Visits (Agricultural Trips)

The agricultural extension worker invites ten to eighteen farmers to visit a farm or two in another region to learn from others' experiences. Such visits are prepared for in advance. In addition to the main goal of allowing farmers to explore particular practices of outstanding farmers, the visits play an important role in strengthening the relations among farmers, especially when they are in the bus together riding from one region to another.

6. Agricultural Courses

PARC's extension workers annually design specialized agricultural programs for a limited number of farmers. The goal is to introduce a specific agricultural technology or expertise. The training course is one link in a comprehensive extension program aimed at these farmers. It is designed to focus on practical components.

7. Media

PARC has recently started to produce extension films, which are used in the extension work for farmers through videotape sessions for groups or local television broadcasts. This is a very successful method that will continue to provide positive results as long as PARC keeps improving its skills in this field.

Success Stories

In the early 1980s the white fly spread throughout the Jordan Valley, inhibiting the cultivation of tomato seedlings unless they were sprayed twice daily. As a result, cultivation costs were very high, the risk of polluting the fruit increased, and productivity decreased. PARC's extension workers faced this problem at the outset of the association's founding. Therefore, they identified as one of their objectives to find a less costly and more secure method for pest management. Extension workers applied the results of an experiment conducted by one of the teachers at the University of Jordan, who recommended the use of mesh sheets to cover the seedlings in order to deny access to this fly, and thereby prevent the transmission of viruses. Following successful trials with this method and a successful demonstration on land belonging to farmers, more demonstrations were implemented in other fields by offering subsidized mesh to farmers for three years. Results were annually documented and published in handouts that were distributed to farmers. Furthermore, a documentary was produced about mesh and was presented at agricultural lectures. But the lack of availability of mesh in the market remained a major obstacle to farmers' until PARC and farmers representatives succeeded in convincing one of the local factories to manufacture it. Now, after ten years, most of the Palestinian districts use mesh, saving tens of thousands of dollars and protecting the environment and the fruits from the risks of insecticide use.

PARC's program of reclaiming and developing sloping rocky highlands is one of its most important projects. It benefits farmers by increasing their income and providing constant employment opportunities. Furthermore, it protects land from confiscation and erosion. However, the farmers in the north of the West Bank are less interested in this program than those in the south. Therefore, PARC has focused on increasing the awareness of farmers about the importance of reclamation through organizing visits by farmers in the north to reclamation projects by farmers in the south. Following each visit, a lecture on land reclamation is held and a documentary shown. Handouts on the steps of reclamation are also distributed. The program, which has been implemented over three years, aims to encourage farmers in the north of the West Bank to reclaim their lands. It has fulfilled its goals, as evidenced by the increased demand for, and investment in, land reclamation, as well as by the achievement of a number of projects established by farmer leaders in the north that have successfully imitated this program.

The Lessons of Experience

Reviewing the past fifteen years of agricultural development in Palestine, we have drawn up the following list of the lessons that have proven most essential to the success of our endeavours:

1. The most important strategy for increasing the effectiveness of the agricultural extension programs is to teach farmers how to teach one another, or how to learn from others, by building strong community leaderships.
2. Developing self-education methods allows shared experience,

knowledge, and know-how to benefit the maximum number of people.
3. Organizing people and farmers in formal and informal frameworks helps solve their problems, as well as sustain educational and developmental work.
4. It is important to connect educational and developmental processes in cultural, social, economic, political, and environmental realms.
5. The participation of beneficiaries and target groups in the planning, managing, and evaluating of programs and projects gives greater opportunities for understanding the circumstances of the target groups.
6. Women are more attracted to awareness and educational programs, and benefit more from them than male farmers in terms of attendance and professionalism.
7. The focus on inherited traditional knowledge and the means of transferring it contributes to its development and its effective transfer between generations.
8. The identification and distribution of responsibilities in farmers' extension and awareness programs among governmental and non-governmental organizations increases the effectiveness of these programs. The shortcomings in this regard between the Ministry of Agriculture and PARC have so far reflected negatively on both the development of the message and the achievement of the goals of the awareness programs.
9. Moreover, the badly defined relationship between PARC and the Farmers' Union has not allowed each of their roles to be clarified. Instead of playing a role in general policy planning, the Farmers' Union has simply been employed to connect PARC with the union's members.
10. One of PARC's strengths is its grass-roots focus. It gives PARC flexibility in its work and access to a vast target group. However, this has not been reflected until now in the establishment of a serious framework for the most marginalized and impoverished groups. PARC is still targeting general groups such as farmers of rain-fed land, rather than smaller sub-groups within this population.

Closing Remarks

The Nuweiba Seminar

Jean-Paul Hautecoeur

In spring 1999, all the authors represented in this volume met at the Nuweiba seminar in Sinai, Egypt. The aims of the meeting were to reach a common understanding on what we started out by calling 'an ecological approach to adult basic education,' to reveal differences, and to spell out the prospects for future action and cooperation. The participants in the seminar wanted the conclusion of the publication that was being prepared to reflect the Nuweiba meeting and the genuine interaction that it would bring about among researchers from a dozen countries. I shall therefore try to remain as faithful as possible to the spirit and the letter of the meeting, and to refer to the particularity of each written contribution.

We split into language groups, Arabic, English, and French, before coming together. The composition that follows is therefore compiled from a number of parts, with the freedom that distinguishes an essay from a report. I have had to remain silent on many of the questions raised, especially those concerning how to get things done – the strategies for action. Bits and pieces of the answers have been included in the text, but do not amount to the kind of operational instructions that are generally expected from a discussion of education. A number of authors went into the exercise of analysing the meaning of various ecological approaches. I have not continued the exercise, being the least well placed of them to conclude it satisfactorily, given the distance which separates us at the UNESCO Institute for Education from people's everyday experience.

The concluding chapter consists of four sections: a reminder of the diversity of regional contexts in which the authors work; the current issue of linking ecology and education; a reconsideration of the initial notions inherited from earlier ALPHA research; and an overview commentary on ecological education.

What Brought Us to Nuweiba?

At the opening of the seminar, the designer of the ALPHA 2000 project could well have replied: three invitations – the first, from the UNESCO Institute for Education, to follow up a proposal for cooperative research between two regions (Europe and North America, and the Arab States); the second, from a small Egyptian enterprise (Community and Institutional Development) which was engaged in the unequal struggle for sustainable living with the very poor; and the third, from the spirits of ancestors and the natural world, the guardians of a magnificent location that is under threat, between the desert and the Coral Sea: Nuweiba, in the Sinai.

All the authors, with the exception of Jan Keller, who was absent, were meeting for the first time in Nuweiba. They stated their expectations, which can be summed up as follows:

- *learning to appreciate* differences and to understand them through dialogue;
- *making links*, especially between ideas and experience;
- *sharing* through bounty and generosity;
- *strengthening* joint responsibility in the different projects;
- *disseminating* our work; and
- *consolidating* an incipient network so as to better deal with crises, to resist aggression and to guarantee a fairer future for the world.

In short, the aim was to set out a clear ecological purpose for education, and to make a commitment to it in order to radically change our ways of thinking and behaving.

Regional Contexts

Let us start with the geopolitical and cultural peculiarities of what the authors said, as expressed by the authors themselves. They represent the perceptible background for the concerns raised by each author; they are the source and the stuff of his or her actions, experience, dreams, and goals.

In the Palestinian Territories, recent history has been that of occupation. People live as refugees on the plots of land that have not been confiscated. Water, land, and energy resources have become scarce. Traditional economic activities, especially agriculture, face serious obstacles. The whole way of life and social organization are 'controlled from outside,' dislocated, and monitored. In the face of this helpless confusion, educational schemes to teach farmers how to adapt agricultural methods to the natural and cultural environment, and to improve production, have also to address the needs of social cohesion, cultural traditions, and communication and liaison between communities. The major role played by women is stressed in all these cooperative service activities for the community. The main focus is on endogenous resources, on preserving them and making active use of them, and on the inhabitants' will to survive.

The attempts at survival within the Territories and outside, in exile, have led to a rediscovery of the wealth of the internal heritage, the moral culture bequeathed by ancestors, and the practical knowledge, the 'communications knowledge' of simple people's experience, all of which casts doubt on the pejorative labels attached to the people, including that of illiteracy. Learning necessarily occurs through what may be termed the dialogue of identity, and through the expression and sharing of experience in a common language, Arabic.

Egypt faces the threat of terrorism in some regions. A secular tradition of ethnic and religious tolerance is seriously affected. Alexandria is no longer a prosperous cosmopolitan city nor an international cultural capital. Its environmental problems are acute, caused by both poverty and overpopulation, and by the inactivity of the local authorities and the inadequacy of the legal system. The same applies to Cairo, where the collection and treatment of refuse is largely left to the initiative of certain communities, as are essential health and education services. There is a gulf between the elite who are attracted by Western culture and alien ways of thinking, and the poor, whose way of life is dismissed by the elite and whose practical skills are ignored. In rural areas, widespread illiteracy, outmoded agricultural technologies, rudimentary means of communication, a high rate of population growth, and lack of openings for young people are some of the causes of the impoverishment of the population, of urban migration, exhaustion of natural resources, and of other environmental disasters.

Against this background of generalized erosion, endogenous development initiatives have to set out to tap community resources while respecting the local social structures and cultural traditions that are the foundation of community cohesion and permit participation. Indigenous knowledge has to be actively used and updated. Educational activities need to be incorporated into projects for survival and improvement of the quality of life, and conducted whenever possible by members of the local community and community organizations.

There were other contributions from the Arab Region: from Yemen, Saudi Arabia, Tunisia, and Morocco. Four of the five researchers from these countries were women. It is regrettable that they were not able to take part in our work until the end, which would have deepened our knowledge of the region and enabled us to give greater space to the voices of women.

In North America, the colonization of indigenous peoples is not entirely a thing of the past. Formal and adult education continues to pay little regard to the customs, ways of life, and cultural resources of indigenous communities (nor to those of poor whites). They also help to drive communities apart, in a devastated environment. However, in Nunavut, Canada, the new political autonomy is accompanied by a cultural renewal that is radically changing certain educational practices. Among the Metis of Canada, vernacular speech and a hidden historical identity are resurfacing wherever literacy is at last entrusted to the communities.

In some impoverished regions, such as the Appalachians in the United States, mass culture, formal education, and a way of life controlled from outside are killing off the regional culture. A primary economy built on the extraction of natural resources, and reliance on a single crop, are having disastrous effects on employment, the natural environment, and social cohesion, which had been based on local roots. Two opposing development scenarios can be imagined: one is tied to the dominant economy of production and consumerism, in which the land and the regional heritage are obsolete economic factors; and the second is closely tied to the land, the local culture, and the potential of its natural and human resources. This second alternative scenario runs counter to dominant practice. Its promoters are counting heavily on down-to-earth education to reinvigorate the community economy and to restore common sense in an environment that has been regained.

In Canada, as in most of the countries in the North, there is a dense network of voluntary associations working on defending citizens' rights, the environment, and the quality of life. They are playing an increasingly important extra-parliamentary political role, especially since the launch of an economic offensive in favour of globalization in tandem with an aggressive neo-liberal ideology, which have been able to seduce national governments. Many hard-won rights are under threat – the right to information for all, the right to work, social equity, the right to a decent life in a stable environment, political participation, etc. NGOs are major players in the active education of citizens and in debates on important social issues, while the media play a crucial technical role.

From Europe also there were a number of different points of view. Overall, the creation of a collective European identity by means of supra-national institutions and a common market must not be allowed to destroy regional identities and the many different cultures. Whereas the tourist industries have long been turning regional heritages into marketable commodities, with serious ecological dangers, local communities need to rediscover the value of their heritage in order to restore regional solidarity and to put forward proposals for local development that look beyond nuclear power stations, dams, land-fill refuse dumps, and amusement parks. Environmental education can therefore fulfil a threefold function of reconstructing regional identities in a territory governed by the laws of the single market, rebuilding local solidarity to aid the very poor, and creating a sustainable framework for interaction among individuals, communities, and their environments through local development projects.

An example was given, in an urban context, of the commercial value of the scarce green spaces that have been eroded by speculation and building – in Lancaster, as in Alexandria. Environmental self-education can mobilize concerned people, local knowledge, and power relationships in order to protect a right, a common good, and a non–profit-making activity of great applied value (gardening, for example). In Lancaster, as in Alexandria, the local elites have sacrificed the environment and the public good to market forces (in their own interests). Community education and voluntary exchanges of skills cannot then be content to share information and to sit and wait. They have to counter-attack, to try rapidly to reverse political decisions, to act strategically, and to bet on winning in a game that seems at first unequal. The environment of our lives is too seriously threatened to expect education merely to be a long-term, distant, and politically neutral investment. What is at stake is a life of democracy, sustainability, and solidarity: a rare and priceless commodity.

In Central Europe, there is the historical peculiarity of the state centralism of the former regimes, with the corollary both of the dependence of individuals and social groups on state services, and of their disillusionment with political elites and political-party statements (a phenomenon that has now become widespread throughout Europe). NGO networks are recent creations and lack roots, it seems, in national, regional, and local public life. Ecological associations are often likened to tiny radical groups by a political class that has little time for democratic debate. Living conditions are deteriorating for most of the population. What is called the transition to democracy appears to many to mean the impossibility of joining in the 'market democracy.'

The search for a 'third way,' an alternative to authoritarian socialism and neo-liberal economism, is reflected in the many experiments with regional revival. In these movements, voluntary associations find their support among public institutions, local authorities, professional groups, and European programs, and among traditional social structures that outlived the communist regimes. Sustainable development projects draw both on the cultural heritage and traditional solidarities, and on the new information technologies. Education plays a key part in them, tapping into both traditional experience and new occupational knowledge. Above all, education too is experimental. It interacts with everyday life, using available resources, in an environment that has once again become familiar, in which people are learning to live differently, as they used to, or even far better.

To sum up:

- A tidal wave threatens from all sides: economic *globalization*, which is endangering cultures, societies, and the environment. The Multilateral Agreement on Investment is emblematic of this.
- The new world order is, however, not doing away with *specific regional problems:* mass poverty, social inequality and discrimination, occupation/deportation, mass culture, productivism and consumerism, overpopulation, uncontrolled urbanization, destruction of heritages and ecosystems, and moral crises.
- On all sides, there is *resistance* to ways of thinking imposed from outside and to external control of resources (either by national elites, neo-capitalism, Western culture, occupiers, or experts) through information, community education, autonomous organizations, appropriate technologies, and small-scale solidarity initiatives aiming at a global perspective and sustainability.
- The *global aspect* of survival and endogenous development is built on culture (heritage and identity), local resources, community

values and solidarity, and symbolic capital. The *sustainable aspect* seeks to maintain the links among the generations, among species in a given area, and among diverse communities, by means of traditional and technically advanced communication.
- The powers that impose themselves are opposed by the *right*, the equal right, to life, to improvement in the quality of life, to citizenship of the community and the planet. Non-formal education and voluntary organizations are preparing the way, keeping watch, but cannot embody this right. Local, national and international institutions must guarantee such rights. From past experience, these institutions are proving to be either obsolete, restricted, lacking autonomy, or insufficiently powerful.
- *Community education,* in all the situations we have encountered, has more functions than merely passing on and exchanging knowledge, skills, and the ability 'to be.' It is also reviving erstwhile knowledge, inventing solutions to current problems using available resources, and restoring value and meaning where they are in danger of being lost. It must guarantee the continuity of the group in the ecosystem, and hence constantly recreate value, meaning, and links.
- Ethical questions cut across the whole gamut of visions, projects, and actions. What is particular to an *ecological vision*, unlike economic calculations, is perhaps the reference to the Other, to what is alien and different, and reverence for the Other, as part of a whole that must be protected and reconstructed in the face of terrible danger.

Why Link Ecology and Education Now?

One expression from the Delors Commission on Education for the Twenty-First Century has become a byword: 'education throughout life and within society.' One essential element, however, is missing, as in most of our anthropocentric utterances: the environment. A society makes its nest in its surrounding countryside, from which human beings feed themselves, where they relax, dream, and meditate, discover the universe, and are free to be inventive. The Fifth International Conference on Adult Education opened its Declaration with a reminder of this: 'Adult education ... is a powerful concept for fostering ecologically sustainable development.'

For a long time, education was cut off from life, as though it were in a laboratory or a prison. Schools were scrupulously separated from the family and from peers, from the kitchen and the workshop, from vernacular language and customary interaction, from the familiar landscape of the community. In short, schools were cut off from the immediate culture and from nature, often with the blessing of God. In many countries, schooling was decreed to be compulsory, like national military service and, in some, the right to vote. Today, schools often are institutions which provide legitimacy for social hierarchies (though they were supposed to ensure equal opportunities), outmoded rites of passage, and 'historic' disciplines: square, overcrowded edifices surrounded by asphalt, full of resentment among those who work inside them, and full too of ugliness, violence, and even fear. In some failing states, and in the poorest areas of the rich countries, schools are falling into ruin.

Criticism of education and the crisis in its institutions have opened the way to a reunification between education and its social, cultural, and natural environment. Separation and discrimination between genders and among ages, classes, and cultural and religious communities are today questioned in many countries, and have sometimes even become illegal. States no longer have a monopoly, *de jure* or *de facto*, over education. Some education is being given back to civil society, to communities, to enterprise, where it had in fact never ceased, and where knowledge and skills suited to the context have to a greater or lesser degree been preserved, despite being dismissed or prohibited. This movement to restore some educational activities to their varying contexts is ecological. It is hence free, as has been said above, to guarantee the continuity of the group in the ecosystem, and hence continually to recreate value, meaning, and links.

At the same time, the market is absorbing these liberated educational services and products, along with all other cultural manifestations. Education is suddenly undergoing a radical change: through information and communications technology, it is being subjected to short-term market values, technical efficiency, and cultural standardization. It is no longer sacrosanct, except for the most prestigious and expensive items: the New. The picture is one of creation – dramatic spectacle, fantasy, endless repetition, insignificance – and the scrap heap. Machine images – machines taking over the imagination, self-production of artefacts, kitsch, virtual consumption, and – flash, bang, wallop – instant communication! Nothing is ever a failure. In the post-economy, learning consists of making everything vanish: matter, work, products, interaction, and failure. Or rather, the added value accumulated by the work of others is spirited away and burned without a backward glance or a trace of emotion. Virtual education is the direct antithesis of sustainability. And close to being black magic.

In education, ecology functions as an antidote to the instant learning of the new. Its global vision encourages the making of links, the discovery of forgotten associations. Isolation leads to the illusion of the self, to egocentrism, and degenerates into tyranny over one's neighbours. Ecology in education encourages the recognition of difference, the learning of how to live with others, with all other living creatures. Ecology also encourages us to look beyond the barriers of anthropocentrism, the vanity of rationalism, the diktats of the written word, the neutralization of sensitivity through disciplines. Ecology is not a discipline, but rather a current of sensitivity running through all fields of knowledge. It is a liaison – in the romantic, the grammatical, and the musical sense – experimental, curious, willing to surrender to great beauty and great simplicity. It is a sensitivity that sharpens the ear, non-verbal communication, and the imagination.

We are concerned less with ecological education – or environmental education – as though it were some distinct subject with its own tools, teachers, and traditions. That new discipline is now taught at universities, and it is necessary (V. Gurova). But we mean ecology in education throughout life. We refer to ecological approaches to social relations, cultural interactions, and relationships with the biophysical environment. Our school is the world, everyday life. We are building a vision of the world, we are seeking the means to preserve and improve it.

Basic Education? Literacy? What Are We to Call What We Do?

The original research proposal read as follows: 'Ecological Approaches to Adult Basic Education' (see Introduction). (In French: 'Approches écologiques de la formation de base.') We had to find a title in Arabic for the seminars and the subsequent publication. If possible, we wanted to find a common expression that respected diversity of practices and linguistic usage.

Originally, ALPHA was almost exclusively concerned with *literacy* in industrialized countries. When the spectrum was broadened and diversified (the real situation is neither homogeneous nor confined), bringing in popular education and community education in varying contexts, we borrowed the notion of *basic education*. In French we chose the expression 'formation de base' rather than 'éducation de base' because the latter has connotations of the schoolroom and the curriculum for children, even if modified for adults. 'Formation' is also used in reference to the world of work, and in the expression 'formation professionnelle,' rendered in English as 'vocational education' and/or 'vocational training.' At a disturbing time of mass unemployment, the term 'training' invested literacy with the goal of social reintegration. Later, when it became obvious that 'literacy,' the need for which was a supreme disqualification in the rich countries, only led to jobs by chance, and even less often to the minimum wage, the term 'reintegration' was scrupulously replaced by 'employability.' In other words, it was no earthly use.

Basic education, in its current senses, goes beyond literacy in the sense of initiation into writing (the alphabetic code and, by extension, other codes) in schools and outside, at work and in life. The French *formation* is derived from 'form,' and all learning is a process of forming, or shaping the physique, emotions, aesthetic sense, morals, and intelligence, with connotations of the forming of the physical world. As for the term 'basic,' it relates to the foundations of society, to the bases of cultural memory, to continuity, and to values that are sacrosanct, or at least commonly agreed upon. Basic education (with its inferences of training and *formation*) always refers to one place, one social group, and one cultural history: a notion grounded in an ecological approach to education.

We have explored the complexity of this expression in order to make a critical point. Literacy and formal education are generally imposed from outside the community, as legalized offensives to change culture and re-educate, as though previous learning had been unsuitable, and the original social context dysfunctional or even pernicious. Like the social services, education starts by isolating the individual from the original milieu or group to which he or she belongs. All of the interactions and references of that community are neutralized.

In adult literacy, in the countries of the North, tests and diagnoses are then carried out, and 'learners' are put into categories and subjected to the rules of methodology. Some people succeed: they pursue their studies, get a job, and find love and fulfilment. They bear witness to the idea that the past was awful. Many 'benefit' from the experience by recreating a welcoming environment and taking over the initiative. They are the ones who take what they can from it, often preferring to keep quiet about the outcome – for making do, getting along, is a semi-private affair. Many others leave. It is said that they drop out. For all that, they are not finished with. There will be other attempts to involve them, other courses, a 'third chance,' since illiteracy, the experts and the politicians say, is dangerous, costly, and hugely wasteful. Much is said about it in economic terms. Instead of correcting it, we have to prevent it. And then steps are taken to intervene in the family and the community. There are many educational social workers who do so with zeal.

Adel Abu Zahra spoke in such terms. Education directed at the poor, or at the South by the North, is an imposition of re-education, as though people had to be reintegrated because they have marginalized themselves – through traditionalism, incompetence, outmoded social structures, and religiosity, it is said. But people are not answerable for poverty, illiteracy, and environmental degradation. Their knowledge and skills have become obscured, just like their identities and persons. They knew how to pass on their cultural heritage, and how to conserve the resources in their ecosystem. Their sayings provide the proof. They have been sentenced to change and to disregarding their own experience, despite the destructive effects of Western methods of production and consumption. Serge Wagner gave examples from among the indigenous peoples of Canada. Anthony Flaccavento showed the degree to which the people in his region have been dispossessed of the most ordinary skills, such as how to delight in wild strawberries. Munir Fasheh recalled the time of the *intifada* in the Palestinian Territories, during which the schools were closed. No bad thing, he said, since children went back to their own affairs, to their mothers and their experiments.

How could the concept of education be liberated, in the various languages? All the authors agreed on a common vision of *education in the community*, what we called at the outset an 'ecological approach.' However, although we shared a global ecological vision of education, the notion of 'basic education' did not take account of such a vision. The use of the word 'education' in English once more tied the concept to educational institutions. In Arabic, 'basic' was not understood in the sense explained above. 'Basic education' rather evoked compulsory formal primary education, which has nothing at all to do with the critical, creative approach of out-of-school education that is sensitive to the global environment. As for literacy, all were agreed that it was very important, especially among women in Yemen, the Territories, Egypt, or Tunisia, where children, and particularly girls, have no access to schools. However, it had to be remembered that schools have solved nothing, and that literacy goes the way of schooling, abandoning its pupils in many cases on the edges of poverty. Literacy cannot be isolated from life or from local endogenous development activities.

We therefore decided to call all of what we do *ecological approaches* to education, and our common vision of the processes and purposes of education in the community, *ecological education*. It needed to be defined, shared, and implemented.

What Do We Mean by Ecological Education?

The English-language working group gave the following definition during the seminar: 'a continuous process of learning, including education and training, enabling people to think and act more responsibly and creatively in the context of their environment, their culture, and their community.'

Ecological education has a local basis, being founded on what people are – on their social origins and cultural heritage, and on their experience – and on the characteristics and boundaries of their bio-region. Ecological education is also part of the worldwide perspective of sustainable living, typified by respect for bio-cultural diversity, equitable interactions between the different sections of the community and of humanity, economic solidarity which creates added value at the local level, and regeneration of ecosystems – of all resources (A. Flaccavento). To quote Salah Arafa: 'The environment is made up of all the resources which surround us, including people. All awareness-raising, education, and training programs should have a bearing on the protection of these resources and on the way in which they can be used most efficiently, for the benefit of present and future generations.'

Ecological education founded on sustainability takes place throughout life, prolonging the legacy of the ancestors and preparing the future even unto the seventh generation, as the American Indians used to say (according to M. Fasheh). It applies to human activities as a whole, including everyday activities and the domestic economy, where knowledge is often oral or even implicit, acquired and transmitted through practice. In the traditional division of work, women initiate many of these activities. Women are effectively at the forefront of ecological education, as the authors Kamel, Daiq, and Sarsour have stressed.

While formal education is essentially a thing of public or private educational institutions, ecological approaches to education are above all a thing of the civil society (NGOs and informal community associations and organizations). These voluntary, changing structures of social life can respond rapidly to emerging local problems. They are familiar with local customs, and know how to use or get around local power structures; and they can mobilize a great deal of energy and skills through cooperation. But also, they are attached by an identity link to the territory that they occupy, cultivate, and protect. This link must be maintained and renewed. By networking, these organizations can play a similar role in safeguarding the heritage on a larger scale (B. Sarwer-Foner, J. Keller, D. Barton, I. Mihaly, and V. Nagy Czanka).

We have already noted that ecological education presupposes a holistic vision – 'perceiving life as a whole' (H. El-Geretly) – unlike specific disciplines and institutions, which are by definition limited. It has a trans-disciplinary purpose, as the Hamburg International Conference on Adult Education indicated in its *Agenda for the Future*:

> We commit ourselves to:
> 35. Promoting the competence and involvement of civil society in dealing with environmental and development problems:
> ...
> e) by integrating environmental and development issues into all sectors of adult learning and developing an ecological approach to lifelong learning.

The holistic dimension is dynamic and practical, and not transcendental as one fundamentalist branch of the ecological movement would prefer. A series of key words at Nuweiba reflects this voluntary, creative process of association among the parts of a whole: linking – connecting – activating – sharing; dialogue – commitment – participation. The environment as we understand it actively brings together ideas, bodies, and phenomena in space and time: nature, culture, and society are interwoven. Ecological education is addressed to all social actors, spilling like water across boundaries of age, gender, class, and power. This pragmatic aim must break with ideological syncretism, which sets out to persuade as many people as possible regardless of differences and costs. While classes and cultures find it difficult to live together and seek to exclude each other, the overall target of ecological activities can be seen as an enlargement of the scale of geography, culture, ethics, and imagination. Paolo Orefice called this 'the construction of personal and collective identity, and the building of world citizenship.' I shall quote a shortened version of what he said: 'In the commitment to global development directed towards the right to be different and the protection of differences, and by rediscovering these differences by living more closely together with them, people can attain an identity as a species which shows greater solidarity and makes them more fertile and creative.'

Ecological education cannot be neutral in its beliefs, unlike former precepts of positivist science or the spirit of conquest of technicist ideologies. This ethical dimension – 'generosity, at the heart of Arab culture' – which is embodied in all our relationships with the environment, was heavily stressed by the Arab researchers. Education is incarnated in cultures, and displays values, however contradictory or conflictual they may be. Ecological education specifically consists of recognizing these values in all their differences and contexts, confronting them with real situations, testing them in the resolution of common problems, and transforming them into democratic decision-making. Civic issues such as relating to others with dignity, respect for diversity or tolerance, equity before the law, reciprocity in interactions, transparency of information, and solidarity in adversity, sometimes come up against cultural traditions. An ecological approach to these obstacles and prohibitions consists in bringing them into the open and contrasting them, in an intercultural dialogue, with the rights and obligations of everyone, making reference to the principle of responsibility. Ethical issues can, from an ecological point of view, be transposed to the civic code. Their purpose is to be discussed, resolved, and applied.

While ecological education aims at the recognition of differences, it also sets out to build bridges between rich and poor. Its moral and political commitment is targeted primarily at the poor and the damned of the earth, in justice out of principle, and in the pursuit of sustainable living out of both generosity and necessity. A series of glaring questions is raised by several authors: Who controls the resources? Who takes the decisions about the issues crucial to the community, the region, and the country? To what end? On the one hand, poverty is growing in all regions, especially in the South, threatening the environment and life. Its consequences are drastic and universal. On the other, the knowledge, skills, and organizations of ordinary people are systematically being demeaned or ignored, and replaced by 'outside ways of thinking' at prohibitive cost (knowledge, technologies, services, staff, and capital are all imported). At worst, and this is becoming increasingly common, the poor themselves are displaced, deported, made to vanish. Ecological education necessarily actively defends human rights in protecting the lives of peoples and minority cultures in their own environments (L. Kamel). It does so by informing and educating decision-makers; by exploiting national and international legal institutions (A. Abu Zahra);

and by public demonstrations which go as far as civil disobedience (in times of peace, and where possible – see B. Sarwer-Foner). We are a long way from academic literacy for the purposes of subjection and social control (S. Wagner).

Ecological education inevitably runs up against the question of the means of resisting domination, organizing autonomy, and experimenting with alternatives to unequal development. In this book and throughout the ALPHA collection, it has been stressed many times that the means and the resources are to be found in the experience of the people and in the inheritance of the communities, including their economies. Ecological education cannot be carried out by transferring knowledge and strategies from rich to poor, from North to South. Since time immemorial it has been practised by communities which have experience of useful production, of equality in commercial dealings, of conservation and recycling, of transmission of knowledge, and also of the ritualized art of 'squandering' during celebrations (regenerative squandering). These practices may also need to be updated, improved, put in a wider context and communicated. Research and initiatives nonetheless come back to indigenous organizations (L. Kamel, S. Arafa). If the latter find it beneficial to associate themselves with outside agencies, that can best be achieved through networking in an ecological chain, and not in the outside market (I. Daiq and S. Sarsour; A. Flaccavento). Information and means of communication are accessible at modest cost in alternative networks, as a number of monographs have demonstrated.

Finally, ecological education is incomplete unless both art in the classical sense and the popular arts are reintroduced into projects to revive the heritage of communities and of all of humanity. Nowadays, we are accustomed to the commercialization of cultural creations, in the form of kitsch, alien art forms, clichés, and ephemeral images: 'The superficial treatment of reality that characterizes the mass media, that takes no account of the depth of history, of its diverse shades, or of the particularity of our cultural character,' writes Hassan El-Geretly. Popular arts (crafts) are vanishing in the rich countries, or are 'delocalized,' which means devalued, their skilled artisans exploited and subjected to the rules of the global market. They have been relatively well preserved in Central and Eastern Europe (thanks to the Iron Curtain), and they are still practised in countries that have been spared the worst of capitalist destruction. Their days are numbered.

Classical arts are also disappearing from our everyday lives: in the North, they have been absorbed into the luxury market; in the cities of many countries in the South, they are succumbing to urban impoverishment, overpopulation, urban decay, and pollution of air, land, and water. Everyday existence is globally devoid of artistic expression and participation, which are henceforth confined to museums of various sorts (to attract tourists), a few rich districts, and reservations. Active art, which has always been closely associated with religion, as in the times when individual and collective life had a sacred element, has vanished with the death of God. Our souls cry out.

Hence the attraction of 'nature' to our contemporaries, albeit mythologized and seriously endangered. Hence also the rise of ecological movements throughout the world, the urgent and growing demand for radical change in our way of life. Hence the ecological ferment in our education, which needs to be conducted quite differently, and in which art plays a regenerative role, being intimately associated with learning about how to express the imagination, about emotions, and about how to give and to share. 'Art as an expression of the space occupied in our lives by the imagination and the emotions ... A language guaranteeing equality and respect for the lives of peoples, which enables us to receive and transmit simultaneously in order to avoid prejudice and prejudgment' (H. El-Geretly).

It is a very different kind of literacy that is the aim of ecological education: discovery of the abundance of our heritage and the fragility of our environment; speech which is both respectful of others and creative; and a recreation in our lives of sanctified spaces, with ethical, civic, and aesthetic meaning. It is a huge, fascinating, and immediate task. It deserves to be taken up here, in the cooperative approach of the ALPHA projects. Its title might be 'Learning the Art of Living,' or something like that.

Notes on Contributors

Salah Arafa is a professor of physics at the American University in Cairo. He earned a master's degree in nuclear physics in 1966, and a doctorate from the University of Cairo in 1969. Dr Arafa is widely reputed for his work in science and in community development. He is a pioneer in environmental work and action-research in the implementation of renewable energy resource techniques and waste recycling. His work led to the founding of the Integrated Rural Technology Centre for Training and Production (IRTECTAP) at the village of Basaisa, in the heart of the Nile Delta, and the New Basaisa Community, in Sinai, Egypt.

David Barton, a literacy specialist, is a professor of language and literacy with the Department of Linguistics at Lancaster University (United Kingdom). He is interested in all aspects of reading and writing, in adults and children, in school and in everyday life. Co-editor of several books and many articles, he is the author of *Literacy: An Introduction to the Ecology of Written Language* (Blackwell, 1994) and, with Mary Hamilton, *Local Literacies: Reading and Writing in One Community* (Routledge, 1998).

Michal Bartos is the head of the Centre for Environmental Education in Slunakov in the Czech Republic. He graduated from the Faculty of Natural Sciences at the University of Palacky in Olomouc, specializing in environmental protection. He has worked at the new Department of the Environment for the municipality of Olomouc since 1990, concentrating on public ecological education. A member of the Czech Association of Environmentalists, he is the director of the Citizen's Association for Environmental Education of Slunakov. He frequently travels to Denmark and the Netherlands, where he focuses on relations between administrations and the public.

Ismail Daiq is a founding member and the general director of the Palestinian Agricultural Relief Committees (PARC). Since 1983, he has occupied several positions within this organization. He is currently a doctoral candidate in agronomy at the University Hohenheim in Germany. He has been a speaker at many regional and international conferences on agricultural development. He regularly publishes articles and research reports on the ecological approach to rural development methods.

Hassan El-Geretly is a theatre director, and has worked in film production. In 1987, he founded El-Warsha, an independent company that produces contemporary theatre works inspired by popular Egyptian traditions, a process that requires research and training with and among masters of popular traditions. In recent years, El-Warsha has incorporated social action and training/education into its endeavours, in order to create a distinctive cultural milieu that draws on the collaboration of creative artists in Egypt, the Arab world, and beyond.

Munir Fasheh was born in Jerusalem (Palestine) in 1941. Expelled with his family in 1948, he has since lived in Ramallah on the West Bank. He holds a doctoral degree in education, and has taught mathematics and physics in schools and universities, mainly at the Birzeit University in Palestine. He was in charge of mathematics instruction in West Bank schools for five years (1973–8) and taught mathematics to illiterate adults. In 1989 Munir Fasheh established the Tamer Institute for Community Education in Palestine. For the past two years, he has been Visiting Scholar at Harvard University. He has published six books in Arabic, and more than forty articles in Arabic and English on mathematics, education, society, and religion.

Anthony Flaccavento has been executive director of Appalachian Sustainable Development since its founding in 1995. Prior to that he worked on social justice and human needs issues for more than ten years in the Appalachian region. Educated in agriculture, ecology, and rural development, he has published several articles on these topics, along with a chapter in the book *Rural Sustainable Development in America*. Anthony Flaccavento is married with three children and runs a small commercial organic farm.

Viara Gurova is an associate professor at the Faculty of Education of the University of Sofia. For a number of years, she has been contributing to the work of UNESCO and the European Union on the improvement of the quality of teaching and learning, the rights of children, the prevention of drug abuse among young people, and adult education. She has published many articles and two books: *Education in the World: Issues and Perspectives* and *Andragogy or the Art of Teaching Adults*. Her work concerns especially the organization and management of education, and models of teaching and educational intervention.

Jean-Paul Hautecoeur was a senior researcher at the UNESCO Institute for Education from 1990 to 2000. He coordinated a research program on literacy and basic education, and edited the UIE ALPHA series on community basic education. Before 1990 he taught sociology in several Canadian universities and coordinated the ALPHA program at the Quebec Ministry of Education. He is the author of the following publications: *L'Acadie du discours* (Québec City: Les Presses de l'Université Laval, 1975), *Analphabétisme et alphabétisation au Québec* (Québec City: Official Publications Office, 1978), and *Anonymus autoportaits* (Montréal: Éditions Saint-Martin, 1986). He has written numerous articles on literacy and adult basic education in industrialized countries.

Laila Iskandar Kamel has worked with grass-roots communities in Egypt since 1982. She holds a master's degree in education and a doctorate in international education development. Her main areas of intervention have been in poverty alleviation and economic empowerment for women, primary health care, and community mobilization. She is a member of various non-profit organizations and consultant to international development agencies. She is now the managing director of Community and Institutional Development (CID), a private firm which she founded in 1996 with four professionals from the private sector in Egypt.

Jan Keller is a historian and a sociologist. He teaches general sociology at the Faculty of Letters at the University of Brno in the Czech Republic. He is the author of several works, including *An Introduction to Sociology*

(Prague, 1992); *Society with Limited Rationality* (Brno, 1992); *The Twelve Errors of Sociology* (Prague, 1995); *Sociology of Organization and Bureaucracy* (Prague, 1996); and *Sociology and Ecology* (Prague, 1997).

Ildiko Mihaly has a degree in Hungarian language and literature and psychology from the University of Letters of Budapest. She began her career as a journalist on the daily *Magyar Nemzet*. In the 1970s she was a secondary-school teacher and then, in the 1980s, worked as a researcher at the National Institute of Pedagogy and the National Institute of Vocational Education. In the 1990s, Ms Mihaly became a principal adviser to the ministries of labour and education. She has published a number of articles on the psychology and sociology of education.

Valeria Nagy Czanka has been a metalworker, and then a group leader and coordinator with several organizations in the District of Somogy. In the 1990s she became president of the Banya Panorama Association, and then president of the Zselic Development Association. She has been awarded numerous prizes for her commitment to development in the Zselic region, including the Somogy Citizens' Prize in 1996, and the Pro Regio Prize in 1997.

Paolo Orefice is dean of the Faculty of Education Sciences at the University of Florence. He directs several national and regional projects, as well as a number of European projects. He is currently a member of the board of governors of the UNESCO Institute for Education. Among his most recent contributions to the field of environmental pedagogy in adult education are *Didactique de l'environnement* (La Nuova Italia, 1993); *Modèle territorial de programmation éducative et didactique: Images d'une expérience de recherche participante dans les Campi Flegrei* (Naples: Liguori 1997); and, in collaboration, *Itinéraires méditerranéens pour l'éducation environnementale et culturelle du citoyen européen* (Éditions Pacini, 1997).

Shawkat Sarsour has occupied since 1993 a range of posts within the Palestinian Agricultural Relief Committees (PARC). A graduate of the University of Jordan, he is an agricultural expert, and specializes in strategic planning and the management of agricultural development. He has conducted numerous studies on extension techniques, for which he regularly publishes the findings.

Brian Sarwer-Foner holds a Master of Science degree, and is currently persuing his Ph.D. in communications at McGill University in Montréal, Canada. An environmental consultant and ecology activist, he ran as a candidate for the Green Party in the 1997 and 2000 Canadian federal elections. The father of two children, he loves nature and scuba diving, and plays the saxophone and the clarinet.

Serge Wagner is a tenured professor of education at the Université du Québec à Montréal, where he founded an adult education and literacy research laboratory. He has worked in literacy and adult education for thirty years and has helped to set up a number of literacy projects and voluntary organizations both within and outside Quebec. He is the author of books and articles on adult education and literacy, and a former member of the board of governors of the UNESCO Institute for Education.

Adel Abu Zahra is a professor of behavioural sciences in Alexandria. In 1974 he earned a master's degree in psychology and completed his doctorate in 1978. Dr Abu Zahra has been involved in volunteer community service since 1974. He founded NGOs devoted to the classical arts, the environment, consumer protection, women's rights, and the preservation of historical buildings. He is a regular newspaper and magazine correspondent, has hosted a television series since 1992, and is a frequent participant in international meetings. He has also worked as a counsellor and researcher for several environmental and human development organizations.

Lisa Zucker has led a dual career, combining sculpture with academics. She received her doctorate at Stanford University in 1990 and taught theory of representation at l'Université de Montréal until 1997, speaking frequently at the International Philosophical Seminar on social issues in contemporary aesthetics. Her early sculptural work was in clay, but changed to bronze after her studio collapsed in the California earthquake of 1989.